WALKING THE SACRED PATH

A Life Lived for Mother Earth

ZELIMA XOCHIQUETZAL AND ELISE D. GARCÍA

SOR JUANA PRESS

San Antonio, Texas

About Sor Juana Press

Sor Juana Press is a project of Santuario Sisterfarm, a nonprofit organization rooted in the Texas Hill Country and grounded in the rich multicultural legacy of the Borderlands. Founded in 2002, Santuario Sisterfarm is a sanctuary for cultivating diversity and living in right relationship with the whole Earth community.

Sor Juana Press is dedicated to publishing the works of women—particularly women of color and women religious—on topics rooted in women's spirituality and relationship with Earth, *la Tierra, nuestra madre.*

The Press invokes the name and honors the memory of Sor Juana Inés de la Cruz (1648-1695), a Mexican nun, scholar, poet, playwright, musician, and scientist—a woman with a *sed de conocer* (thirst for knowing)—who was silenced for advocating women's education. She is the first writer in the Americas to speak out in favor of a woman's right to learn and express concern about human depredation of the environment.

Other Books by Sor Juana Press

THE OHTLI ENCUENTRO: WOMEN OF COLOR SHARE PATHWAYS TO LEADERSHIP by Elise D. García (2005).

CRUCIBLE FOR CHANGE: ENGAGING IMPASSE THROUGH COMMUNAL CONTEMPLATION AND DIALOGUE, edited by Nancy Sylvester, IHM and Mary Jo Klick (2004).

ENCOUNTERING MYSTERY IN THE WILDERNESS: ONE WOMAN'S VISION QUEST by Margaret Galiardi, O.P. (Issue No. 4, April 2004).

EARTH, OUR HOME: BIBLICAL WITNESS IN THE HEBREW SCRIPTURES by Sarah Ann Sharkey, O.P. (Issue No. 3, February 2004).

PERMACULTURE: FINDING OUR OWN VINES AND FIG TREES by Carol Coston, O.P. (Issue No. 2, August 2003).

EARTH SPIRITUALITY: IN THE CATHOLIC AND DOMINICAN TRADITIONS by Sharon Therese Zayac, O.P. (Issue No. 1, June 2003).

Dedicated to Mother Earth

Acknowledgements

My deepest gratitude goes to my mother, Esmeralda, my first uncondi-tional love; Peter Rogers, Ph.D., for I would not be here without him and will always love him; and the sisters in the Milpitas County Jail between 1974 and 1977, who taught me about love and respect in such a deep way, I integrated each of them into who I am.

I'm very grateful, also, to Liz Krainer, who has been there for me through so much, and to so many others for their wonderful friendship and help along the way. This includes each one of the friends mentioned in this book, as well as my dear friends Dollie Beck, Lon Brodsky, Alicia Casares, Coyote, Patrick Delaney, Tracy Delaney, Jill Lessing, Lanny Lewis, Joyce Meyers, Carolina Pesqueira, Delia Ruíz, Maynard Stout, Elana Summers, Marion Tolson, and Gina Varelli; and so many others whose names remain in my heart.

I send love and gratitude to my first teacher, Micaela, and to each of those wonderful women who followed: Sister Nazareth, Sister Agnes, and Mildred Jackson. I also acknowledge the debt of thanks I owe to Jamie Sams for the Sacred Path Cards, which have helped me so much in my healing work.

Finally, I acknowledge the insanity and violence that has run through my family for generations. I have made peace and connected with my ances-tors, who teach and guide me from their knowledge and their mistakes. I real-ize that this insanity and violence is in our genes and in our blood, and I pray for healing for all—past, present, and future generations.

~Zelima Xochiquetzal

I am immensely grateful to my co-editors, Carol Coston, O.P. and Maureen Kelleher, R.S.H.M., for their yeowoman's work in editing the man-uscript, and to the several dear friends who read it at various stages of com-pletion, offering helpful insights and comments, including Melba Beine, O.P.,

M.D.; María Antonietta Berriozábal; Derre Ferdon; Rosemary Ferguson, O.P.; Arlene Flaherty, O.P.; and Esther Kennedy, O.P.

To Carol Coston, I also owe my deepest appreciation for her patient and loving support and friendship through arduous months of writing. It's fair to say that this book would not exist without her steady supply of healing food and drink, and warm encouragement.

~Elise D. García

TABLE OF CONTENTS

Foreword viii

Introduction xi

Part One: The Sacred Path
Chapter 1: *Micaela, Mi Micaelita* 3
Chapter 2: Nicaragua: *Bella y Violenta* 9
Chapter 3: Coming of Age in the U.S. 29
Chapter 4: Marriage at Eighteen 51
Chapter 5: Coming Out & Coming Alive 65
Chapter 6: Re-Awakening to the Sacred Path 93
Chapter 7: Medicine Wheel 135
Chapter 8: Medicine Journey 151
Chapter 9: Shamanic Death 177

Part Two: Healing Ways
Animal Stories 227
Gathering Healing Energy 232
Dance of the Soul 234
Working with the Stone People 235
Working with the Light 236
Herbal Remedies 237
Prayer for Love 242

Endnotes 243

FOREWORD

At the end of May 2004, I joined Elise D. García on a trip to Arizona where I met Zelima Xochiquetzal for the first time. I had already heard much about her, but now I was seeing with my own eyes the way Zelima lived, at home on Mother Earth and in communion with our Creator. I also met all the creatures—her animal family of birds and dogs and cats of all sizes and personalities—who shared her life and home in the desert.

In the dry heat and blinding sun of the day and chilly cold nights with jolting winds, we lived for a couple of days with Zelima in the desert where her small camper and dome sit. The basic necessities we all take for granted—potable water, electricity, a toilet, or place to bathe—are absent. Yet, in this environment I met an incredibly powerful and beautiful woman who years ago was lured to the desert from the depths of her heart. Although a grave injustice has prevented Zelima from living on her own land and in her own house, this desert is her beloved home.

In the midst of the harshness of her living conditions, Zelima one morning prepared a special breakfast of handmade corn tortillas and Nicaraguan

eggs. We ate outside the small camper next to the propane tanks in a cool spot protected from the bright morning sun. I can still taste the delicious food, and tears well in my eyes as I recall the feeling in my heart of deep gratitude and pure joy at the gifts of simplicity, generosity, and hospitality I had received.

Zelima and María getting acquainted

In that dusty, desolate, windy, and seemingly barren terrain, we celebrated a sacred ritual of sharing; Zelima's meal fed my soul.

Her welcoming spirit, smile, love for her family of feathered and furred creatures, and joy at seeing her friend, Elise, made of my brief time with Zelima a visit to Holy Ground. I did not yet know the details of her life story, as chronicled in this book. But after reading about the terror she experienced as a little girl and the painful journey that eventually brought her to the desert, I was humbled. Zelima's journey from her childhood home in Nicaragua and to this home in Arizona is an extraordinary testament to the fortitude, patience, wisdom, and integrity of a woman who has had the courage to delve into her own soul and follow the sacred path that beckons.

I had another opportunity to be with Zelima in the spring of 2005 when she came to Santuario Sisterfarm for some days of rest and to give a workshop as part of our *Latinas in the Borderlands* program, teaching us her powerful healing practices. It was a deeply spiritual experience.

Gracias, Zelima, por darnos parte de tu vida, tus conocimientos y tu historia. (Thank you, Zelima, for giving us part of your life, your knowledge, and your story.)

In this chronicle there is yet another gift. It is the friendship, the sharing of spiritual gifts, and the collaboration between two exceptional women, Zelima and Elise. This book is a fruit of that friendship. Zelima's painful life story and healing gifts are extraordinary, but we would not know of them without Elise's penetrating eyes and intuitive heart. Where there is mystery, we need visionaries and translators to interpret the mysteries for us. Elise's profound wisdom, patience, and keen talent for the written word have made this book possible.

Gracias, Elise, por tu entendimiento, tu trabajo y tu espíritu de generosidad. (Thank you, Elise, for your understanding, your work, and your spirit of generosity.)

In Zelima's story, which tells of excruciating violence and suffering, she speaks of a pain so deep it made a hole that "connected with the Infinite," becoming a channel where the healing energy came through. There is hope in these words for all who suffer around the world and for all who struggle so painfully for peace and justice.

These are disturbing times, violent times, pain-filled times. Yet even in the midst of all the pain and suffering, I see countless individuals and organizations valiantly working to find solutions and new ways of being human— respectful of each other and all life forms on Mother Earth.

Zelima's story is a powerful allegory for these times and for Mother Earth, herself. In both, we see so much suffering, yet so many signs that we are at a momentous time in history—a transformative time when we are being called into radical equality with each other and all life forms on Earth, in love and forgiveness.

Santuario Sisterfarm and Sor Juana Press are honored to present Zelima's story to you. We hope you find reflections in it of your own goodness and your own gifts. We also hope, if you find reflections of your own pain and suffering, that the healing ways will comfort you and that you, too, will discover in the depths of your suffering a hole so deep it connects with the Infinite.

María Antonietta Berriozábal
President of the Board of Directors
Santuario Sisterfarm

INTRODUCTION

Just as Zelima would say that a stone I picked up and put in my pocket actually *called* me to it, I sense that this book is not so much something I chose to help bring to life as something that has chosen me.

It beckoned some five years ago, in April 2000, when I first met Zelima Xochiquetzal, a Nicaragua-born healer, or *curandera*, as a participant in a one-day class she gave on gathering healing energy from Mother Earth and Sky. Something about her presence and person impressed me greatly. Zelima not only spoke of our Oneness with all creation, an Earth ethic I value and believe in, but also seemed to live and breathe that ethic. Her whole being exuded a deep inner knowing that her life was intrinsically connected to all life.

After the workshop, on a whim, I offered to accompany the driver who was taking Zelima back to the airport, more than an hour's drive down a snowy mountain. I sat in the back seat and at some point on our way down the mountain, I was prompted to scribble a note and slip it in the side pocket of her suitcase. It said, "If you ever decide to write the story of your life, I'd be glad to help in any way I can."

A few weeks passed. I had forgotten all about my impulsive note-writing, when a large manila envelope addressed to me in an unfamiliar handwriting landed in my mailbox. It was stuffed with the first ten or so pages of Zelima's book, written in long hand on legal paper. In her cover letter, Zelima wrote that she had just gone through her suitcase again and discovered my note. She said she was delighted by my offer of assistance and was taking me up on it, enclosing the first installment.

In this casual way, a relationship started and grew even as the idea of the book—after three or four more installments were added to the first—soon faded away. Zelima was confronted by a number of trials, fanned by economic poverty, and our telephone conversations increasingly focused on those struggles and on strategies for overcoming them. But each of the conversations revealed more and more of who Zelima is—both the difficult raw facts of a life faced with many challenges, as well as the extraordinary gifts and encounters of a life full of riches. Like a double-strand of DNA, with its always-locked pairs of bases, in Zelima's life, the extraordinary gifts seemed to be in lockstep with the challenges.

As time went on, Zelima would often begin our telephone conversations with the phrase, "I was told to tell you this …" What she was told to tell me might be something that was happening deep in Mother Earth; it might be instructions on how to do "absent healing;" it might be how Jesus came to her in the night; or it might be an insight that the "Stone People" were revealing to her. Regardless of what was happening to her, Zelima shared what she was learning from her "voices," from "Spirit," from the "oracles," from the "Stone People," from the trees, the birds, the wind, the stars, all kinds of animals, Mother Earth, and, yes, from her beloved friend, Jesus.

Whatever she was learning she would share generously, saying, "It's time, it's time, it's time." It is time, she said, for all she has learned and knows to be shared.

I realize now that it took entering into the story of Zelima, with its Job-like trials and revelations, to get to a place where I could begin to sense what it is that this book was yearning to say. Despite the hardships she was experiencing and the persistent questions that arose in our conversations of why life had to be so difficult, they always brought me to a deeper place. Her struggles, her life, her "sacred path" were always framed in the largest possible context—always connected to the struggles of our living planet, Earth, and to the struggles of all humanity and creation.

Zelima's story is *our* story. It is the story of one human being living a life in keen awareness that she was born of and is totally dependent on Earth, that she is spiritually and physically one with Earth, and that, as part of the Earth community, she is also in communion with the sun and moon and stars and distant galaxies.

As are we.

This, more than anything, is what Zelima has to teach us—with her body, with her life.

I believe that there are people alive today (as others have been in past centuries) who, through the very way they live their lives are helping us, as a species, to take the next evolutionary step in human consciousness. Through the changes in perception that they cultivate in their own bodies— different ways of seeing, hearing, feeling—they are forging, at the cellular level, new ways of being human for all of us.[1] As the theory of non-locality in the new physics teaches us, where a change in one particle can be instantaneously perceived and occur in another particle on the other side of the world, we do not need to know of this work to be impacted by it.[2] But it helps.

I believe that Zelima is one of those people, forging new ways of being human for all of us—with all the wonder and imperfection that each of our lives contains.

This is her story, as told to me in writings, phone conversations, and tape recordings. It begins in Nicaragua, where she was born in 1940, and was first taught the ways of Mother Earth by a remarkable *India*, who took care of her. It ends in the White Mountains of Arizona where she now lives in a dome tent on the land, offering loving shelter to a number of abandoned dogs, cats, and a rabbit—and healing from an illness diagnosed in December 2002 as pancreatic cancer that had progressed to the liver.

Part One is the story of a life spent transmuting unspeakable cruelty and hardship into love—and, eventually, into a life lived for Mother Earth. Part Two is a sharing of herbal remedies, animal stories, and the ways Zelima has been taught to gather energy from the Earth, the sun, the wind, the moon, and stars; to communicate with the Stone People; and to heal with the Light— teachings that are coming to you now, because it is time.

~ Elise D. García

PART ONE
THE SACRED PATH

Chapter 1

MICAELA, MI MICAELITA

From hearing the adults talk, I understood that I was going to *el hospital*. They were going to give me *una operación* that would take care of the little *bolitas* (balls) that were growing on my lower eyelids. No one talked to me about it. I wasn't yet two years old, so they probably didn't even think of telling me.

Whatever they were going to do in *el hospital* did not make Micaela happy. Today, Micaela was not her usual self. I sensed and retain the memory of her feelings—I now know that she was thinking and praying about what to do. That was Saturday. On Monday, I was to go to *el hospital*.

On Sunday, Micaela started dressing me without the usual humor and teasing. She seemed intent on something, and said we were going to *la procesión*. In Nicaragua, on special saints' days, we had processions on the streets with *los Indios* playing drums, and many people dancing and fulfilling the *promesas* they made when their prayers were answered. There was much music and beautiful smells of incense and tropical flowers.

Catholic icons and statues were carried through the streets. My favorite was a life-size statue of Jesus on the cross. Always carried on a cart, Jesus looked so beautiful to me that I didn't see him as sad or suffering. I just saw this beauty that gave me a feeling that I realized much later was peace.

With me holding onto Micaela's long Indian skirt, we went to the street where *la procesión* would pass. We found a place to stand in the front row and watched the people dance, the statues being carried on strong shoulders, the drums beating.

First, came a beautiful statue of *la Virgen María* dressed in a long white satin gown, with a baby blue satin mantle draped over her head and down her shoulders. Then came other saints. Finally, I saw the beautiful Jesus on the cross with garlands of flowers strung around him, their petals beige and light yellow speckled with brown spots. The fragrance of the flowers was so strong that I started inhaling them while they were half a block away!

I remember it so well. As Jesus neared us, I looked up at him and as he passed before us, two fragrant flowers fell to my feet from the garland around his neck. Before I knew what was happening, Micaela had picked up the two perfumed flowers and was rubbing the petals over the *bolitas* on my lower eyelids, over my upper eyelids, and then all over my closed eyes!

We walked home more slowly than we had walked to *la procesión*, but Micaela still didn't tease or joke with me—and she still had that intent look about her, though it was softer. I remember having a light supper and warm milk in a gourd. Then Micaela put me to bed, with a prayer and no laughing.

When I woke up on Monday morning, Micaela was smiling and teasing me, and there was a scent of perfume in the house. Soon, I heard the adults talking, saying the *bolitas* on my eyelids were gone! No *hospital*. No *operación*.

Something was different in the house that day. I liked the feeling. Much later, I recognized that it was a feeling of peace.

Until I was in my middle fifties, I had tiny little scars on my lower eyelids; then they went away. I wasn't supposed to forget that experience. For a long time I had forgotten. And then I saw my little scars, and I remembered.

INDIA GUACHAPEADA

Whenever Micaela would take me to visit her family or her friends, they would say, pointing to me, "*Y esa India*, where did you get her?" Micaela and the other Native people who helped raise me, drilled into me that I was Indian. They called me *India guachapeada* or "splattered" Indian. "You're never going to pass as white," they would say, taking me in as one of their own.

The Native people loved me, and they made sure that I loved them, doing extraordinary, unforgettable things for me. For example, I never liked playing with toys (except a little black doll I had—but I never considered her to be a toy; she was my little friend). I liked the real thing, not toys. Micaela's nephew, Alejandro, who was very poor, built me a little wood stove with his own money, his own hands. I could get dough from the women in the kitchen and bake bread in this little oven. I could get little pieces of meat and cook them on the stove. I loved that little stove.

4

I did not see much of my parents when we lived in Nicaragua. They gave me over to Micaela, who took care of me. When I was born, Micaela looked into my mother's face and laughed, *"¡Esta es mi hija!"* (This one's my daughter!) Micaela got away with things because of her magic. She and my mother would have fights and Micaela would walk out, carrying her *motete*, her bundle of things wrapped in Indian cloth, with her parrot perched on her head.

But even during these fights, when Micaela wasn't working for my mother, she would come to my school and bring me something to drink. It was a Catholic school and there would be breaks when people could bring us refreshments from home. Micaela would always show up to tend to me. It was just a matter of time before my mother would beg Micaela to come back; she had a hold on my mother.

I don't remember eating at the table with the rest of the family until I was close to four years old. Before that, it was more fun. Micaela would take me to *el patio*. We would sit on the ground and Micaela brought my food in two gourds—a long one for drinking and a round one to eat from. Each gourd sat in a matching holder, also made from gourds.

Eating like that with Micaela was one of the times when I could feel that certain *something* about her. It was inside her and invisibly around her. I could feel it. It was good.

Micaela didn't let many people see that part of her. Perhaps only her niece, Olga, her nephew, Alejandro, and I saw it. She appeared to others as a poor, barefoot Indian—uneducated, illiterate, and therefore, ignorant. And, interestingly, she was a midget, which was very unusual among Native peoples. Micaela liked it that way; most people were not allowed to see deep into her eyes.

Micaela's job was to take care of me, and I believe our relationship was destined. She and I were the "Little Sisters." The path of the "Little Sisters" was to be my spiritual path, and looking back, I see that it began with Micaela—she initiated me.

The Path of the Little Sisters teaches that things would eventually happen on Mother Earth that have never happened before. Because no one would know what was going to occur next on Earth, and what steps we would need to take, all of us would be like babies on this path. We would need to let the Creator and Mother Earth guide our steps.

It would be a time when the female energy would be much needed. The Mother would call her daughters for this work.

Later, I was given instructions to guide me on this path. I was to be humble and, as a Little Sister, not allow myself to be controlled or dominated because I had to be able to follow the guidance of the Creator and Mother Earth.

I was told that the Little Sisters are sometimes big sister and little sister and sometimes mother and daughter, and that the littlest one is always the oldest. That was part of the magic with Micaela—she was the littlest. Because she was a midget, I was taller than Micaela when I was seven. My son's hand at the age of three, when years later we visited, was already the same size as Micaela's. Sometimes, because Micaela called me her daughter, we also were mother and daughter.

Micaela was teaching me this path, and I believe it was to prepare me for these times—the times we are in right now. There is something happening on Earth right now that we are totally unprepared for because it has never happened before. We are not going to be able to think our way out of it. But there is a way to live through this, and it has to do with allowing ourselves to be guided. To be a little one again, to become like little children, allowing each step to be guided.

DON'T KICK THE SALT

Micaela's way of teaching me this path was not with words but through touch. When she touched me, I would see picture images that would convey the teachings. Although Native beliefs were no longer punishable by fire, by death, as they were in earlier times, the people still held a lot of fear, so there had to be another way to pass on the beautiful knowledge. Touch was one of the ways.

Here is my favorite example of how Micaela did this: When I was very little and couldn't talk much, we were sitting in Nicaragua in *el patio*. There was a big yard in the middle. That's the way the houses were built. We were sitting there and I didn't have any shoes on. I was either in training pants or a diaper. We were eating green mangos and salt—that's a favorite in Nicaragua—when I dropped and spilled my little pinch of salt. I started crying and screaming and kicking the salt.

Ever so swiftly, Micaela reached over, touched my arm, and said, "*No patees la sal.*" (Don't kick the salt.) And when she touched me, I instantly saw a wide-screen image of the beautiful ocean before me. I saw that the ocean was sacred and that the salt came from the ocean. "*Don't kick the salt.*" The *salt* is sacred. In that instant, I made the connection.

REVERSALS

Micaela also taught me to do some things in reverse. She still wore her indigenous dress (I didn't know any other Native women who did), but some days when she would pick up her parrot and put it on her shoulder to start the day, her clothes were on inside out. My mother would say, "That's because when they get dirty on one side, she'll...." But that wasn't it, because Micaela was never dirty. She was a very clean person. She just put on her clothes inside out from time to time, and I find that now I sometimes do it, too, unconsciously.

Micaela never explained why. There is no way she could have; it was too dangerous. But I know that reversals are something significant. It feels really, really good when reversals happen to me. I think it is a way of putting me in balance or in greater balance. That may not be all of it, but it definitely has something to do with balance.

LEARNING THE WAY

Micaela was my first and most influential spiritual teacher. The way she taught me—by osmosis—prepared me to learn from the Stone People, from the trees, from the wind, from the sun, from the moon and stars. When Micaela touched me, and said those words about the salt, I could see those pictures, and I *knew.* Whenever I touch a tree, or a stone, or reach up toward the sky, the energy comes through me by osmosis. I see it sometimes, looking like a "bubble, bubble, bubble, bubble" that enters and heals, and I feel more and more the intensity of the life force in my body. It is a way of collecting energy that is available to all of us. Indeed, it is our *birthright.*

CHAPTER 2

NICARAGUA, *BELLA Y VIOLENTA*

y first home in Managua, Nicaragua, was in *el barrio de San Antonio*. I don't know if I was born in that house, which was long with many rooms surrounding *el patio*, but I remember crawling in it. The earth of *el patio* was very pretty and felt pleasing to my eyes. There were fruit trees. My favorite was the Breadfruit tree. Even now, I long for that soft, white, fluffy fruit. People would remove the green peel, slice it, and fry it. To me, it is the most delicious bread I've ever tasted.

On his feast day, our *Iglesia de San Antonio* would give away tiny little loaves of bread—so small I could hold them in my little hands. They were supposed to remind us to be kind to those who didn't have enough to eat. In that house, near the church of San Antonio, I saw very little kindness—and much cruelty. On occasion there was a dash of humor.

By the time I was born, on March 31, 1940, my parents, Juan Humberto and Esmeralda Sánchez, were doing very well. I found out years later, when Mami was dying, that when they were a young couple, they would save whatever little amount they could from selling the food Mami cooked to buy a little gold so Papi could begin making jewelry. Mami had tears in her eyes when she told me this. Papi was a gifted artist and Mami an excellent business woman. In time, they rose from poverty to owning *the* place in Managua to buy quality jewelry—*La Joyería Sánchez* (Sánchez Jewelers), which was also the sole distributor of Swiss watches in Nicaragua.

9

By the time I was born, they had a cook, three servants to clean the house, a seamstress, and nannies to take care of us.

MAMI AND MY SIBLINGS

From the earliest time I can remember, when I was still crawling, my siblings let me know that they did not like me. In fact, they *hated* me.

Hiram, me in Zela's lap, and Ivan

Throughout my childhood, they would tell me how awful I was when I was little, when we lived in Nicaragua. My sister, Zela, was the oldest, followed by Hiram and Ivan. There had been another, older, sister named Zelima. But she died of unexplained causes when she was around eight months old. I was named after her.

My siblings' hatred was very real. It showed in their eyes and actions that they were children who had been severely abused—physically, emotionally, and mentally. Children who had been told repeatedly, for several months, that a baby was coming soon and that if they didn't obey, the baby would get everything—and they would get nothing. When I was finally born, my brothers and sister were told that now that the baby was here, if they didn't obey, the baby would get everything, and they would get nothing.

My great auntie, Tía Yita, later told me that I was set up for punishment from the start. By the time I was born, my brothers and sister were waiting for me. *"Te estaban esperando, m'ija."*

My first clear memory of standing up as a child was when I was up against a wall. My brothers and sister were coming at me with anger, hitting me. I cried, and the tears felt so hot, they burned. My eyes started to itch and I rubbed them, trying to ease the itch. I remember my siblings saying, "Look at her, she's faking! She's rubbing her eyes to make it look like she's crying!" I was to hear that often, each time I was hurt bad enough to cry and to have the tears burn, making my eyes itch so that I would rub them to stop it. Perhaps that's why the *bolitas* grew on my lower eyelids.

I didn't spend much time with my parents during those years, and what time I did spend with them made me anxious and fearful. Whenever I saw my mother and father, I would also usually hear my siblings screaming, crying, begging not to get beaten, and running around, knowing there was no escape. I would run toward them, wanting them not to be hurt. A few times when I could, as my mother got ready to beat them because of something they had done, I ran up to her and said, "I did it, Mami!" Mami then said, "Oh, okay," and put away the belt. My siblings escaped a beating, but they hated me even more.

Their faces, full of fear and tears, haunted me much of my life. My mother would whip them with the leather belt, and sometimes, after beating them, Mami would fall to the floor unconscious. Some of the household members would then get the *agua florída* (healing cologne) and splash it on the inside of her lower arms and the back of her neck, and she would wake up and then go lie down. Zela, Hiram, and Ivan would be left alone with their wounds.

I remember one time when Mami was screaming and looking for the belt. My brothers and sister were running around, crying because they were going to get whipped. I was still learning to walk. But I remember seeing the belt on a chair and the next thing I knew, I was sitting on it. Mami kept screaming, looking for the belt. She finally got tired and gave up. When Mami went to her room, Papi came to me and said, "You can give me the belt, now."
I lifted up my little behind, and he took the belt and left. It's the only time as a child that I remember liking my father.

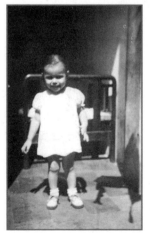

My parents would spend time with me when they wanted to teach my siblings "a lesson." They would give me all the toys and give my siblings none, telling them that they had not been behaving as they should, "so that's what they got—*nada*." I don't remember ever using any of the toys and special things my parents gave me. I think they took them away from me once the "lesson" was over.

It didn't take me long to see what was going on. In my baby mind, I saw that when my

In *el barrio de San Antonio*

parents "did this" (gave me all the toys), it was "to do that" (punish my siblings), and "to make them this way" (sad and angry at the loss, and jealous of me). Much later, I learned that parents used this method, thinking it would keep their kids in line and make them behave. This was common practice in Nicaragua at that time.

HIRAM AND ME

Hiram, who was around six years older than I, was the child my mother beat up the most when he was little (until we moved to the States and my sister Lotus was born; she got it even worse). Mami beat him and beat him. The worse thing she ever did to him involved me.

I was in the backyard in *el patio* where I used to play with red ants. This is something my mother never understood and I don't quite understand either: the ants would never bite me. When I was just barely walking, I would put my feet on the ground in *el patio* and these red ants would crawl all over my legs and tickle me. I would play with them and let them crawl all over my hands and arms.

My brother, Hiram, in Nicaragua

My brother Hiram would take off his shoes and pull up his pant legs so the red ants would crawl on him, too. But the ants would bite him to pieces! He would stomp them and end up screaming and crying. I see all this in pictures since I was too young to think about it. I see that I would then go back to playing with the ants, and a few days later Hiram would come, try it again—and get bitten again.

It was one of those days when I was playing with the red ants that my mother and Tía Hilda came out to *el patio*. My mother said, "*M'ija*, come make *pipí* in the potty." So I went over and urinated in the little *basinilla*.

Soon after, I heard my brother Hiram screaming. They brought him outside, kicking and screaming. I heard my mother say to someone, "Get the *molenillo!*" The wooden egg beaters they used to keep our mouths open whenever they gave us medicine we didn't want. Two people wrestled Hiram to the ground, sat on him, and held down his arms. My mother poured my urine from the *basinilla* into a glass, and then down Hiram's throat.

I couldn't talk; I was barely walking. But Hiram hated me for that and talked about it for years after. "They made me drink your *urine!*" he would say in a rage.

Despite this and all that happened later between us, I know we *wanted* to love each other and that my brother Hiram and I *could* have loved each other. But my mother wouldn't let us.

I'll always remember this incident. I was sick in bed, as I was most of the time in Nicaragua—sick with fevers. This time I was sleeping in my mother's bedroom. It had a balcony and I hadn't seen the outdoors for I don't know how long because my mother thought the air might harm me. Suddenly, I heard the drumming of the *gigantes*, the *gordos*—enormous, fat giant figures manipulated under covers by men—advertising the *lotería*. The giants represented the huge amount of money you could win if you played the lottery. I loved them! When I heard their drumming, I turned to my brother, Hiram, who was in the room, and said, "José *¡allí van los gordos de la lotería!*" We called him José at the time.

Hiram said, "You want to see them, right?"

"*Sí...*"

"*Te voy a cubrir bien, bien, bien para que los veas.*" (I'm going to cover you really really well, so you can see them.) Hiram wrapped me up in all these sheets, and carried me to the balcony so I could see them. We were just at the balcony when the daughter of one of the servants came in and yelled, "*¡Ay!* You have the *niña* on the balcony!"

The girl ran downstairs and told her mother who told her to run and get my mother. Mami came rushing in, her eyes ablaze, her face contorted. She started beating Hiram with her purse, with its leather straps; she pinched his face, she socked him. I don't know how long she beat him.

When she was done, she made Hiram kneel on floor with his arms out, right in front of me. Then she lay down in bed with me. I looked at Hiram and felt the blood draining out of me. I kept looking at him, feeling this horrible sadness.

My mother caught the expression on my face and said, "What's the matter with you? Why are you looking like that? You look terrible."

"Because José is kneeling down like that and he's hurting."

She felt my forehead and said, "Oh, my God, *estás prendida con fiebre!*" (You're burning with fever!) She turned to Hiram and said, "Now see what you did to her?" And she started to beat him again.

I don't remember anything after that. I passed out and went into a coma; I stayed gone for three days.

EL JUICIO (JUDGMENT DAY)

I don't remember my father ever beating us when we were in Nicaragua—that would come later. Although my siblings always got it, my mother only hit me once in Nicaragua. I remember it clearly. I was around four years old; Papi, Ivan, and Zela were already in the United States.

Mami was in her room, combing her hair. I had just heard the Indian women talking about *el Juicio*—Judgment Day—the time when the world would come to an end. Something about that talk among the *Indias* riveted me. Something in me connected with the idea of the end of the world. I remember thinking to myself, "I have to find out when it's going to happen. I have to find out how much time I have." I was not conscious of why this was so important to me, only that I had to find out.

Mami had long, long hair and in those days they didn't have brushes in Nicaragua, only very big combs. So, she was combing her long hair with the big comb when I came racing into her room.

"Mamita," I asked, "*¿Cuando es el Juicio?*" (When is the end of the world?)

My mother looked at me. Without warning, she smacked my arm with the comb so hard, it left a stinging red mark. "Don't ever talk about that again!" she said, glaring at me. Tears filled my eyes as I slinked out óf her room, holding my arm. The red mark was burning like the warning about discussing *el Juicio*. But I had to find out. I had to know how much time I had. So, despite my mother's warning, I went back to where the *Indias* were talking and asked, "*¿Y cuando es el Juicio? ¿En cuanto tiempo?*" (How soon?)

They looked at me. "*M'ija*," one of them finally said. "*¿Y tu porqué quieres saber?*" (Why do you want to know?)

"*Quiero saber cuanto tiempo tengo. Cuantos años voy a tener cuando llega el Juicio.*" (I want to know how much time I have. How old I'll be when the end of the world comes.)

"*Vas a tener ochenta y cuatro años.*" (You're going to be eighty-four years old.)

The answer satisfied me. "*Bueno*," I said, as I left. Being eighty-four years old sounded far enough away that I would have time. Time for *what*, did not enter my conscious mind.

MICAELA'S MAGIC

The only other time in Nicaragua when my mother was about to hit me happened when both of us were at her office in the jewelry store. I don't remember what I did but she looked at me with those eyes and said, "When we get home, you're going to get hit with the *coyunda*, or "cat of nine tails."
Nine pieces of leather bound together and used specifically for whipping children, a common practice at that time in Nicaragua.

In the garden of our house
in *La Hormiga de Oro*

I was scared, so scared! As we neared the house, while we were still half a block away, I saw Micaela. She had come out to meet us. Micaela had never done this before, and never did again. Terrified, I blurted, "*Micaela, mi mamá me va a pegar con la coyunda!*" (Micaela, my mother is going to hit me with the *coyunda*!)

Micaela, in her magical way, just came up to me and said nonchalantly, "Oh, no, no, no. Come, come. *Vamos, vamos.*" She took my hand and off we went, leaving my mother. By the time I saw her again later that day, my mother had forgotten all about the fact that she was going to beat me. Micaela's magic saved me from that whipping.

TÍA HILDA

Tía Hilda, Mami's sister, lived with us for a time. When I was between two and three years old, I heard a few times about Tía Hilda's husband. I think his name was Simón. The adults were saying how Simón hurt Tía a lot. He would get drunk and beat her up really bad. Tía Hilda's brothers finally took Tía out of her husband's home, and protected her until Simón moved away and left Tía alone. That's why she came to live with us. Simón never bothered her again after that.

I remember one funny story about Tía Hilda and Simón. When Tía lived at the family home in Masatepe, Simón was courting her. Tía was in *la sala*, the living room, sitting in her special sewing chair, embroidering. Next to her, on a small table, were her sewing basket and colorful threads. She had her favorite thimble on her finger and was not expecting company. Focused on her needle work, she did not know that Simón was standing in the back of the room, admiring her.

Tía needed to expel gas. Feeling very comfortable, *se tiró un pedo.* She farted.

Simón cleared his throat. Tía recognized him instantly and automatically flicked her hand and threw her thimble to the floor, thinking she could disguise the sound of her fart. As she did so, she meant to say, "Oh, I dropped my thimble!" But instead, the words that came out of her mouth were *"se me cayó el pedo!"* (I dropped my fart!)

TíA HILDA AND TERESA

As I write, the face of Teresa, a Native slave girl, appears in my mind. She belonged to Tía Hilda. For a long, long time, many *Indias* had to give their children away just so the children could have food and shelter. Tía Hilda had very little money and so she and her children, Hector Luís, Armando, and Alejandrina, lived with us. Papá Juan, my grandfather, who lived in Masatepe, would travel a couple of days by horseback to bring her money.

I remember Tía Hilda would shed a lot of tears, wringing her hands as she jumped up and down, and then would walk around in a circle, crying out to God for *misericordia* (mercy) and help with her *desesperación*. After that, she would go and beat up Teresa, who was probably eight years old—or younger.

There were times when she was first evil with Teresa, and then would cry, jump in circles, shake, and beg God for *misericordia* and help with her *desesperación*.

Teresa was really screaming this one time. By then I was walking and remember crossing *el patio*, which was kind of dark. A kerosene lamp was lit in Tía Hilda's room, and the light cast shadows against the wall. I could see Tía Hilda banging Teresa's head against the wall. Soon, Teresa stopped screaming. Tía Hilda stopped. My heart stopped. Step by step, I moved closer until I was close enough to see the blood coming down Teresa's face.

I loved Teresa. Her face at that moment stays in my mind.

Next, I am aware that Tía Hilda is putting a large round porcelain bowl, *un basín*, for washing the face and body, down on the floor. Somehow, she was holding Teresa, washing her head with the water in *el basín*. At some point, when I looked at *el basín*, I saw red liquid in it. I believed it was filled with Teresa's blood, and my mind went blank. It wasn't until many years later that

I realized it was not all Teresa's blood in *el basín*, but a mixture of blood and water.

A few nights later, Papá Juan rode in, and went straight to Tía Hilda, scolding her severely. He was very angry. Tía Hilda shed tears, jumped in circles, and begged God for *misericordia* and help with her *desesperación*.

Then, days later it seems, Teresa's mother came from out of town and she and Tía Hilda sat down to talk. I saw Teresa sitting on the curb of *el patio*. I was filled with fear, but something within calmed my fear and helped me walk toward her and go sit next to Teresa. No words were spoken as I could not yet talk. But we were sitting there together when Teresa's mother approached us. I remember her smiling face and was filled with fear again as she beckoned Teresa in a frightfully sweet voice, "*Ven aquí, mi hijita.*"

Moving towards her mother, Teresa cried, "*¡No, mamá, no!*" When she was within grabbing distance, her mother's face turned ugly, her eyes fierce. She pulled Teresa toward her with one hand, while the other hand appeared out from behind her back gripping a *coyunda*, the dreaded "cat of nine tails."

The mother then whipped and whipped Teresa. When she stopped, Teresa was on her back on the ground, her legs kicking from the pain. I felt something draining down from my head, all the way down my body, arms, and legs, and felt myself urinating out of control.

After a while, Tía Hilda, her kids, and Teresa moved to their own house. Times were still hard financially for Tía. But things got a little better for Teresa. She was still smacked on the face and head, got shaken and her hair pulled, but for the next few years I lived in Nicaragua, Teresa did not get those horrible beatings anymore.

TÍA HILDA TRIES TO GET HAPPY

When Tía and her family moved from our house in the San Antonio *barrio* to a place a few blocks away, Mami was worried because Tía was crying and crying and very depressed. Finally, Mami said, "*Mira*, Hilda, you need to get happy. Why don't you buy a bottle of *ron*, take a few drinks, and get happy?" Tía didn't look interested.

A few weeks later, our family went to Tía's place. She did not answer the door, so Mami walked in. We followed her. We found Tía close to the door, lying on the floor with her face down, her right hand holding an open bottle of *ron* on the floor beside her. Tía's face was soaked in tears mixed with dirt.

Mami screamed, "*¡Hilda! ¿Qué estás haciendo?*" (What are you doing?) Between screams, cries, and sobs, Tía answered, "*¡Me estóy poniendo alegre!*" (I'm making myself happy!)

Tía Hilda decided that she did not like that kind of happiness—nor *el licór.*

Eventually Tía's household moved to Masatepe. She got a job as a teacher in a school for poor children. One time when I was in Masatepe, visiting my great aunt, Tía Yita, Tía Hilda came to visit. She looked very nervous, shedding tears, wringing her hands, and shuffling her feet. Tía Yita's daughter, Miriam, went to her and took her aside to talk. I could see Tía Hilda was in a state of *desesperación.* She had removed all her eyebrows and had a thin pencil line in their place. That day was the first time I felt a conscious sadness for Tía Hilda. I was about three years old.

TÍO ALFONSO, *EL BUENO*

My favorite uncle, Tío Alfonso, never married. He was very handsome. Sometimes, he would get very drunk and stay with us for a while.

Mami seemed to care a lot for her brother. Tío was taken care of during those drunk times. Meals would be brought to him, and there was a caring feeling in the house when he was there that I didn't feel at any other time in our house.

When Tío was drunk, I was not allowed to be in the room alone with him, only with Mami there. Once, when he was drunk, Mami and I entered the room. When he saw me, he got all happy and stumbled toward me to hug me. Mami immediately pulled me away and Tío fell down. Mami helped him up, sat him down, and we left the room.

I only knew a few words at that time, so my thinking was different then. It was like a wave, a knowing feeling in me that caused me to believe that Tío Alfonso would not have hurt me. He was drunk, but his heart felt good to me. I did not have the same feeling about him that I had when I was around my father—that strange feeling in my stomach that made my skin move. Tío's smell, whether he was drunk or not, was all right with me. But I never liked Papi's smell. Not ever. I would feel a little upset when I'd be close to Papi's smell. I would feel a slight nausea.

So Tío would get through his drunk period and spend time with Mami and the family. When Tío was around, Mami didn't go into her violent rages. Tío never stayed for very long though.

Once, during a visit, Tío brought me a deer as a pet. I loved the deer. The deer really liked me, too. But, somehow, that wave of feeling told me the deer wanted to leave. I was so little, those thoughts just came and went. I didn't know about solutions.

One day, someone left the front door open. The deer ran through *el patio, la sala,* and out the front door. It got killed by a car. It took me several minutes to hear and understand that the deer was dead and gone.

I cried and cried. An adult said that the deer was wild; naturally, he could not be happy in *el patio.* The deer ran, wanting the space of the wild. I think that was the first time that I actually thought "solution." I wished the deer could have been in the wild instead of in *el patio.*

During his next visit, Tío Alfonso heard about the death of the deer and sought me out. He said he was sad to hear about my deer friend, and he talked to me as if I were somebody, like an adult, even. Afterwards, I went looking for Micaela, feeling like I was somebody.

Tío's last drunk was before he brought me the deer. He never got drunk again.

When we moved to the house by *La Hormiga de Oro,* Tío's visits became infrequent. Mami was very proud of him, though. He had found a good government job in Costa Rica.

Tío came to visit for the last time a few weeks before we left Nicaragua to go to the United States. We never saw him again. He would write to Mami, though, and tell her how he loved Costa Rica; this was home, now. Costa Rica liked him, too: He was promoted in his job and was now traveling throughout Central America, and sometimes to Mexico, representing Costa Rica. Mami said Tío was like an ambassador now.

When I was about twelve years old, Tío stopped writing. No one in the family knew what happened to him.

A few years later, word came from Tía Hilda that Tío Alfonso had died. She learned that Tío some time earlier had confessed to the authorities that he had killed a man, and that he wanted to be incarcerated. The authorities checked out Tío's story but could not find the man or his body, or any evidence of a murder, or even that such a man existed. They refused to prosecute Tío.

But Tío insisted that he had killed a man and demanded to be incarcerated. On his demand, the authorities put Tío in a jail cell, leaving the door unlocked. He was in a cell by himself and knew he was free to leave anytime. But Tío remained in that cell until he died.

Years later my daughter, Wanda, was going through some old family photographs when she called to ask me about a family member she didn't recognize. "Mom, who *is* this queen?" she asked. "He looks just like my beautiful gay son." I had no idea. The next time I saw her, she had the photo in hand.

It was Tío Alfonso.

THE ROOSTER & THE HEN

I started talking with animals early, when I was around three years old. People said animals were dumb, but I never believed them because I experienced their intelligence. And for that reason, I didn't fear them, either. I remember hearing relatives telling my mother things like, "Don't go see your cousins now because there's a lion loose out there." And I would think to myself, "The lion wouldn't hurt me because I would talk to him."

When I was around four or five years old, my mother gave me two little chicks—a hen and a rooster. We'd sit and talk for long periods and they'd follow me around everywhere. We were a team! They grew bigger, and we continued to hang around, playing, talking, running, doing things, always together.

One morning, I was sitting on the ground with my two little friends, talking, when the new cook showed up. She came right up to where I was sitting with my friends, talking, and then suddenly reached down and grabbed the hen by the neck. "We're going to have her for lunch," she said, heading back into the kitchen.

"Noooo!" I screamed, racing after her. I tried to grab the hen away from the cook, but she pushed me away. As I fell back, the cook quickly shuffled her hands and rung the hen's neck. Right there, in front of me, she killed my little friend. And when she was done, she threw the dead chicken at me.

I was in such a state of shock, no tears came. I just remember holding onto my little friend and hugging her dead body. The next thing I remember is being up on the roof of the house next to the water cistern. I don't remember how I managed to get up there or how long I was there before a couple of men I didn't know found me, crouched over, holding my chicken. When they brought me to my mother, she grabbed the chicken out of my arms and scolded me severely. It was on her orders that the cook had killed the little hen, she told me. I was put to bed that night without dinner.

Two or three days later, my mother came to me and said, "Today we're having the rooster for lunch—and I don't want any *problemas, me oyes* (do you hear me)?"

They killed my little rooster, and at lunch time my mother came and got me. I had to eat him. So, I sat there, totally numb, eating my rooster. The only thought that went through my head was, "Well, my little friend tastes good."

It wasn't until I was in my thirties that I could again talk with animals. But it was never the same. Something inside me was killed when my little hen and rooster were killed, and I have never gotten over it. I have never allowed myself to go through what I'm going through right now, remembering. I have never been able to cry about it—until now.

MAMI, WHO DANCED WITH THE SNAKES

When she was very little, no more than a toddler, Mami had this relationship with snakes. It really scared her parents. Snakes always seemed to find her, wherever she was—and the snakes would dance with her.

Tía Yita told me that my grandparents were desperate, wanting to get rid of the snakes. So, on several occasions the whole family would leave the house for days at a time. They would sprinkle sawdust all over the floor of the house, thinking that by the time they got back they would be able to see the tracks of any snakes that came in, and find them wherever they were.

The family would come back home and, invariably, they would find no snake tracks in the sawdust. They'd settle in and a short while later, they'd go to my mother's room where, to their horror, they would find little Esmeralda dancing with the snakes! The snakes would weave back and forth, and my mother would be swaying with them. They never could figure out how the snakes got in.

There was something else that scared my grandparents. Mami could see things. From the time she was very little, she could see things that were going to happen in the future. And whatever she saw, always came true. She used to climb up a certain tree and sit there, and that's where she would see into the future.

One day, when she was four years old, sitting in her tree, Mami had the most horrific vision. There was an *Indio* that Mami loved dearly; he also loved her and took good care of her. In her vision, she saw four men grab her beloved *Indio*, chopping him to death with machetes.

Mami fell out of the tree and was kicking and screaming and crying, horrified by her vision. When people rushed over to see what had happened to her, Mami cried out what she'd seen in her vision. Later that evening, the *Indio* was brought home dead, wrapped in a blood-soaked blanket, having been hacked to death with machetes.

After this incident, my grandparents decided they *had* to find a medicine man who could take away their daughter Esmeralda's powers. But before they found somebody, Mami foresaw her own mother's death. Her family assured her that this vision could not be true. "Look at how healthy your mother is! Look at how strong she is!" Her mother did not die right away, within hours of Mami's vision as had happened with the *Indio*. But a few years later, her mother got sick with cancer and died when Mami was only nine.

My grandparents soon found a medicine man, a *curandero*, who took away her powers. But something else happened to Mami. When the powers were taken away, my mother was left open and vulnerable—she became a blank open space into which evil spirits entered. That's what my Tía Yita believed. So did Mami, much later in life, close to when she died. And that's what I believe happened, too.

I could sense it from the time I was little, long before I knew what had happened to her. Something was terribly wrong with my mother. I would watch Mami and she would be talking to me and all of a sudden her eyes would go blank. I would look at her, keep looking at her, right into her face, and her eyes would be completely blank. She got that way each time she had her evil episodes and went into her violence. Mami would also get that look when she would tell stories—she would fabricate these elaborate stories. I always knew they were not true because of the look in her eyes. She was going someplace that was obviously real to her—but not to anyone else. Much later, I would do the same thing.

A few years after Mami's powers were taken away, her mother, Hortensia—the strong, healthy one—got sick with cancer. Hortensia ran a little store out of her house, mostly for the Native people who would come to buy things. They often had no money and my grandmother would let them buy on credit. She never made any money running that store because she never got paid back in full; she just broke even. But she kept it going because the people needed it. *Her* people. My grandmother never tried to run away from her own Native roots; she was proud of them.

When Hortensia got sick with cancer, my grandfather, Papá Juan, deserted her. It was Mami who took care of my grandmother. According to my Tía Yita, "That little girl worked and worked and worked and never left her mother's side." Tía Yita said, "Your Mami would cry when she would see her father pass by the street where they lived, right on the sidewalk, right in front of the door of their house, with a woman on his arm—and sometimes two women on his arms. Laughing and drunk."

That's when my mother began to hate my grandfather. I knew she didn't like him because whenever he came over on horseback from Masatepe, she'd be very cold, ice cold with him.

When Mami's mother, Hortensia, died, *Indios* came streaming down from all over the hills to pay their respects.

Papi's Papá

In the days when my father was born, the Catholic Church had a great hold on the people. There was deep fear of punishment for sins, especially the great sins where sinners in their wickedness would come face-to-face with the devil. Among those great sins were heresy, witchcraft, and a woman having sex with a priest. Those sins brought eternal damnation to the sinners and suffering not only to their children but also their grandchildren, great grandchildren, and future generations.

Just hearing that there could be a woman who would take part in such wickedness as having sex with a priest would leave one wondering, "Has she no fear? How could she walk into the hellfire and damnation like that?"

As a child in Nicaragua, I heard a story about such a woman once. I don't remember whose house we were in—perhaps relatives. I just remember that it was in Managua, and it was dark already. I see *Indias* sitting on the floor by *el patio*. They had heard of a woman who had sinned with a priest. The energy of disbelief and deep dark fear filled the air.

A few years later, when we were living in the States, I found out that my grandfather, Papi's father, was a Catholic priest. Perhaps it was the simple way my parents told me this shocking news (they did some things right!), but

I didn't feel any of the fire of hell, the damnation, or the dark fear in the air. Although over the years, it was something I would give thought to every now and then, wondering, especially, about my grandmother—how it was for her, how she lived.

Papi's parents died before any of us were born. We never knew them. Only one of the children, Tío Virgilio, the youngest, had a photograph of their father. None had a photograph of their mother. When I was grown, I heard that they all wished that they had a photo of their mother; none, however, had any desire to have a photo of their father.

Papi would occasionally tell us stories about his parents, Papá y Mamá. The same two or three stories were repeated each time. Only one story, the one about his mother, was pleasant. The others were very sad, yet Papi added humor to them.

Papi's stories about his father, the priest, were about the whippings they would get, severe whippings that sometimes made them pass out. Papá would always tell Papi, "I'm going to whip you so God won't have to punish you. You should be grateful that you only have to deal with being whipped by me, and not with the greater punishments of God!"

The two stories Papi told most about his father went like this.

Once, Papi's father told him to get *un basín* and all the necessary items so Papi could wash his father's feet and cut his toenails. In those days, people cut their toenails with a sharp blade that looked like a pocketknife. Papi obeyed, gathering all the things he needed. He soaked his father's feet in the *basín*, dried them, and reached for the blade to cut the toenails. But the blade slipped out of Papi's hand, and cut his father's big toe!

After declaring the kindness he was about to render by whipping Papi, and thus sparing him the wrath of God, Papá beat Papi until he fell unconscious. Papi would always laugh telling this story, recalling his father's priestly sermon about the "kindness" he was about to render by whipping him.

The other story is about a time when Papi and his brother, my Tío Pedrito, were sent on errands by their father. They enjoyed themselves so much that they were late heading home, and knew they would be in serious trouble. By this age, however, they had discovered that their father could become easily confused. So they planned a strategy to confuse *el señor*.

It was dark when they got home. Papi went to the door and knocked while Pedrito hid in the bushes. Papá answered the door with the leather belt in his hand. "Where is Pedro?" he asked. Papi pointed behind him and said,

"He's back there somewhere." His father said, "Go get Pedro and bring him here!"

Papi left and took Pedrito's place. Pedrito knocked on the door. His father answered with the leather in his hand. Seeing only Pedrito, he asked, "Where is Juan Humberto?" Pedrito pointed behind him and said, "He's back there somewhere." Papá ordered Pedrito to go get Juan Humberto. This went on until their father got confused and tired, and finally went to bed. The boys snuck in, went to bed, and were up early the next morning and out in the fields at work when Papá rose to ride his horse into town, to tend to his church and priestly duties. The boys were victorious that time, and enjoyed reminiscing about that story.

PAPI'S MAMÁ

The story Papi used to tell about his mother was hilarious because of the faces he would make as he told it. Sometimes we laughed so hard our eyes would close and we'd miss the next face and beg Papi please to repeat it, so we could see the next face.

Papi and Pedrito were still pretty little. They were in their hut in *el campo*. It was dark. The candles—made of mutton fat and poured into clay jars with wicks—were lit, and the boys were sitting on the bench next to the dining table. Their mother was feeding them supper, warm milk served in a round gourd with bread.

Papi looked at his bread and then looked at Pedrito's bread. Pedrito's bread looked so much bigger, Papi hung his head and felt sad. Pedrito and their mother stopped and looked at Papi. Papi sniffled a little and put much emotion into his little face. Their mother asked Papi what was wrong. Without looking up, Papi told her that Pedrito's bread was bigger than his. Their mother said, "¡Ay, dios mío!" She took Pedrito's bread and exchanged it with Papi's.

Papi lifted his head and, happily, looked at the bread by his bowl and then looked at Pedrito's bread. Papi again hung his head and started sniffling and simpering. Their mother asked, "Now, what's the matter?"

Papi whimpered, "Pedrito's bread is bigger than mine."

Without a word, their mother gently took Papi's bread and exchanged it with Pedrito's. Without a word, Papi took the bread, crumbled pieces in the milk and started eating. His mother smiled. Papi smiled.

Papi and Pedrito's stories were only about each other. They never told stories about the other siblings, who were, from oldest to youngest, Erlinda, Berta, Lola, Ernesto (who became a movie star in Mexico and would have nothing to do with the family ever again), and Virgilio.

MAMI Y PAPI

From time to time, Native women would come to the jewelry store my parents owned to see Mami with their newborn babies. "This baby belongs to your husband," they would say. "I didn't want to do this." They would tell her that they needed help. She would always look at the baby to find the resemblance, and then she always would help—for years she would help them.

After Papi left for the States, my mother set up a big room in our house where people who didn't have anything to eat could come and be served dinner. One time a frail old lady came to our house and said to me, "*M'ijita, soy una viejita de setenta y ocho años y no he comido.*" (Little one, I'm a seventy-eight-year-old lady and I haven't eaten.)

I ran to Mami and said, breathlessly, "*¡Mami, hay una viejita de setenta y ocho años y no ha comido!*" (Mami, there's a little old lady who's seventy-eight years old and she hasn't eaten!) Mami said to me, "*Si tiene setenta y ocho años, ella sí ha comido....*" (If she's seventy-eight years old, she definitely has eaten....)

ADIOS, NICARAGUA; MICAELA, ADIOS

I was nearly four when Papi, for political reasons, left for the United States, taking my sister, Zela, and my brother, Ivan. Mami, Hiram, and I stayed behind. My parents were opposed to the dictator, Anastasio Somoza, Sr., and Papi was spending most of his time in jail. He would have been killed already if it hadn't been for the fact that Papi was an illegitimate cousin of *el General* Somoza. They had played together and had some closeness as children. However, it began to look as if Papi were pressing his luck if he stayed any longer. My parents had been preparing for Papi's departure for a while

Four years later, in 1948, my mother and Hiram and I also moved away. My father had been calling and calling my mother, urging her to come join him. He had been having a hard time making it in the States and since they had done so well together in Nicaragua, he thought they would be successful again once she joined him. She finally agreed, and so I had to leave Micaela, the dearest one in my life, and my Nicaraguan home with all the fragrances of the tropical fruits and flowers, my wild animal friends, and the ocean with all the precious colorful seashells.

A few months before we left Nicaragua to join Zela, Ivan, and my father in the United States, I was sitting quietly at home, looking outside at the narrow, unpaved streets. I could smell the Earth and the scent of the vanilla, strawberry, and prune ice cream wafting out of the candy store at the corner. Suddenly, the whole panorama in front of me changed. The narrow unpaved streets turned very wide and everything was paved in concrete. There were no pungent smells of Earth or of fruits and flowers, or of food cooking on street corners. I did not see or feel the familiar sun. And there was something else in the vision. It made everything look gray. Later, I learned that it was called "fog."

CHAPTER 3

COMING OF AGE IN THE U.S.

My parents thought they could make it in the States because they made quality jewelry. But it didn't work out that way.

It is part of the culture for Indian people to have gold—although it means something very different than what it means to most North Americans. So no matter how poor they were, the *Indios* managed to get and keep quality gold. The same was true of Nicaraguans as a whole, and *La Joyería Sánchez* was the place to go. By the time we got to the States, however, the mass production of jewelry had started and people were more focused on cost than quality.

We first went to Long Beach, California, where my father had been living, but in less than a year, we all moved to San Francisco, where we had family, to see if we could do better there. We stayed with my father's aunts, Tía Goyita (and her husband Carlos) and Tía Lolita, all of whom lived with Tía Goyita's daughter, Delia. Soon after, we moved to a boarding house where the six of us lived in one room, sharing a bathroom with the rest of the tenants. My first Christmas in the States was spent in that boarding house. I had been used to getting tricycles and all kinds of things. That Christmas, I got some plastic toys from the five-and-dime store.

The only bright light in those desperate days was that it was a time— the only time—when I felt love from my sister, Zela. She seemed genuinely happy to see me when we moved to the States, and when we were in that one room in the boarding house, she and I would sleep in the same bed.

At some point when we were living in the boarding house, my mother went back to Nicaragua for a couple of months to take care of business. When she was gone, my father would make me sleep with him. I would beg him to let me sleep in the other bed with my sister, Zela. But he would make me sleep with him—and he would molest me.

I wanted to vomit whenever I smelled him. One morning I remember waking up feeling sick. My brother had come down with the flu; I just felt sick. I tried to get up to go to the bathroom but my legs wouldn't carry me. I fell down and had pain. That's all I remember; I was probably nine.

SÁNCHEZ STREET

From the boarding house, we moved to Sánchez Street in the Mission area, where my parents set up a store in front of the building where we lived. The house had no bathtub or refrigerator. In Nicaragua, we were among the first to have refrigeration.

My father and mother kept struggling, but no one wanted to buy Papi's jewelry. It was too expensive. So, he tried to make it repairing watches and then as a factory employee. My sister, Lotus, was born when we lived in this house. It was 1950; she was born thirteen days before I turned ten. Lotus and I were the only siblings in my family who genuinely loved each other.

GERMANIA STREET

Soon after Lotus was born, we moved to Germania Street where we lived for three or four months in a house in an alley, surrounded by abandoned buildings. All I remember from the short time we were there was an incident with my father.

My parents had sent me to the corner store to get something. I saw a friend there and stopped to talk. I guess I must have taken too long, because Papi came looking for me. He came into the store and I smiled when I saw him, but with one very hard slap, he smacked the smile off my face. Angrily grabbing my arm, he pulled me out of the store toward the alley. That's when he tried to take me into one of the abandoned buildings. As little as I was, I had just turned ten, I knew that he must have checked out these abandoned buildings before. I also knew that if he were able to get into one of the buildings, he would have beaten and sexually molested me. However, that day, the abandoned buildings were all bolted shut and I escaped the punishment.

30

Every time I went into the corner store after that, the Chinese guy who worked there would laugh at me and say, "Here comes daddy..."

DIVISADERO STREET

I turned eleven not long after we got to Divisadero. Except for the time when he smacked me at the store, I had never seen my father beat any of us, until we were at Divisadero Street. Years later I learned that he had beaten my sister, Zela, when they were living in southern California before the rest of us came to the States. Zela was having her period and my father wanted to give her an enema. She refused, so he beat her. But I never saw him hit anyone until we were at Divisadero. Twice I saw him hit my brothers because they had gotten into some kind of trouble on the streets. Each time, he made them take off their shirts and kneel. He whipped their bare backs with a belt.

I also remember my father talking about how he beat my brother Ivan because he wouldn't stop laughing. Ivan had a great laugh. It was a tickling, wheezing laugh and I loved it when we laughed together. Ivan actually tried to stand up for me when we were in the States. He took me on his paper route early in the morning in the little red wagon, and I loved it when we used to laugh together. One time when Ivan was laughing, Papi told him to stop. When he wouldn't or couldn't, Papi beat him and beat him until he finally stopped laughing. Papi would later brag about how he beat the laughter out of Ivan.

Sometime while we were there, on Divisadero, my father abandoned us. He left under the pretense of going on a business trip to Nicaragua, but he never came back, leaving my mother behind with five children and no job. His brother, my Tío Virgilio, was a Somozista

My brother, Ivan

and he had persuaded Somoza to allow my father back as long as Papi promised to keep his mouth shut and stay out of trouble.

For a while, he sent my mother Nicaraguan cheese to sell. But that didn't last long and soon she had to go out and find a job, speaking no English. That's when my mother started beating me, smacking me across the

31

face. It's also when I began to be a servant in my own home. I had been going to St. Dominic's School and had to rush home to take care of my little sister, Lotus. My mother was working and my sister Zela had gotten married and left home. I would start the cooking, wash the clothes, and iron my brothers' shirts. I had no time for homework, and started having blackouts in school.

I remember times when my teacher was at one end of the blackboard, beginning a problem. I would concentrate hard because I wanted very much to understand what the nun was saying. The next thing I knew, she would be at the other end of the board and I had no idea what had happened in between. A therapist later told me that this is what happens to much abused children.

It was also this year, when I was eleven, that I was wetting my bed every night. In Nicaragua I had had kidney problems and experienced bedwetting. But now it happened every night—and as punishment, my mother would not let me change the sheets. I had to sleep in the urine-soaked sheets night after night. I was so miserable, I used to get a board and go into the closet and bang my head with it to try to knock myself out. I prayed and prayed that I would wake up and stop wetting the bed. I even tried tying the *basinilla* (chamber pot) onto my rear end, but it didn't work. I had awful blisters, full of pus, all over my butt; the scars remained for years.

I remember coming home after school one day and as I started to go through my mother's bedroom to get to mine, my mother and my sister and brothers were in there, waiting for me. My mother held a dead mouse by the tail, which they said they found in my bed. They taunted me, saying it had died from the fumes. "That's how disgusting you are," they said. "Not even a mouse can live with you." It hurt so bad, there was nothing I could do except look at the dead mouse, walk past them, and lie down on my stinking bed. Eventually, the mattress rotted.

We lived above an antique store on Divisadero. An old man named Mr. Miller owned it and one day when I went next door to do the laundry at the laundromat, he started to talk to me. He talked to me as if I were a real person. He asked me about my report card. No one ever cared about my report card or asked me about it. I began to visit him at the antique store, the back door of which led to our back yard. I ran out into the yard whenever my mother called, because I wasn't allowed out of the house. He started taking such an interest in me, started to give me little presents, started to give me advice…and started to molest me.

32

I kept going back to see him. For nearly one year, I kept going back. I felt sure that Mr. Miller cared for me. He kept telling me to "watch out" for this and "don't do" that, giving me gifts, and talking to me like a real person. Yet here he was *molesting* me. I knew what he was doing was wrong and that it had to stop. But I didn't know how to stop it. I was confused and full of guilt because I knew this was a sin—a *big* sin. To make matters worse, I was going to communion every week, without having confessed this big sin—a huge sin! I was terrified of going to hell, terrified of confessing, terrified of stopping.

I wrote a poem when I was eleven that captures what I was feeling.

Darkness is a child,
Who in her solitude,
Thoughts run wild.
Love and hate!
Love and hate!
O run child,
Meet your fate.

You must flee
Never to return,
Try to drown the inner fire,
Don't let it burn.

You must leave this place,
So you may find,
This world, this life,
This God, is also kind…

Somewhere, you will find the light,
And no more must your rushed
Emotions fight,
For your tense being will be calm,
Knowing no more must your face escape
The dreaded, fierce, fiery palm.

During this dark time, I read a book about Saint Maria Goretti. I don't know how I came across it; I must have picked it up at the school library. But I loved her. Maria Goretti was not yet twelve when she told a man she would rather die than have somebody defile her body, and was stabbed to death as a result. I read her story over and over and over again. In my English sentences at school, it was "Maria Goretti this" and "Maria Goretti that." My teacher said, "You really like Maria Goretti, don't you?" She is the first saint I completely loved.

I think Saint Maria Goretti helped me break from Mr. Miller. From reading about her and praying to her, I had strong feelings of wanting to be pure. In my own way, I had been trying to stop seeing Mr. Miller. I knew I couldn't tell my mother because she would be sure to blame me for it and then I would really get it, but I once tried telling the lady next door. I said, "Mr. Miller does nasty things." She didn't believe me, however, saying "Oh, he's such a nice man!"

I knew the only way to end it—to stop the cycle of seeing him in order to get attention only then to get molested—would be to do something that would make me afraid of ever seeing him again. So, one day I went downstairs to the store when only his wife was there, and I told her everything. I told her that Mr. Miller did nasty things, that he showed me nasty pictures, and did things he shouldn't do to little girls. She looked at me with disbelief, and her first response was to say it couldn't be so. But then I told her things that he had told me about *her*—sexual things.

That's when she knew I was telling the truth. It must have been devastating for her, but she was very nice and said, "I'm sorry, dear. Thank you for telling me. I will take care of it."

The next time I went to confession, I confessed everything. I'm not even sure what I said, but I put words to what had been going on and felt so much better afterwards. It was *over*. I never went back to see Mr. Miller again. After that, when I took the staircase down from our apartment, I went right, towards the laundromat, instead of left, towards the antique store. If Mr. Miller ever accidentally looked up and saw me, he turned his head. He did not want to see me.

Turning to Violence

It was during this time, my eleventh year, that I began to like violence.

I had made friends with a neighborhood girl named Darlene. I wasn't allowed to go out except to do the laundry, so she would come over. She came every day, and every day I would beat her up.

Darlene kept coming back because she had no one else to play with—and because she was used to getting beaten. Her mother was a serious drunk who used to beat her all the time. They were Jehovah's Witnesses and lived above Kingdom Hall, so they would go to all meetings.

One morning I woke up thinking, "I don't ever want to beat Darlene again." It was an awareness that just came spontaneously as I woke up. "I will never beat her up again," I thought. It made me feel good to think that thought and to say it to myself.

Later, when Darlene came over, I said, "Darlene, I have a surprise for you!"

She said, "You're going to beat me up."

"No," I said, "I'm never going to beat you up again or hurt you in any way."

"Really?" she said.

"Really."

It turned into a wonderful friendship. Not only did I stop beating her, I became her protector.

One day when I was at the laundromat, I saw Darlene running down the street, her eyes were wild. A group of kids was chasing her. Before I knew it, I ran across the street and stood in front of her, between her and the kids. They all stopped, probably too stunned to know what to do. In a firm voice, I said, "Darlene, go into your house." Then I turned to the kids and, again, in a firm voice, poured out my heart. "Why do you want to hurt her?" I said. "She's got enough problems without you hurting her. You don't know what she goes through. Why do you want to hurt her? You better not ever hurt her! You hurt her, you're going to have to deal with me."

They looked at me like, who *is* this girl? At the head of the pack was a young Black boy. Something about what I said or how I said it touched that little kid.

"What does she go through?" he asked.

I said, "She gets beat up all the time. She doesn't need to get beat up. Her mama beats her every day."

The next thing I remember, the boy turned around and all the others followed. They never bothered Darlene again.

When my father used to buy me comic books, I liked all the super heroes, but my favorite was Mighty Mouse. Mighty Mouse was doing a really important job—taking care of the little mice that no one cared about. I wanted to be Mighty Mouse. When no one was around, I'd stick out my chest in front of my mother's vanity, like Mighty Mouse, and flex my muscles. I knew that when I rescued Darlene, I was being Mighty Mouse.

LIVING WITH MY MARRIED SISTER AT ESQUINA STREET

Sometime after my father abandoned us, my mother, now desperate and destitute, moved all of us, Hiram, Ivan, Lotus, and myself, to Esquina Street, near Cow Palace, to live with my sister, Zela, and her Polish-American husband. Zela had gotten married a year or so earlier, when she was eighteen.

Before my father abandoned us, Zela had fallen in love. She fell

Papi and I smile for the camera

deeply in love with a Nicaraguan boy, but my parents disapproved of the match. They put so much pressure on the young couple, they finally split up. It broke Zela's heart, and I think it broke his heart, too. They both married on the rebound.

Zela's life had always been hard, being beaten by my mother when she was a child and then by my father when she was a teenager. She doesn't remember much of her childhood except for a few searing experiences, like the time when she was only two or three and my parents burned her feet over red-hot coals because she wandered a block or two too far away from home. This was a common punishment in Nicaragua in those days. The other experience she remembers is when her appendix ruptured. The doctor came over and when he saw the condition she was in, he had to operate then and there. There was no way to get an ambulance to rush her to the hospital, so he operated on her where she was, on a cot in the patio—and without anesthesia. Zela remembers alcohol being poured on the open wound and biting on a pillow. Zela took all that. I can't even imagine it.

Right after she graduated from high school, Zela started working to help support us, and then she married this guy and got pregnant. That's when she changed. She had treated me decently ever since we came to the

36

States, *until* she got pregnant and had her baby. Then, she treated me like dirt. It was back to how it was when we were kids.

Later, I understood what happened to her because the same thing happened to me. I loved my baby sister, Lotus, dearly, but when I got pregnant, I couldn't stand to be around her. Fortunately, I recognized what was going on, so even though I had the same impulse as Zela, I was able to control it. And, fortunately, when my baby was born, those feelings ended and I couldn't wait to see Lotus again.

That's not how it turned out with Zela, however.

My mother was now living under my sister's thumb. The tables were turned. Mami was completely dependent on Zela and my older brothers, and although I had been my mother's favorite child, now that my sister and brothers controlled her, she would beat me for their benefit. It happened every day, never stopping.

I was in sixth grade, going to public school—Kate Kennedy Elementary School—and continued to suffer blackouts that to this day confound me. For example, I had grown grotesquely fat when I was eleven, living on Divisadero Street. But by the time I was at Kate Kennedy's, I was back to normal size. I have no memory of losing weight—just of being fat and then not. At first, the kids at school didn't like me but then I became popular. I actually had some friends and I used to hate to go home. I remember getting on the school bus and becoming very, very sad because of what was waiting for me at home—nothing but abuse and beatings.

We lived in a three-bedroom house. My sister and her husband had one room. My two brothers had another, and my mother, Lotus, and I shared the third bedroom. Lotus was in a crib and I slept on a navy cot. It was very uncomfortable. One day my mother and Zela started to take care of babies. They added several cribs to our room. When my mother had enough money from the babysitting, she bought two twin beds. I thought one was for me, so I started arranging the beds, and making her bed and what I thought was my bed.

"That's not your bed!" Mami said when she came in. "Put them back together like I had them."

She could see the disappointment in my face, so she went after me with a flyswatter, swatting even my face. She could be sparked just like that. I'll never forget that flyswatter, the sting.

It was around this time that my mother's beatings became frightening for other reasons. When she would beat me, she would get on top of me to hit me. She would grab my face with her hands and tell me, "I don't like that expression on your face! Take that expression off your face!" And with her hands, she would contort my face. She would twist my face to get a new expression. This happened several times when I was twelve and again when I was thirteen; maybe even when I was fourteen. I would look at her when she was on top of me. Her mouth would twist and contort and her tongue would hang out and she would make this ungodly sound.

One time, when she was on top of me like that, she was beating me and rubbing against me. I didn't know what was going on. Her eyes were rolling, her face contorting, her tongue hanging out, and she was rubbing and rubbing against me. I think she had a climax. I'm still not sure what happened, but it stays in my mind because of the sounds she made. Her face was ugly, though. Ugly.

One day, as I was washing out the tub and refilling it to take a bath, my mother grabbed me by the hair and slapped my face. Her face was contorted, her mouth curled, her eyes wild. She dragged me out of the bathroom by my hair and dropped me on the bed. Then my sister Zela went in, and took her bath.

The morning after that incident, I decided to die. I couldn't take it anymore and decided there was no sense in going on. There was only one way out—to die. I had heard friends say that if you took twenty aspirins, it would kill you. I heard it on the school bus one day, and it had been on my mind a lot. "Twenty aspirins would kill me."

So that morning, I woke up very early and went into the bathroom. I knelt down to pray and said, "God, I'm going to kill myself. I know I'm going to hell for this, but I also know that hell could not be worse than this." I took the bottle of aspirin out of the cabinet and started to take every pill. It was my first suicide attempt.

It took me a while. I had to drink lots of water, but I kept swallowing pills until I polished off the bottle. I was twelve years old and I thought that as soon as I finished taking the aspirin, I would drop dead. So I sat there, waiting to drop dead. I started to get a little anxious when nothing happened. I was hoping it would all be over with before the rest of the family got up. But the clock ticked on, and nothing happened. Soon everyone was up. I was still alive!

I went about the day as if nothing had happened, boarding the bus to go to school. However, right before we pulled into the school parking lot, I turned green. My friends asked me what was going on. I told them what I had done, but said, "Please, don't tell anyone," and started to vomit. Of course, my friends immediately ran and told the principal.

An ambulance took me to the hospital. I was falling asleep and they kept trying to keep me awake. At some point, when I was lying on a hospital bed, I felt someone punch my arm. I opened my eyes and saw my mother. She was furious. "You did this to hurt me. Now I'm going to kill myself—and it will be *your* fault."

I passed out again, and later awakened to see a doctor hovering over me. The first thing he said was, "Who is the boy?" I looked at him blankly. He saw that I was clueless and then said, "Okay, sweetheart, don't worry. We're going to take care of you...."

At home, I had left a note, saying, "I can't take this anymore. I can't take the way I'm treated and I want to die." When I was released from the hospital, Zela was at home crying, saying that I was blaming her. My mother said, "Zelima is stupid, crazy, lazy, and not worth even crying for." She told me I was a disgrace to the family and that I would be punished for this.

THE ORPHANAGE

It was now Christmas time in the house at Esquina Street and my baby sister, Lotus, who was around two, was drawn to the cheap shiny Christmas balls hanging on the tree. She walked over to touch one, and it fell and broke.

My big brother-in-law took off his belt and said, "Now you've had it." He was about to beat Lotus with the belt when I got in front of him and said, "No, you won't. NO!"

He yelled, "Get out of the way."

"No! Don't hit her," I insisted. He lunged to push me out of the way—and then drew back. It must have been the way I looked at him. He must have seen that I was ready to kill him. I *was* ready to kill him. He put away the belt.

A little later, when my sister and my mother and brothers got home from shopping, my brother-in-law was waiting for them. He

My little sister, Lotus

39

said to Zela, "I'm sorry, but your family is going to have to leave. I cannot live with Zelima. They've got to go. They can't stay here, anymore."

That's when my brother Hiram took off his belt and gave it to him, saying, "Here. Take her into the bedroom and do *whatever* you want with her. We won't stop you."

I'll never forget that word. *"Whatever."* That meant everything. Whatever he wanted to do with me he could do, and it was my own brother telling him so.

My brother-in-law knew better than to take up the offer. I was scared of him, that's for sure. But I was also ready to kill him—and he knew it. So he just said, casually, "Nah, nah. I don't want to do that."

My mother didn't say a word. She was terrified. What could she do? She was already a servant in my sister's house. We were right at the beginning of what was going to be a long, long time when my brothers and sister got even with my mother, paying her back for what she did to them when they were little. They got *so* even with my mother. She suffered, suffered, suffered with them. I saw this and made up my mind that I would never seek vengeance. I would rather die than seek vengeance on anybody. I saw that vengeance was ugly, as ugly as the other—perhaps even uglier.

Nobody said anything to me after this. I thought everyone had forgotten all about it when a few days later, I was told, "You're leaving."

"What?"

"You're going to Mt. St. Joseph's with the nuns."

It wasn't until we drove up into the hills and I saw the sign that I realized Mt. St. Joseph's was an orphanage. Mami and Zela took me, depositing me there without a word of farewell. They walked in with me and walked out without me, leaving me in the care of a nun who started spelling out orders: "This is your dorm. You will get up at 4:30 a.m. You will… "

I had to get up at 4:30 in the morning to get the kindergarten girls up and make sure they washed their faces and brushed their teeth and were ready for breakfast. Then I had to get myself ready for school. Every once in a while my family came to take me home. But when I was home, they turned me back into a servant.

I was in seventh grade, and since the orphanage school only went to sixth grade, I had to go to a school outside the orphanage. One day, on my way to school, I called my mother. She said, "Where are you calling from?"

"A phone booth."

"A phone booth! Where are you?" she demanded.

"On my way to school."

"On your way to school?"

"I take a bus."

"You take the bus? What??"

And that was it. They thought I was confined to the orphanage at all times. They did not want me outside anywhere. They did not want me taking a bus or going anywhere. They wanted me enclosed.

So I was taken out of the orphanage and put into a Catholic boarding school—Immaculate Conception. I wasn't there for very long, however. The feel of the whole place was different. It was a gentle place, and I fell in love with a very kind nun who was good to me. I ran away. It wasn't because I wanted to run away. In my needy child's mind, it was because I wanted the nun to ask me to come back. I wanted someone to say, "I want you. Come back!"

It didn't happen. Instead, I got kicked out and landed back home.

Then, of course, I got a beating for running away. This time, my mother said, "You will not go to school. You will not go anywhere. You will not watch television. You will not read. You will not go out to play. You will not receive phone calls. You will not look out the window. You will not go out in the backyard. You are going to work. At home."

That's when I became a full-time servant and a prisoner in my own home.

About a week later, my brother Hiram came into my room and said, "You're sleeping eight hours a night. That's too much for you. From now on, you will sleep six hours a night. You will have fifteen minutes to brush your teeth, ten minutes to get dressed, and then—get to work. Clean the house, do the laundry, cook. You are the servant here."

CALLING THE DEVIL

During this time, while I was the servant, my mother would slap me across the face with an open palm and then with the side of her hand. Every day. She would get that look, those eyes. Her face would contort and she would tell me that I was *mierda* (shit). "Do you hear me? *Eres mierda, eres mierda, eres mierda. ¿Me oyes? ¿Me oyes? ¿Me oyes?* Do you hear me? *Mierda, mierda, mierda.*" She would repeat it over and over, beating me. *Eres mierda, eres mierda, eres mierda.* I did grow up thinking I was a piece of shit.

Mami also repeatedly told me, "The devil is going to get you." With everything that had gone on in my life, this was a threat that really got to me. I was *so* scared. For a time, I was scared to go to sleep, scared to get up, scared to walk into an empty room, scared to do anything.

Finally, I'd had it. I couldn't live with the fear anymore; it was paralyzing me. So, I decided to get it over with—*and call the devil.* I went into my closet and closed the door. All alone, in the dark, where I couldn't see a thing and where the devil surely would have no trouble "getting" me, I said, "Okay, devil. Let me see you." I waited. "I want to see your face," I said. I waited. Nothing happened. "Let me see you!" I taunted.

I waited and waited and waited. But the devil never came. After that, I wasn't *as* afraid.

WALLER STREET

I'm not sure exactly how long I was the servant in my sister's house but I know that it would have lasted a lot longer except for the fact that Ivan told my mother she could get into trouble with the law for keeping me out of school. I was enrolled in James Denman Junior High School, having missed most of the seventh grade. Soon after this, my mother and my sister, Lotus, and I moved to our own apartment on Waller Street. My brothers had already left home. Hiram was in the Army, having been drafted as soon as he turned eighteen. Ivan, who was around two years younger than Hiram, was in jail. He and a couple of other teenage boys, who made a sport of "rolling queers," had made the local news. It was a gruesome story of brutality, and Ivan was serving time in jail for it.

We weren't at Waller Street for very long. But I'm still haunted by memories of what my mother did there to my little sister, Lotus. My mother started beating Lotus when she was a baby, when she was barely walking. But when we lived at Waller Street, the beatings became brutal.

The memory that haunts me is of my mother dragging Lotus up the stairs of the apartment building. It happened often. I remember begging, "Mamita, Mamita, no! No, Mami, no!" Ignoring me, my mother would drag Lotus up these dark steps that I think led up to the roof. I can still hear my sister's screams. By the time they returned, Lotus would be all black and blue and bleeding. I can remember my hands shaking as I tried to stop the blood from flowing out of her nose and lips.

HUNTER'S POINT PROJECTS

My mother was a seasonal worker at a factory. Although Hiram sent her an allotment from his Army pay, she still didn't have enough money to pay the rent. So we ended up in the Projects—Hunter's Point Projects—perhaps the biggest and toughest ghetto in San Francisco at the time, and the site of one of the worst stories of violence involving my mother and my little sister.

Lotus was around three or four, not yet in school, when my mother walked into her room and caught her playing with herself. Mami yelled and started beating her, so I rushed in. "Lotus was doing something *terrible*, something *nasty*!" Mami yelled as she beat her. Then she turned and picked up a newspaper. She started to roll it. When she had it tightly rolled, she put a match to it, turning it into a burning torch.

Mami thrust the torch in my hands and, prying my sister's legs open, told me to burn her vagina. Terrified, I refused, and backed away. My mother then grabbed the torch out of my hands to do it herself. But between trying, with one hand, to pry my sister's little legs open while holding the torch in the other, the fire burned down to her hands and she had to put it out. The image is seared in my mind, as it must have been in my baby sister's— because she did, eventually, go insane.

GANGS AND CATHERINE

At James Denman Junior High, I got mixed up with *pachucas*—gangs of Latina girls, mostly Chicanas. It was in secret because my mother wouldn't allow me to have any friends, "good" or "bad." I hung out with my tough little friends at school and, somehow, also managed to spend a little bit of time with them after school. I started to like violence again, and I would throw myself into any fight with the best of them.

One of my friends—not a gang member—was a little girl named Catherine. I always had some kind of love for people who were not popular and here was this little girl who wore very thick glasses, spoke in a strange hoarse voice, and had a haircut that looked like her parents had just put a bowl over her head and cut it. Nobody else at school would talk to her, but I always did.

One day after school, as I was going home, I saw a crowd of kids gathered. There was a big fight going on, so I ran over, eager to throw myself into it.

But when I pushed my way through the crowd of kids, I saw that it was Catherine they had ganged up on. Her glasses were on the ground, broken. Her nose and her mouth were bleeding. My friend Grace, much bigger than Catherine, was punching her one more time before they all ran off. I was stunned, and then felt sick to my stomach. Catherine! When I saw two girls going over to help her, I backed away and ran straight home.

That night, I thought about what had happened. All night, I couldn't get it out of my mind. The next day I told my mother, "I think I need to go back to St. Dominic's." That was the grammar school I had attended before we moved away from Divisadero.

"I can't afford to send you," my mother replied.

"I'll go talk to the Sister," I said.

The principal was Sister Nazareth and, next to Micaela, she became my most important teacher. I went to visit her and told her, "I'm getting in trouble. I'm in with bad company. I saw something horrible." We talked, and I explained what happened to Catherine and how I didn't want to go back to that way of being. "I want to come back to St. Dominic's," I said, asking if there was anything I could do to be admitted even though my mother had no money to pay for it.

"Can I work for this?" I asked.

"Yes, you can," Sister Nazareth said.

Sister Nazareth worked it out so that I helped in the cafeteria and with some cleaning around the school. In order to get to St. Dominic's from the Projects, I had to take a bus and transfer twice. It took more than an hour each way.

But not long after I went back to St. Dominic's, I started getting into some serious trouble. I was fighting again, and got caught threatening to beat up a girl. Sister Nazareth called me in and gave me a serious scolding. But then she let me go—and didn't tell my mother! I never got in trouble again.

Sister Nazareth[3] was both the principal of the school and my home-room teacher in the eighth grade. She was, to my thirteen-year-old eyes, already old. I loved her. She was sweet and gentle. I remember standing next to her in the schoolyard one day during recess. We were talking, she in her black and white Dominican habit and me, next to her, in my blue pleated skirt, white shirt, and blue tie. As we were talking, I noticed that she was watching a little girl who had been playing with a ball and had lost it when it fell between the schoolyard fence and an adjoining building. Another little girl, a bit older, was trying to help her.

The older girl tried to get the ball for the younger one. She tried all kinds of ways to retrieve it. As I saw Sister watching this scene, I, too, turned to watch. Finally, succeeding in retrieving the ball, the older girl gave it to the happy younger one. That's when Sister Nazareth turned to me and said, "I like her perseverance."

"I like her perseverance." Those words were like magic. They were words of wisdom, words that explained things, loving words that went deep into my soul and have stayed with me all these years. I was so hungry for this kind of wisdom. I held onto it.

VAN BUREN STREET

After I graduated from St. Dominic's, we left the Projects and moved back in with my sister, Zela, and her husband and child. They were living on Van Buren Street, and I was in my freshman year in high school, at St. Vincent's.

I got a work permit right after I turned fifteen and worked all through high school at the Emporium and at Penney's Department Store to pay for the tuition. But my first job was working at a movie theater in skid row. Everything I earned I gave to my family except for the bus fare to get me to and from my job.

I started having a problem at work. The son of the owner kept trying to put the make on me. He'd get me in the back of the theatre and rub against me. I knew I had to quit, and I soon did. When the manager asked me why, I told him. A short while later, the manager called me at home but Zela answered the phone. He told her to tell me to come back, that it would never happen again. But I didn't want to go back, and my family was furious with me because I refused to return to that job.

Before this, when I was bringing home my pay and giving it to them, my sister made a point of letting me know that everything I had was being given to me. If I ate a lemon, I was made aware of it. If I had some toast, I was made aware of it. Now that I was no longer working, she really landed on me. Now she would say, "You are *taking* this from us." Every day, with every single thing I ate or used in that house, I would hear the same thing. "You are *taking* this from us."

One day, as I was getting ready to go look for another job, I poured myself a glass of milk. My sister said, "You know, we're giving this to you. You're not putting anything into the family. Everything you eat comes from us."

I put the glass down, and went to my mother. By now, they had made a servant of Mami. She worked for them. They were abusive and showed her no respect; she was at their mercy, totally dependent on them. I went to her and said, "Mamita, I'm leaving home. I can't live here anymore. I'm going."

My mother got tears in her eyes. She reached into her apron, fumbled around, and pulled out two dollars. It was all she had, and she gave it to me.

I then went over to Mrs. Carpenter's house on Folsom Street. She was the mother of my school friends, Phyllis and Helen. I explained the situation to Mrs. Carpenter and told her that I didn't have a home. A wonderful woman, Mrs. Carpenter listened and then said, "You have a home, sweetie. You just come and stay with us."

I then told her the *whole* story. I told her what was going on with my mother, how my sister was treating her as a servant, and how awful it was. The Carpenters had two flats and had recently put a hole through a wall so they could go in and out of both of them. Mrs. Carpenter said, "We don't need two flats. You tell your mother that we'll close the hole back up, and give her cheap rent if she comes here to live."

I went back and told my mother. She had recently learned about welfare and had gone to apply for it. Just before we moved into the Carpenter's flat, however, she found a job and didn't need to go on welfare. We lived on Folsom Street for the rest of my high school years and even into my first year of marriage.

My mother still beat Lotus. But the last time she tried to beat me was at Folsom Street. I took hold of her arms and held her and said, "*No más, Mamita. No más.*" She never tried to hit me again.

I had made up my mind when I was in high school, seeing how Mami was and how she too was suffering, that I would love her no matter what. Mami was my first unconditional love.

FUZZY

We'd had a dog named Fuzzy since we lived on Esquina Street with my sister, and he was my beloved companion. Fuzzy would know what time I'd be home from school. Every day, he would be looking out the window, waiting for me.

But when we were getting ready to move into the Carpenter's flat, my mother told me we had to get rid of him. Since she couldn't speak English, she made me call the pound. So I was the one who called and made the arrangements for Fuzzy to be taken away. When the guy from the pound came, he said to Fuzzy, "Come on, boy." Fuzzy followed him and hopped in the truck.

I saw them drive off.

It so ravaged my heart, I couldn't speak about it until I was in my fifties; I can barely speak of it today.

ST. VINCENT'S HIGH SCHOOL

I went through my entire high school years at St. Vincent's. There was a nun there I loved dearly. Her name was Sister Agnes. In those days the nuns did not tell you their real names, but since I was special to her, she revealed her real name to me. She told me her name was Mary Jo. I later named my daughter after her—Wanda Jo. When Wanda was young, we called her Jodie, after Sister Agnes.

Sister Agnes was a Daughter of Charity and was very influential in my life. While the other kids were playing, I would stay after school and help her. My mother liked that because she knew I wasn't running around. I helped Sister Agnes with her chores and would go on visits with her to help the poor and to get the things they needed.

"We're going to go begging today," she would say. We'd go to stores to ask for Christmas presents and things that the poor needed. She was good at it and she would get so much. I remember this one man gave her so much stuff and she kept asking, what about this or that. "All right," he said. "Sister, *please* don't come back."

She very humbly said, "Thank you."

"He told you not to come back," I said. She smiled and said, "We won't—for a while."

But then in my junior year, she completely flabbergasted and disappointed me, and I had to break off the relationship. We were riding a street car in San Francisco. She was sitting by the window, and I was sitting next to her. A Black woman was sitting in front of us. All of a sudden, Sister Agnes pointed out the window and said, "Look at that *Black* man with that White woman! Oh, my God!"

I looked at her in shock. "Sister, there's a colored lady sitting in front of us," I whispered. In those days it was impolite to call people "Black."

"I don't care!" Sister Agnes said in a loud voice. "I hope she hears me."

It was completely out of character, because what I loved about Sister Agnes was her sweetness. When we got off the street car, I asked, "Sister, why did you do that?"

"A Black man has no business being with a White woman," she said.

I said, "You don't like Black people?"

"No, they're *black*."

"Then you don't like me?"

"Well, you're brown. Brown's okay."

I said, "And, Gina, she's ...?"

"Oh, Filipinos, they're brown. They're okay."

I said, "Sister, that's *wrong*. What you're saying is wrong."

"This is the way I was brought up." Sister Agnes was from the South. "I think they should go to school together but they should *not* intermarry and they should not be together *socially*."

I didn't say anything more.

Every school day I had spent time with Sister Agnes—as well as most weekends when we would go help a disabled person or baby-sit for poor children. The next day I was so sickened, I couldn't even go see her.

The day after, I talked to my good friend Yvonne, who was Black. I told her what happened. My head was going around in circles. I didn't know what to do.

That day on the bus Sister Agnes had said to me, "Zelima, why are you getting so upset? It's none of your business, anyway." I repeated what she had said to Yvonne. Because she loved me and wanted to let me off the hook, Yvonne said gently, "But you know, Zelima, this really isn't any of your business."

"You bitch!" I yelled. "You mean to tell me we've been friends all these years, and now you're telling me that this is none of my business?"

She looked at me and got tears in her eyes. "I'm sorry," she said. "Yes, of course. It *is* your business."

I never went back to help Sister again. When she would see me, she would say, "Look, there's this to be washed and that to be done. Where are you?" I would say, "Well, I'm obviously not here, Sister." And I would take off.

Finally, one day I went back to see her after school. I had heard from Mrs. Carpenter that when she was in Illinois, or wherever she was from, that they hated Catholics and used to call them "Catlickers." I also had heard that when the Irish first came to the States, they called them "Mics."

So I went to see Sister Agnes. "Sister, somebody told me that in Illinois, or some place like that where they don't like Catholics, they call them, 'Catlickers.' And you're Irish right?

"Yes, I'm Irish."

"Well, somebody told me that in several states they don't like the Irish and they call them, 'Mics.' Why is that?" I asked.

"Well, that's just ignorance!" she said. "That's just ignorance. That's all."

"Sister, isn't hating Black people ignorant?" I asked.

Sister Agnes looked at me. She then lowered her eyes and said, "Zelima, maybe you're right. Maybe you're right. I don't know. Maybe you're right."

I turned and left.

MEETING ELVIE

I was sixteen years old when I met my future husband at a YMCA dance. I had already dated other boys in high school and many of them were dolls—gorgeous. My friends would always kid me about that. But I found out that the guys I dated who weren't so gorgeous were actually more fun. My friends didn't get it and would ask why I was dating these guys that weren't "dolls."

One day, I met this freckle-faced redhead. He was not "a doll," by my friends' standards, but I thought he was really cute. I loved his facial expressions, his wit, and the way he moved his body. He told jokes and made me laugh. Also, he

At 16 when I met Elvie

was interested in *me*. I used to tell my friends in high school that, "Boys talk like this: Me, me, me, me, me, me, me. I, I, I, I, I, I, I."

My friends couldn't believe it when I started going out with him. "He's not a doll!" they said.

"Yeah, but he's cute! He's my red-haired, freckly faced sweetie pie, and I love him," I said. "And this one talks."

Elvie was interested in me and I was interested in him. He wanted to know all about me and where I came from and was fascinated by my background. It was during talks like this that we learned that we were both abused children. He told me about how his father used to beat him with a belt. Almost every day when his father came home from work, as soon as he opened the door, Elvie's mother would say, "Elvie did this and that..." His father would get so angry, and start taking off his belt as he came inside the house. Elvie grew up dreading having his father come home. He also grew to realize that his mother, in her own sweet way, was the one who got him in trouble.

A month after I graduated from high school, we got married.

CHAPTER 4

MARRIAGE AT EIGHTEEN

I got pregnant the first month after Elvie and I married. He was a sweetie. He loved me pregnant and used to tell me jokes, amazing jokes that I still remember. We laughed so much! As abused children, we had a powerful bond, but I think we both expected the other to be stronger. It didn't take long for our brokenness to reveal itself and for us to begin doing things to hurt each other.

Elvie was in the Navy and went to sea soon after we married. I stayed behind, pregnant and living with my mother and Lotus on Folsom Street.

When my sister Zela was pregnant, my mother treated her like a queen because, of course, Zela was supporting her. When I was pregnant, I took care of two other children and helped my mother financially with the money I earned and the money my husband would send. Still, Mami treated me horribly. She no longer physically abused me, but she would abuse me emotionally, making me cry. I would cry and cry and cry.

I did everything I could to try to please her. Mami would come home from work and dinner would be cooked, the house would be spotless, and she'd have a cup of coffee waiting for her. One time she came in and threw the coffee on the floor. She threw one of her tantrums and I don't even remember what she said, but it wounded me deeply. I said, "Mami, if I lose this baby, I'll never forgive you." I felt it had to be affecting my child.

ELVIE SNAPS

Elvie came back from sea duty a few months before I gave birth to our baby girl on Mother's Day, May 10, 1959. We had a beautiful time during the last weeks of my pregnancy. Elvie loved me big—and I got so big! He would rub my tummy. He also was wonderful during my labor. He was delirious with joy over the birth of our baby girl, Wanda Jo, named after Sister Agnes and Hiram's wife, my sister-in-law. The doctors and the nurses all told us, "Don't expect the next baby to be this beautiful because she is unusually beautiful. They don't usually come out like this," they said. So, our daughter had beauty from the time she was born. Elvie was delirious, delirious with joy.

But then one day, while I was still in the hospital and just before he came over to see me, Elvie was talking to some guys on Folsom Street. One of them started to cross the street and a car crashed into him. The guy was thrown up into the air and then back down again. Elvie saw the whole thing and even though the guy survived, Elvie was traumatized. All he could think about after that was death.

When I came home from the hospital with Wanda, Elvie was out of it. I had to take care of the baby *and* Elvie. He was talking crazy, his expressions were crazy—and he stayed crazy for about two months. It wasn't until later that I realized Elvie had suffered a nervous breakdown.

We didn't know anything about psychological treatment at this time. All we knew was that Elvie was acting really strange. I would try to massage him. He'd lie in my arms, and I would stroke his face and his hair. But then he wanted it more and more. It was a real struggle, trying to take care of a very needy baby and a very needy husband. I was also starting to get really scared because the situation was touching off the crazies in me. About two and a half months into this constant care-taking, I said, "Elvie, I can't take this anymore!"

"You're going crazy, and I don't know what to do," I said. "I just don't know what to do with this."

"You're right, baby," he said. "You're right. I'll try to do better."

Elvie did try. He came back, but he was never quite the same after that. The violent accident he witnessed triggered Elvie's mental illness, which started to manifest itself in two ways—into withdrawal and into violence.

Not long after Wanda was born, Elvie went back out to sea and I moved out of my mother's house to an apartment down the block. I couldn't take her meanness anymore—and I was pregnant again.

However, Mami couldn't keep up with the rent, so she and Lotus soon moved into the same apartment building. She was on the first floor and I was on the third, so it was no problem. But I always made sure I never left the baby alone with my mother.

When Elvie came back, we moved into naval housing. It was a nice hilly neighborhood with lot of kids, but it was dangerous because there were blind

Elvie and I

curves and kids were getting hit by cars. I had been told that there had even been one or two deaths by car accidents. Despite my warnings, Wanda kept running into the street. Several times, my neighbors would see her and say, "You're going to have to spank that kid because she's going to get hit by a car!"

I had promised myself that I would never hit my kids. But after these warnings, I smacked Wanda a couple of times on her behind. My neighbors said, "That's not going to do it." One day, Wanda ran out and a car came right at her. I ran to grab her. We both almost got run over. That day, I hit her with a belt and she never ran out again. After that, I would spank Wanda from time to time—and my son, John, too, after he was old enough to get into trouble. Although it was the way most people spanked their kids in those days, nothing brutal, still, I wish I hadn't done it.

Our son, John, was born on Elvie's birthday in 1961. He was our 2nd child, born on Elvie's 22nd birthday, on the 22nd day of January. Even our tax return that year marked the two-ness of it all—$222.22! But Elvie had a really hard time with John. I see now that John's birth brought back the memories of the accident he witnessed when Wanda was born, traumatizing him all over again. He never was able to bond with John as he bonded with Wanda, and John suffered for it.

Elvie completed his last tour of duty sometime after John was born. We were living in naval housing. I remember going all out to welcome him. I even bought a negligee. But when Elvie came home, he wouldn't come near me. He wouldn't touch me. Finally, I asked, "What's going on?" Elvie confessed that he had gone to a whore house while he was away, and was pretty sure he got V.D., venereal disease.

While our husbands were away at sea, several of the Navy wives would immediately start going out with other men. I never did—and all the guys knew it. They envied Elvie because his wife was faithful. I never felt quite the same about Elvie after this. Something broke inside me.

THE CRAZIES BEGIN

My husband left the Navy and started working for Pacific Gas & Electric. As we settled into the routine of family life, with both of us working and raising the kids, the nightmares from our childhoods started creeping in and taking hold. With Elvie, it had been happening for some time now. He would withdraw into himself or he would hit the kids, or both. Then, one day, my crazies came out—*explosively*.

Elvie was watching television—the Shirley Temple Show. I don't know how many times that show was on, but Elvie watched it each time. It was 1962, and we were living in a house across from Esquina Street—that place of nightmares.

Elvie was watching the Shirley Temple Show for the umpteenth time and I was in the kitchen. I heard the kids cry and found out he was hitting them because they were making too much noise while he was watching TV. A wave of unsettled feelings came over me. I went over to Elvie and said, "Something's wrong here. Can we talk?"

"Yeah," he said. "Can you wait until the Shirley Temple Show is over?"

I looked at him and that strange wave of unsettled feelings suddenly exploded. I went into the bedroom—and went into a rampage. Later, I wrote a poem that tells what happened.

and so,
my husband hit the kids
for making noise while he watched
   the shirley temple show
for the umpteenth time,
and i felt like i was
fading out,
and i said to him,
"something is wrong here,
can we talk?"
and he said,
   "can you wait

               till
                    shirley temple's
                              over?"
and i went
   into the bedroom
               and screamed
and threw lamps   and screamed
across the room   and screeeeeeeamed
      and popped pills into
         my mouth
then picked up   not really
a knife for nothing   knowing
   better to do, and   why,
pointed the knife at my stomach
   and wondered what it would be like
to stab myself with it ....

then the ambulance
         came
and they took me away,
   and
the psychiatrist,
   she said i was
sick because i had been screaming
that i would "promise to stay in
         my closet,"
but she thought i meant a different
closet, well, i didn't know what i
meant either, at the time......

and the judge said
i needed to be sent
up to get cured,
and my husband
told the psychiatrist
   i beat my kids,
and my neighbors

        went to the
                psychiatrist
and told her my husband
                was lying,
but she didn't believe
them because they were beatniks
and besides, one of "them," the female,
was a patient of hers, and had been in
this ward just last week, so she (the psychiatrist)
told my neighbor she should not relate with
me anymore because we were not good for
                each other,
and after all, it was me who was in
                not my husband.
so this wagon came
    to transfer
            me and some other women (including the one who said
                she was just writing a book) to a bigger hospital,
and,
    i was acting
            funny, like i didn't
want to go, but i was just acting, i thought,
and this nice lady with a big smile,
told me i was only going to go for a little
ride, and i didn't *think* i was crazy,
but i KNEW she was lying,
                but this kind nurse
who knew me from high school
    because her daughter, peggy, was my best friend,
and peggy and i had been in love with each other
but had to get drunk to say it, anyhow, this nurse said,
"now, please go quietly, i don't want to see you
get forced into the wagon."
i went quietly,
then in that truck with the other
prisoners, or sickies,
    i felt free,

like i had never felt before,
   so i kept playing the game
      for
        one
          eternity.

In the Mental Hospital

I was hospitalized for eight and a half months. I almost made it to the really bad ward, the one no one gets out of. I had a friend named Vickie. Right away, Vickie and I became best friends. She got out and then, when her social worker reported that she was depressed, they went and got her and forced her back in. After an incident in which she threw an ashtray across the social room, the male workers came and got her and threw her into the cell, breaking her front tooth. They then slammed the cell door, breaking her toe. When her family came and saw her, they were enraged and tried to sue. But it didn't go anywhere. The male workers didn't even get fired. Black people had no rights in those days.

Vickie and I realized that anyone who was put into that really bad ward changed. If they had any life left in them, they lost it after they went into that ward, and they never got out. You were automatically put into that ward if you were hospitalized for more than eight months. So Vickie and I stuck together, figuring we'd be very lucky if we both got out. We both did, just under the wire.

I was initially sent to the San Francisco County ward, but then I was transferred to Napa State Hospital. When Elvie heard they were going to send me there, he called his mother, who said, "Come on home, baby." He wrote me a letter saying he had moved to Texas with the kids and would come back when I was released. I wrote back saying I would divorce him if he didn't bring the kids back to San Francisco.

He brought them back and they went to live with my mother, with Elvie sleeping on the couch. After a couple of months of being hospitalized, I was allowed to visit my kids. I loved seeing them whenever I got the weekend leave, but I had a terrible time coping. My mother was at her best when I was in the hospital; she tried hard to be good. But something got triggered in me whenever I was released there. I would eat everything I could find and then would be overwhelmed by the need to sleep. My therapists at the hospital would say, "You begin to get happy, then we let you go home and you come back depressed."

As depressed as I was, as drugged as I was, as crazy as I was, I kept telling myself in the hospital, "You've got kids. You've got kids. You've got kids. You've got to pull yourself together and get out of here." Eventually, I was released—just under the "bad-ward" wire.

When I first got home, I was scared to go outside. I had been in an institution for so long, it was terrifying to be outside again. I told myself that I had to get through this. I would try to take a step toward the door. And if I made it, I would say, "Okay, now take another." When I finally got to the door, I would say, "Now open it." After I opened it, I would say, "Take a step out the door, Zelima. Take one step." I would do that. And then take another step.

Eventually, after days and weeks of taking these baby steps, I was able to go down the block. I knew I had made it when I finally was able to go down the block, catch the bus, and take it to the end of the line and back. After that, I got a clerical job, and once I got a job, I started getting my head back.

HIRAM'S MADNESS

For a brief time, until we could get back on our feet, Elvie and I moved in with my brother, Hiram, and his wife, Wanda. It was like being back at the hospital.

Hiram brutally beat his son and his wife. I later learned that he had once burned his daughter's feet with a hot iron before she was old enough to go to school. My nephew was only in kindergarten when we were there. One day I bought lollipops for all the kids, mine and his and some neighborhood children who were playing with them. Hiram told his son he couldn't have the lollipop—that he ate too much candy—and he took it away from him.

The little boy ended up sneaking a tiny bite of someone else's lollipop and Hiram saw a speck of it sparkling on his son's upper lip. Hiram went into a fury, taking the boy into his bedroom where he whipped him mercilessly with a belt. I reported my brother to the police. But kids had no rights in those days, and the police did nothing.

We got out of there as fast as we could—and soon after, left California and the States.

Papi and Nicaragua

It was 1963. My father had been writing to me, begging me to come home because he was sick and needed me to help take care of him and the business. Papi had been living with a woman but said he was leaving her and that's why he *urgently* needed my help.

The woman, Marta, was one of a long string of my father's women. He was addicted to women. But Marta was hardly a "woman." She was a fifteen-year-old girl, an *hija de casa* or "daughter of the house"—someone in the hierarchy of Nicaraguan households who's above a servant but doesn't hold the position of a member of the family. My father was fifty-five years old when he saw this fifteen year old girl and told the people of the house he wanted her. She became his woman and they had two girls, the older one dying as an infant.

It was Marta my father was supposedly leaving. So, we packed up the car and Elvie and I and the kids drove all the way to Nicaragua. By the time we got there, more than a week later, Marta and my father had gotten back together again. And my father, if he ever had been sick, was doing just fine.

We had spent all the money we had getting to Nicaragua, but from the moment we arrived, it was a disaster. Marta was very jealous of me because she saw my father, with forty years difference in age between them, more as a father than as a husband. She was hostile. And my father was so cruel to us and our kids that we finally left his house to go live with his brother, Tío Virgilio, and his wife.

My Hermanita and the Purisima

Micaela came to see me right after I got to Nicaragua. Everybody told me, "Now look, don't be shocked, Micaela has gone crazy. She can't hold a conversation." So I took a deep breath and prepared myself.

But there was nothing wrong with Micaela! She refused to go into the house because she didn't like it that my father had another woman and, instead, took me to her little hut. Micaela asked about my mother and told me she was going to introduce me to my *hermanita*, my little sister.

My *hermanita* was someone Micaela was raising as a daughter, the way she had raised me. Except this little girl was her niece's daughter, so she could have her in the house and really teach her. I couldn't wait to see my *hermanita*!

59

We got to Micaela's little hut, on the outskirts of Managua, where she had a pig living with her, and that's when I met Olgita—a beautiful Black girl with nappy hair. Micaela laughed, saying, "¡Esta viene de Blufil!" ("This one comes from Blufil!")

Bluefields, a Caribbean port city in the eastern rain forest of Nicaragua, is where the African people stayed after they were brought over on the slave ships. The slave traders tried to sell them but nobody wanted to buy them because they already had the Indians as servant-slaves. Since it was too expensive to take the slaves back, they just dumped them, and the African people did wonderfully there on their own. Because Olgita was Black, Micaela joked that she came from "Blufil."

Before we left Nicaragua to go back to the States, Micaela invited me to a *Purísima* at her home. *La Purísima*, the Holy Virgin, or Mary, Most Pure, is honored once a year in Nicaragua. It's a very big deal, and I learned that Micaela had been holding a *Purísima* for me at her house every year since I left, to pray for me. She saved her little money to put on the *Purísima*, inviting the people in the Indian neighborhood where she lived to come.

When my husband and kids and I arrived for the *Purísima*, all these *Indios* and their naked children came running up to the car, yelling, "Zelimita! Zelimita!" People I had never met had been coming every year to Micaela's *Purísima* to pray for me, the one Micaela called her "daughter."

It was the last time I ever saw Micaela.

Soon after, my Tío Virgilio told my father, "These people want to go home and you need to help them." Grudgingly, he did, giving us enough money to drive back home.

A MOTHER'S NIGHTMARE

Our car made it all the way back to my mother's apartment in San Francisco from Nicaragua, and then broke down. We, too, were broke, our lives totally disrupted after having been gone for so many months. The experience had put a huge strain on our marriage, and now we were totally dependent on my mother until we could find jobs and get our lives back together.

Mami, meanwhile, was furious with me for having seen my father. She took it out on me and the kids, demanding that they stay on the couch all day long. They were only five and three years old.

We had the saddest Christmas in the world that year. Zela came over to receive gifts from my mother for herself and her kids. As one gift after another was dispensed to Zela's kids, we just sat there. There were no gifts for Wanda or John or for me or my husband. At some point, my mother looked at us and, acting surprised, said, "Ah!" covering her mouth with her hand. She took my sister into her bedroom and came back with an envelope with a check for $5 for me and the kids.

Soon after, Mami told me she didn't want my kids there anymore. She wanted us *out*. We had no money, no jobs, and no place to go. I didn't know what to do. Desperate, I called someone at a social service agency. I told them we had no place to stay, no place for the kids. We couldn't even stay in the car because even though it had broken down, it had gotten repossessed.

Whoever answered the phone was very understanding and said, "Don't worry, the children will be safe."

"You're not going to take them away from me are you?" I asked.

"No, no. We'll just keep them in a safe home until you can find your own place." A short while later, the police came. Wanda clung to me as the police tore her away. She cried and cried, "I don't want to go. *Please.* I don't want to go!" The last thing I saw was my children, Wanda and John, being driven away in the back seat of the police car.

The pain was unbearable. For years, I couldn't bear it. My own mother abandoning my children, my own children feeling I was abandoning them—captured in the image of a police car driving off with my kids. If anyone even approached this topic, I would immediately stop them. Years later, I was at my son's house, when John casually said, "Mom, remember that time we went to Juvenile Hall?" I looked at him, burst into tears, and started sobbing. I sobbed and sobbed and sobbed—uncontrollably, inconsolably.

They took my children to the juvenile center where they stayed for two or three days, and then they were placed in a foster home with an awful lady. They were there for three weeks. I saw the kids every chance I got while Elvie and I looked for work.

One day, when we went to visit them, I saw that Wanda had a giant ear infection. Elvie and I had each just found jobs and we were waiting to move into a place that was pending. The pus was running out of her ear and she was in terrible pain. The foster-care lady was repulsed and wouldn't touch Wanda. I grabbed both kids and took Wanda to the emergency room. I asked the doctor to write down the condition in which he found her, explaining that my daughter was in a foster home and that I needed to get her out of there.

We took the kids to a friend's house and I called the social worker and told her what happened, saying, "Thank you, but we'll have a home in a couple of days." As it turned out, the social worker had called the foster home and gotten the same story from the foster mother, so there was no need for the doctor's note. We had the kids back and within a few days, we moved into a house in San Mateo.

THE CRAZIES COME BACK AND THE MARRIAGE COMES TO AN END

We lived in San Mateo for the next few years—the last years of our marriage. There were more episodes and trips to the emergency room in store for us. This whole period is very hazy for me. I don't remember much of what happened or when. All I know is that several psychiatrists wouldn't see me unless I was tranquilized. So, when I wasn't crazy, I was so drugged I could barely function.

I remember being committed several times. The first few times were for one month. Then there was a four-month stay and the last time was the longest—about six months. These hospitalizations were at a day center where I would go all day, every day, for treatment.

The episodes that would lead to treatment would usually begin with my feeling a deep need to sleep. I would want to sleep for days. Then I would get hysterical, crying, and I would get mad at Elvie. He took a lot from me. I know he loved me because he stayed by me through all this; I was the one who eventually left.

What I remember was persistent depression and an inability to do anything. It would be a great achievement just to brush my hair. I would work hard at lifting my arm. When I'd get my arm up, I'd say, "Okay, now push the brush down through your hair." When my arm would come down, I'd then tell myself, "Okay, now do it again."

It was hard to get out of bed, hard to brush my teeth, hard to walk from one end of the room to another. It was impossible to look for a job.

Elvie and I fought a lot. Our fights were usually over money or his hitting the kids. It didn't take much to push me over the edge. The second to the last time I was hospitalized was triggered when I reached into my purse to get two quarters I had saved to buy milk for the kids. The quarters weren't there. Elvie had taken them, my last two quarters. He had fallen into a habit of taking whatever little money we had, including our bonds, and spending it. I went into a rage and landed in the emergency room.

After this incident, I was separated from Elvie for a short time, living with my friend, Joyce. Undergoing treatment at a day center where they had me on so many drugs, I couldn't even button my own blouse and Joyce would have to do it for me. It's all a haze. I really don't know what happened, but while I was living with Joyce, I attempted suicide, swallowing a bunch of pills. Somehow, it was Elvie who found me. In a scene out of my childhood, an ambulance came and rushed me to the hospital where my stomach was pumped.

I returned home to Elvie. Since I was already in for treatment at a day center, I was just committed to a longer stay.

The last time I was hospitalized, I asked my social worker to have my kids put in foster care. Elvie was hitting them over any little thing, and I wasn't able to stop it. The kids were so hyper, I couldn't protect them and I was worried. Wanda and John were placed in a foster home with a couple named the Whitakers. He was Caucasian and she was Hawaiian. They were beautiful people and did a wonderful job with the kids. I would visit them every chance I could—and saw, for the first time, that my kids were calm.

During this time, I was still living with Elvie and going for treatment every day. But one day, we got into a big fight. I got hysterical, and Elvie ended up taking me to the emergency room. This time, though, the psychiatrist wanted to see my husband, too. He asked Elvie about our relationship.

"I guess I do things that irritate her," Elvie said. "Once in a while, I take quarters from her purse."

I heard the psychiatrist say, "Do you enjoy seeing your wife squirm?" He then asked, "Have you ever thought of getting therapy? That perhaps you need it, too?"

Elvie got mad and walked out. That's when the psychiatrist told me that "a big problem is your husband. He can pull all kinds of strings and you don't even know they're being pulled." I had never considered that my problems had anything to do with anyone other than me. And I had no idea I was squirming or having my "strings pulled," although my therapist in the day center, who saw Elvie a couple of times when he would bring me in, once told him, "You're sneaky." Elvie would seem so nice, but he *was* doing his sneaky things. After all, he, too, had been an abused child.

The psychiatrist said he didn't see how these problems would get settled if Elvie didn't get help. Elvie wasn't about to get help and that's when I decided to leave him. It felt like a relief—like I had a chance at life. So, I ended up leaving Elvie, the freckly faced boy who made me laugh, who coped with my insanity and its unreasonable demands, and for whom, after all these years, I still feel love. But leaving him gave me a chance at life—the life I was born to live.

Chapter 5
Coming Out & Coming Alive

W hen I was finally stable enough to be released from the psychi-
atric day center, the social worker handling my case arranged
for me to get some financial help so I could find my own place
and get some job training by attending business school.

At first I moved into a place with a couple of roommates—other single
mothers with children. They were starting to date and wanted me to baby-sit,
but I said, "There's no way I'm going to baby-sit your kids when I don't have
my own!" I had a hard time studying there with all the noise and distrac-
tions. But I was determined to study and, somehow, with the financial help I
was getting, I managed to get a little apartment, get my kids back, and continue going to business school.

That's where I met Lee.

We were both divorced and had kids, but that's where the likenesses
ended! She was tall, blond, blue-eyed, and ten years older than I. And despite
having five kids, Lee was sought after by all kinds of boyfriends. The first
time we spoke on the phone, all she talked about was the guys she was going
out with—this guy and that guy.

"Oh, well," I said to myself, recognizing an attraction I could no longer deny.

For years I had fought my homosexuality. The first time the thought
occurred to me that I might be lesbian was when I was thirteen, living on
Esquina Street. I had a dream in which I was getting married. I was all
dressed in white, walking down the aisle, and there waiting for me at the
altar, also dressed in a white bridal gown, was the actress-comedienne
Imogene Coca!

In high school, I had a crush on a friend. I fought it, admitting it to her
only when I had the excuse of being drunk. The feeling was so strong I even

went to confession about it. The priest told me it was a grievous sin to love another woman, so I fought it. Sometimes I saw or read things about lesbians. It was always horrible and sadistic. Who in the world would want to be the type of person who used whips on another? I didn't want to be like that. I really fought it.

Even after I got married, I would have a yearning just to be held by and caress a woman. I fought that until one day, nearly six years into our marriage, I talked to Elvie about it. He was very understanding, saying, "You have to find out." Elvie even drove me to a meeting of the Daughters of Bilitus! (Of course, Elvie never stopped to think that I might actually leave him; he thought I could be both a lesbian and his wife.) The Daughters of Bilitus was one of the first lesbian organizations in the country, founded in the mid-fifties. At the meeting, I saw what to my eyes were tough, butchy-looking women. I got scared and went home—but the feelings stayed.

With Lee, however, there was no denying it. I was in love. The attraction was intense and there was no sense in even trying to fight it.

We started talking and doing things together. One day we were sitting in my car talking and I decided I had to tell her. It was my first confession to anyone while I was sober besides my husband (and the priest). "I think I'm lesbian," I said.

Lee looked at me and said, "I've had those feelings, too."

I said, "I mean, I am *lesbian*."

She said, "I know what you're talking about…"

I was shocked! This was the mid-sixties, before Stonewall.[4]

So we kept going out and doing things together, and I kept feeling the attraction grow. The first time we got really close was when she took me to this beautiful beach. It got dark and we were lying on the sand, looking at moon. We both had sleeping bags and I started getting into mine when Lee said, "My sleeping bag holds two." We just held hands and looked at the moon.

We kept going out and Lee kept falling asleep. She was exhausted with school and five kids and would fall asleep at the wheel a lot. It worried me— and it was getting harder and harder to say goodnight.

Then, we graduated from business school. About a year had gone by, and we decided we should move in together. We found a beautiful house in Belmont Hills. With both of us working, we could afford the rent. So we moved in, shared the work and the kids and everything, including one room and one bed. At first, it was to "save space"; within a couple of months, we both awakened to the real reason.

Besides Micaela in my childhood, Lee is the most important person in my life. Lee loved me dearly and taught me how to love. My relationship with her was the beginning of finding myself, who I really was.

Lee and I

We were together for about seven years and something really deep happened with us. It never would have lasted that long if it hadn't been so deep because of all we had to deal with— that is, the kids; the school finding out we were gay and calling her husband; Lee's mother, who couldn't stand her ex-son-in-law, allying herself with him to try to take the kids away from Lee; and so much more....

Elvie and I stayed in touch for a while but when I got together with Lee, he stopped seeing the kids. Even when Wanda fell and broke her arm, and cried for her daddy, Elvie wouldn't come see her. His friends told him, but he wouldn't come.

THE CRAZIES CREEP BACK

My first job after business school was working as a secretary at Holly Sugar in San Mateo. Lee also got a secretarial job in San Mateo.

Just a few months after we started living together as a couple, the old feelings of the crazies came creeping back over me. I was craving sleep—a sure sign that the crazies were coming. I was working a lot, but this deep need for sleep wasn't about that. It was a sign that the crazies were coming.

I was terrified. I was so happy with Lee, the last thing I wanted was to be institutionalized again. I kept the dread feelings to myself until I finally had to tell Lee what was going on, concluding, "I'm going to end up in a mental hospital!"

"Why do you have to go to a mental hospital because you're sleepy?" she asked.

"Because I can sleep for days," I said.

"So, why don't you just go ahead and sleep for days?" she asked.

"But what about my kids? Who's going to take care of them?"

"Well, I will," she said.

"And what about the office, my job?"

"I'll just call in and tell them you're sick," she said.

It was that simple. It never dawned on me that I might be able to just give in to the deep need for sleep—and sleep, without being hospitalized!

I slept for three days. When I woke up, I felt so refreshed!

And something else happened in that sleep. I went through a blackness. I went through a blackness and came out knowing something I didn't know before—layers of things that are hard to explain but that I think was the start of my path, my journey, and my struggle to find out, "Who am I?" I swam through the blackness and came out with knowledge I didn't have before—and I learned to love that blackness inside.

Many years later I wrote a poem about what I understood about the blackness. It's called "Joy Goddess."

You came to me Black
Bare skin
Beautiful and strong
Loving being a woman
Grinning joy from ear to ear
Hands resting on your pregnant belly
A red ruby covers your navel
And you are squatting getting ready to give birth
The powers of Joy and the Creation protect you
I wear your image as an amulet
You came to help me in my journey through the Blackness
The fertile knowledge of the Unknown
In my Darkest hour I see the red ruby covering your navel
I see Blackness giving birth to the Sun

GRASPING AT SPIRITUALITY

After the experience of knowing blackness, I started grasping at spirituality. I didn't know what I was doing. Part of me just knew that I was not going to let others define me. I started asking myself, "Who am I? Who am I?" Those questions meant there was somebody in there, inside myself, beyond myself. It was a time of growth, of reaching for a deeper spirituality—but then my religion got in the way.

Catholicism said to me, "You will go to hell. You are living in sin." I felt fearful and starting worrying about what I was doing to my kids, being lesbian. I couldn't fall asleep and suffered from insomnia. One night I woke up holding Lee, and I heard a voice say, "Let go of her, or God will strike you dead."

I believed it!

I was terrified. But I was also exhausted from the constant anxiety. Like the time when I decided to call the devil, I felt that the moment of reckoning had come.

I held Lee even tighter, and said, "*Go ahead.*"

I held on. I held her really tight and—nothing happened! "Hey," I thought to myself. "Nothing happened—and I've got my woman right by my side!"

That day I made up my mind: Whatever the consequences, this felt like me. It was the most beautiful thing I had ever experienced, and something this beautiful had to be sacred. I told myself, "I don't believe in anything in the Catholic Church."

I put my fingers in my ears and said, "I don't believe in the Catholic Church. I don't believe in Jesus. I don't believe in the Catholic Church. I don't believe in Jesus. I don't believe in *anything* about the Catholic Church...." I kept repeating it, so I could shake the church off me.

That worked for a time, but after a while, I started having a feeling that I needed some kind of connection to the Creator. So, Lee and I started going to this and that church. We went to synagogues and different places of worship. Everything was fine but nothing gave me the feeling that the Catholic Church had given me when I believed. I couldn't feel that way now in the Catholic Church, but I remembered how I had felt when I believed—and it was that feeling I was missing.

VIOLENCE GRIPS

Lee and I were deeply in love but it was a struggle, juggling school and full-time jobs with the responsibilities of a household of seven kids, ranging in ages from six to sixteen. We had to get up at 5:00 a.m. to get to work on time. When we got home, we were usually up until midnight taking care of everyone's needs. Although we had a washer and dryer, our volume of laundry was so large, we had to go to a laundromat.

Lee's five kids were not used to doing anything around the house. Her ex-husband had insisted she be a slave. There were times when she was asleep and one of the kids would call from the bedroom, "Mom, I want a glass of water!" Her husband would wake her up and make her go get it. She was like a servant with the kids; they dominated her and never lifted a finger to help around the house. Lee and I were doing everything and it was wearing us out.

I finally told Lee, "This has to change. We can't keep going like this." I said, "All the kids are old enough to help in some way."

So we started giving them chores, appropriate to their ages.

Around that time, there was an incident with her fifteen-year-old, who was really angry because his shirt had two buttons missing. We were on our way to work, when he tossed it to Lee and said, "Sew this!"

I said, "No, you don't. This will not continue. You will not speak to your mother like that."

·This boy and I had already had one battle where I pushed him up against the wall for beating up his younger brother. There was a lot of violence among the kids, especially between the older boy and his eleven-year-old brother. Eventually, after punching his sixteen-year-old sister really hard in the stomach, the older boy had to leave and go live with his father, but at the time Lee's children were upset because they had to help out around the house and were getting disciplined. We spent a lot of time together and actually had fun times with each other. I grew to love the kids, but there was a lot of violence among them and in time, it set off my violence. I'm not excusing it; I know I'm responsible.

I remember hitting the kids several times with the belt. Afterwards my heart started hurting all the way to my back. I don't ever remember being without fear and anxiety in my life, but now I also started to feel shame.

These incidents stand out: I remember seeing bruises on the arm of Lee's thirteen-year-old girl, thinking she had done it to herself until the sinking realization came that I had caused them. I remember going to the humane society to pick up our dog, who kept running away, and whipping him really hard until I suddenly realized what I was doing and dropped the belt. "What the hell am I doing?" I said.

I also remember taking the belt to Lee's youngest boy. At some point I just saw my arm going up and down, effortlessly. That's when I became aware of how hard I was hitting him and dropped the belt. "What the hell am I doing?" I said, again.

At that point, I made a decision. Like the decision I made when I was eleven years old with Darlene, I decided: "I will never hit the kids again." I told Lee that I had just hit her youngest really hard, and that I thought I had done it before without realizing how hard I was hitting them. "But," I said, "I don't ever want to hit them again."

I kept my promise. But what happened is I started to hallucinate. When the urge to get violent would come over me, I would say, "No! No! No!" I would start shaking with fear and then hallucinate. Some of the hallucinations were fine; I actually enjoyed them. But some scared me, like hallucinations of great big snakes.

It was around 1968. I had started taking psychology classes at night at a junior college, which opened up a new world of learning and understanding. Because Lee and I were going through so much, trying to raise seven kids, dealing with threats from her mother and ex-husband to take away the kids because of our relationship, keeping full-time jobs—and dealing with my recurring crazies—we decided to get some help by seeing a therapist.

I was in a cycle of either wanting to sleep, get violent, or be really depressed. Our therapist told us that she had experimented with a drug given to epileptics and thought it would help me. I took it, and for three months I was in heaven! I felt calm and didn't feel any urge toward violence—all of this without the big heavy-duty drugs they used to give me in the hospital to calm me down. It was wonderful! But then it wore off.

The therapist increased the dosage, but it didn't help at all. In fact, after being on those drugs, I either had a huge amount of energy or was really depressed. The therapist was very Freudian and we were always dealing in intellectual abstractions. That didn't help any more than the drugs did, so we stopped seeing her. But by now, I was shaking a lot and hallucinating. It got really bad when I started seeing things on TV that weren't happening. I caught myself "going into" the TV and becoming one of the characters, usually a man.

Lee would tell me that I would do strange things. We'd be really happy, joking, and then I'd turn to her and say, "You fucking bitch!" It was totally out of character since I was sweet with her, as she was with me. She told me how my expression changed.

I was involved in Action Now, a Black civil rights group, and one day I was at the house of one of the members, my friend Connie, and we were watching TV. I started saying, "Look at what he's doing," describing what was happening. Connie stopped me, and said, "Honey, that's not what's happening, baby. Where are you getting that, child? That's not the program. Baby, that didn't happen. The program is completely different."

I trusted Connie, and I knew I needed to get help. At school, I talked to my psychology teacher and told her that I needed to see a therapist. I told her I needed to see someone who would see me without drugs. (That was what had kept me from seeing a shrink; they always wanted to put me on drugs, which made me feel synthetic and not like I was made of flesh and blood.) I also told her I was a homosexual and that I didn't want to see anyone who thought that homosexuality was my problem. "It's not my problem. This is who I am," I said.

My teacher listened and then told me she knew someone. "Let me talk to him," she said. The following week, she gave me Peter's phone number.

HEALING WITH PETER

Peter had wavy, almost curly blond hair, and I later learned from him that he had a harelip[5] that had been operated on. That explained the unusual way he talked, although I simply thought he had a very attractive accent! Peter wore a beard, was of average height and build, and had very expressive, penetrating eyes.

The first thing Peter told me was, "I do not use medication to treat my patients. I refuse." I asked him how he felt about homosexuals. He said he thought there was no difference, that homosexuals were equal to heterosexuals. I got that issue settled right away. No one was going to try to heal me of the best thing I'd ever known!

I had gone to that first session all dressed in black—black pants, black shirt, black vest, black boots. I had long hair, but I wore a short curly wig. Peter told me later that I scared the shit out of him!

The second time I saw him, I was really depressed. Peter caught on right away. He said, "Now, Zelima, the first time I saw you, you were the Black Knight. And now, you're an invalid. What's going on here?"

Peter had a way with me. Each time I saw him after that he said, "Who are you now?"

"What do you mean, who am I?"

He said, "Well, you're different from the last three times I saw you."

Lee started telling me how I changed. I'd be one way, one type of person, and then I'd be somebody else. I started realizing, "I'm different people." I started being conscious of these different people, these "multiple personalities," and as I kept seeing Peter, we kept going from one to another and another and another and another. I could feel these characters inside me and see what they looked like in my mind's eye.

There were so many! I lost count. Then they stopped appearing. For a few weeks, when no more personalities appeared, I thought I was making great progress! Then, another personality showed up. I called him "Devil-Angel"—a male who looked something like Peter. He had wings, a halo, and a pitchfork—like the devil. Sometimes he would almost fly, and other times he would pace up and down with his pitchfork, snarling.

So many personalities had emerged over the weeks and months since I started seeing Peter, I was ashamed to tell him that yet another had popped up. I was disappointed in myself and thought he would be disappointed in me because I had been doing so well. I kept it from him for about three weeks. When I finally confessed, I stuttered all over the place and put my hands over my face. "Another one has come out," I said.

"How long has it been?" Peter asked.

"About three weeks."

"And you never told me? Why didn't you tell me?" he asked.

"Because I'm ashamed," I said. "I'm disappointing myself and I thought you would be disappointed in me."

"You know what, Zelima?" Peter said. "You can keep opening the drawer and pulling them out forever. That's what you're doing. You're opening the drawer and you're pulling them out. That's all there is to it."

When he said that, something went click inside me. I felt it in my gut, in my head, and in my bones. Somehow what he said made so much sense to me, I stopped pulling them out! "Devil-Angel" was the last personality to come out. Something clicked inside me and I healed. Some of my friends find it hard to believe that it could happen just like that. But it did. Of course, I still had to work with all the personalities I had, but no more came out.

That's how Peter would work with me. He was always direct, pointing things out simply. And once I understood, I would get better. When I confessed to him about my violence and how ashamed I was that I had hit Lee's kids, Peter said, "Well, that's all you knew." I hadn't thought about it that way and I started to feel better, appreciating the fact that I had the sense somehow to know it's not right and to try to stop it.[6]

In my work with Peter I learned how schizophrenia was handled in Tibet. Holy people would work with the schizophrenics and help them express the voices they were hearing. Peter and I talked about this and about how, instead of killing off my personalities, I could make them a part of myself.[7] There was a lot I liked about my personalities—they just needed a little polishing! So, I decided I wouldn't kill them off, but make them a part of me.

One of my personalities was called, "Sal." (This was actually a nickname friends gave me when I was in high school. I didn't like it very much but it was better than "Zel," which is the first nickname they gave me.) I went through a really crazy period when I kept trying to kill Sal. I felt that if I didn't, Sal would kill me. I remember calling Peter twice in the middle of the night to help me through this crisis. He urged me to call him again if I needed to, saying this was very difficult stuff to get through alone. Getting through this was a big part of my healing and it came to a head during a battle between Sal and Zelima—and a "Miss X" who came to guide me. I now recognize that "Miss X" was Great Mystery. That's who Miss X was.

During that period when I was trying to kill Sal, Miss X came in one desperate moment. I forget what triggered the event or how I was going to do it, but I was going to kill Sal. I was ready to kill Sal. Of course, killing Sal meant killing myself. In the middle of this desperate moment, I heard a voice, a very sweet voice, say, "Zelima, I love you. I love you. I love you. I love you." She said everything so sweetly, repeating and repeating the phrase, I went into a trance. I felt complete trust, as she kept saying more sweet things. Miss X told me how good I was and sweetly, gently, softly kept repeating, "I love you, Zelima. I love you, Zelima. I love you, Zelima. I love you, Sal."

"SAL?" I yelled, jumping up. "WHAT DO YOU MEAN, 'SAL'"?

Her voice gently lulled me back, saying, "I love you, Zelima. I love you, Zelima. I love you, Sal. I love you, Zelima. I love you, Sal." With that gentle voice I stopped fighting Sal and started on the path of recognizing that Sal and I were the same person.

Miss X came to me so gently. I know that when Spirit comes in that way, it's always gentle. Everyone I've ever known who has an experience like that has the same feeling of peacefulness. You don't get scared. I remember how Miss X calmed me. It happened in such a knowing way. She sounded so gentle, so trusting. Something changed me, opening me to the realization that Sal and I were the same.

Later, while I was still in therapy, I wrote a play with all my personalities as characters. I wish I still had it, but it burned in a fire. The play starts out with one character saying, "Oh no, she's at it again! She's trying to kill us all! The bitch!"

I don't remember the whole play—but it had a lot of characters! One was a male who stuttered as I did when things got shaky. He would keep interrupting, saying, "I-I-I-I'm s-s-s-sorry to i-i-i-interrupt th-th-this c-c-c-conversation."

Two other characters I remember were called "Seven" and "Eleven." They always repeated what the other had said. If Seven said, "Let's eat." Eleven would say, "Let's eat." In the play, I captured a breakthrough moment that actually occurred between these two personalities when one day, instead of repeating what Seven had just said, Eleven said something else.

"Why did you say that?" Seven demanded. "You didn't repeat what I said. You said something else!"

Eleven answered, "Well, that's what makes you, Seven, and me, Eleven."

Writing that play helped me heal. Several years later, in the early seventies, some of my friends and I performed the play for a few other friends. We all laughed and my friends said the play helped them deal with different aspects of themselves! It was very cleansing for me, a real healing experience.

The other big issue I had was that I used to manipulate. I didn't even know what it was until I saw Peter. I remember telling him how I handled a particular situation, describing how I said this and then did that, thinking I had done a great job.

"That's manipulation," he said. "What's that?" I asked. He explained it to me—and then kept bringing it up. Everything I did was manipulation! I didn't know that I could be and act out of my center. A lot of times when I didn't know how to act or say the right things, I would just copy what others did.

Soon, I started understanding and then would catch myself, "Oh, oh. This is manipulation." The way I described it to Peter was that I felt I had puppets on both hands with strings. My hands were attached to those strings and I couldn't leave them. But then, I decided to take one of my little fingers off the string. I felt what it was like to have a free finger. Then, I took another one off. Two fingers free! That was my freedom. It took a while.

Two of my gifts from Spirit have been having beautiful friends—true and loyal friends I could be myself with—and having a sense of humor! I would say to my friends, "I'm working with my manipulation, friends. If you catch me, let me know." I remember one of them saying, after I described my ways of manipulating, "Hey! That looks good. You sure you want to get rid of that?"

Our code for manipulation was to put a hand out and wiggle a few fingers. I would say, "Olga, how did you get a date with her?" She'd wiggle her fingers!

I kept seeing Peter regularly until 1970 or 1971, and then I'd see him every once in a while for a couple of years after that. I tried to get my kids to see him, but they didn't want to go. Peter and I had code names for each other. I called him "Super Shrink" and he called me "Super Dyke." We remained friends, reconnecting again very recently, just months before he died of a massive heart attack in October of 2004. He was a beautiful man.

Peter also was very interesting. He and his parents survived the Holocaust by going underground, hiding in and around Berlin for three and a half years until the liberation in 1945. He was malnourished as a boy and I think one of his legs was shorter than the other as a result.[8] His parents, who were German Jews, changed their names when they got here because they were still living in fear. Peter's father let him choose the name and because Peter liked Roy Rogers, that became his family's surname.[9]

I don't think I could have survived without Peter. I owe my life to him in many ways. And all the changes I went through with Peter took place while I was with Lee. She was a wonderful support through it all. She saw my different personalities before I knew what was happening. And she took my meanness. She would tell me afterwards what I had said or done, but I usually didn't remember. One day, however, after I started therapy with Peter, I caught myself. I could feel the shift to another personality and I became aware of saying to Lee, "You fucking bitch!"

It must have been in the way I glanced at her that brought me back into full consciousness. I saw the hurt in her eyes and I heard the ugly, awful things I was saying. I saw both pain and compassion in her eyes—pain in being hurt and compassion toward me. I stopped and said, "Baby, I'm sorry. I just heard what I was saying. I'm really, really sorry."

It never happened again. We could still get into arguments, but that cruelty with no awareness never returned. It was her eyes that pulled me back—her eyes, reflecting both pain and compassion.

I couldn't have made it without her.

GOING UP IN THE WORLD

A year or two into living with Lee, while I was dealing with my crazies and multiple personalities and our constant struggles with Lee's mother and her efforts to take away the children, I got a job at Agfa-Gaevert Film, as credit manager. I took care of the books and got really good at it. My boss was a very kind man named Mr. Heller. He was a staunch Catholic and he insisted on having these conversations with me where I would tell him what I thought. He carried a rosary and he would touch it when we talked. He used to say, "I love your intelligence."

One time, Mr. Heller saw a file I was carrying. It was one of the interviews I was doing for a new Kinsey report on the sexual behavior of homosexuals. I had met a guy at a party who was working on the report and he asked me if I would be interested in conducting the interviews. I was to interview people of different races. It was part-time work, and it paid $50 an hour![10]

Mr. Heller saw the file and was shocked. He said, "Zelima, I understand why you're working in the Civil Rights Movement, but with homosexuals? Why?"

"Because I'm a homosexual," I said.

"You are a homosexual?" he asked. He was stunned. "I don't know what to say about that." Finally, he said, "I still love you." And he went into his office.

The next day, his assistant, Myra, a very fine Jewish woman, came to me and said, "Mr. Heller told me you are a homosexual. I want you to know that my respect and feelings for you are not diminished in the least." After this exchange, Myra and her husband became our first best "couple" friends.

Sometime after this exchange, Mr. Heller told Myra that he didn't know what to do. For the first time in his life, he was having doubts about the Catholic Church. He said he couldn't imagine that Zelima wouldn't be allowed into the gates of heaven.

It was 1969 and Lee and I were getting ready to buy the house in Belmont Hills where we'd been living. When I came home from work, I would look at the house with its beautiful stairs and think, "We're doing this. I'm so proud." But I also noticed I was starting to get bleeding ulcers.

Mr. Heller had arranged for me to go to special classes offered exclusively to people sent by companies. I was excited. It was a time when the Civil Rights Movement was strong and communist conspiracy theories were rampant and here I was, a person of color and a woman, going up in the world!

I went to the class and soon found out it was all about how to give more work to your subordinates and keep the unions out. "The most conscientious employee, the one you can load lots of work on," we were instructed, "is a divorced mother with children or a family man with a mortgage." Everyone was taking notes, and I was just listening, my eyes open wide. An older woman in the class came over to me. She must have seen the puzzled look on my face. "Can you believe what they're saying?" she asked.

"No, I feel confused."

After that class, I decided to quit. Something else was calling me. Even though I loved the house we were going to buy, I had a yearning to do something more with my life. So Lee and I talked. We talked about going to college. We talked about what we could study, and what we could do. "Let's do it," she finally said. "Let's go."

We didn't buy the house. Instead, I wrote many pages to my boss, explaining that I was quitting and that I was going to go back to school and into the field of psychology, which I thought would be more emotionally rewarding than what I had been doing. Mr. Heller was in shock. "Do you know you're up for a big raise?" he asked.

"No," I said, "but it doesn't make any difference. I need to do this."

Mr. Heller stayed in touch with me for some time. On more than one occasion, he sent me checks with a cover note saying, "I don't imagine you're overflowing with money." I later learned that he and his company had hired people who were obvious homosexuals.

Micaela Says Goodbye

One weekend when Lee and I were still living in Belmont Hills, we drove to Daly City, choosing to go by the route we loved best, by the ocean. As we drove along the beautiful hills overlooking the ocean, I suddenly felt this deep, deep sadness and tears just started flowing out of my eyes. The heavy feeling that flooded over me was that Micaela had died. Lee looked at me and said, "Honey, what's happening?"

"Micaela died."

"No, baby, I don't think so," Lee said with great tenderness. "I think if she died she would let you know."

"I think that's what's happening. She's letting me know."

Two weeks later, Lee and I took my mother to the beach. At some point, Mami said, "Oh, Zelima, I got a letter from Nicaragua. Micaela died."

Again, the tears started pouring down my cheeks. I went to bathroom and cried and cried. Lee came to me. She said, beautifully, "Just know that Micaela came to see you. She came to say goodbye to you."

It was a Sunday when Mami told me. I had to go to work the next day. I didn't know how I was going to be able to do it. I can't remember why now, but there was something I had to do at work the next day that was very important, so I couldn't just call in sick. I remember praying to Micaela that Monday morning, saying, "Micaela, please help me." Within a half hour, I felt a calmness settle in and went to work. I remember later that morning going to a truck to get coffee and a donut, saying, "Thank you, Micaela."

Micaela stayed with me for three days. On the afternoon of the third day, I went to the truck to get a cup of coffee and felt a sense of relief. I thanked Micaela, again, and she left quietly, leaving me with a deep feeling of peacefulness.

Going to College

Lee and I enrolled at San Jose State University. I studied psychology and she occupational therapy. We moved, renting a house near campus so we could walk to school, and we managed it all with a combination of economic opportunity grants, partial welfare, and work-study programs.

I loved my work-study program because it involved working in mental hospitals with so-called "mentally retarded" kids and adults. It was like a nightmare when I first went in—awful! But it took me to another side of things. I learned I could communicate with these "mentally retarded" people.

The management didn't want the employees to sit with the patients, but I always did. I watched TV with them and made friends. I used their bathroom and my co-workers would say about me, "How could she use the same bathroom?" But my friends and I would talk a lot in the bathroom! I think the doctors must have hated their jobs because they would not even look at the people in their care.

There was an incident one time when a little girl I really loved came up to me and said, "You want to see my new dolly?" I said, "Sure, honey." She raised it up to show me and I said, "How beautiful!" At that point, one of the attendants came by, grabbed the dolly out of the little girl's hands and pulled the head off. I was outraged! I wanted to smack her against the wall. Instead,I went back to sit and watch TV with my friends.

But I was still furious at the attendant and, as we were watching the TV, they could feel my rage. When I got up to go to the bathroom, they all followed me, including a man in his seventies who never spoke. He always just stood around with his mouth gaping wide open, tongue hanging out, and eyes looking up. As I was splashing some cold water on my face, the guy said, "Don't worry. She's leaving on Tuesday, and won't be here any more."

I was taken aback. "How do you know?" I asked, looking at him curiously.

"I know," he said. The man then turned and went back to the living room, where he again stood silently with his mouth wide open, his eyes gazing up, and his tongue hanging down.

Sure enough, on Tuesday the attendant left.

COMING OUT TO MY FAMILY

My mother found out very soon that I was in a lesbian relationship with Lee. I was living with Lee and was in love with her, and there was no way I could hide it. It turned out to be one of the times when my mother was really sweet.

Her first response, however, was to say, "¡Ay, m'ija! ¿Cómo puedes hacer eso?" (How can you do that?) But in time, Lee won her over. Mami said, "Me parece que lo mas importante es tu felicidad. ¿'Tas feliz? Pues bueno." (I think the most important thing is your happiness. You're happy? Well, then, good.)

By this time, my relationship with my mother had gotten better. As I said earlier, I was determined to love Mami no matter what, but it's also true that there was more than one aspect to my mother which made it possible for me to love her. Despite all she had done and all that had happened to her, there was an innocent part to Mami.

I remember when we first came to this country in 1948. My father, Zela, and Ivan were living in Long Beach when we joined them, and I had my first experience with racial discrimination and prejudice.

I couldn't speak English and a group of kids would gang up on me at recess and say, "Thees ees how Zelima talks..." But one day, after they got through with their usual harassment of me, a girl who was playing dodge ball turned to me and gestured if I wanted to play with her. We played and played, enjoying each other immensely, and she became my friend.

One day, as she and I were playing, going up the steps of the slide, an Albino boy at the top looked down at her and said, "No niggers here." I knew that the word "niggers" had something to do with "black" from the Spanish word *negro*. My friend tried to get past him, but he insisted, "No niggers here!" I then got a hold of his leg and pinched him so hard, he yelled and went down the slide. Then we went up and slid down.

When I got home, I told my mother what happened. "Why did he do that?" I asked her. My mother looked at me, her eyes round and innocent and totally perplexed. "*Pues, no sé,*" she said. (Well, I don't know.) She then ventured, "Maybe it's because Black people can take the sun and the little Albino boy has to be careful with the sun and maybe he was just jealous of her." She was totally nonplussed. "*No sé,*" she finally shrugged.

"I don't know." It was the best answer a child could receive to explain racial prejudice. If she didn't know, it was because it was something unknowable. That kind of behavior just could not be explained.

A few years after Lee and I were together, an article about us as "Lesbian Mothers" appeared in the San Francisco Chronicle. The day it came out, I got a call from my brother, Hiram, who said, in a very aggressive tone of voice, "I want to talk to you." I was on my way to my mother's house, so he met me there. I had the newspaper folded in my hand, but when I walked into the house, the paper was on the table, open to the page with the story about us, our faces all over it.

I slammed my copy of the paper on the table and growled to Hiram, "Is this what you want to talk to me about?"

Hiram looked at me, backing away, and said, hesitantly, "Yea."

My brothers had stopped hitting me when I was sixteen. That's when I started screaming at them and being aggressive back. There was something in my tone of voice that scared them and they never again laid a hand on me. I had that tone of voice now.

"What do you want to say about it?" I hissed.

"Well, is it true?" he asked.

"Read it!" I said pushing the paper toward him. "It's all true."

"Well, I read it."

"Do you have anything to say about it?" I demanded.

He looked down and shrugged, finally saying, "No, I don't have anything to say about it." And we then went on to talk about something else!

Later, his wife, Wanda, told me that Hiram had said to her, "There have been a lot of creative homosexuals in the world." He actually accepted Lee, and we had a good relationship for a while. But a few years after this Hiram became a born-again Christian and got after me again.

As for my mother, Lee had won her heart. But she was influenced by my brother, so when questions came up from time to time she would waver. One time she told me, "*Así se pone uno cuando lee libros sucios.*" (That's what happens to you when you read dirty books.)

"*Mami, yo nunca he leído un libro sucio.*" (Mami, I have *never* read a dirty book.) I said, "This is who I am. For the first time in my life I know who I am and I'm not going to change. All I'm being is myself. This is who I am. This is how God created me."

"*Pero m'ija, tu crees que tu eres hombre?*" (But what do you think? Do you think you're a man?)

"*Todos tenemos hombre y mujer adentro. Pero yo se como expresarlo,*" I said. (We all have male and female within us. I just know how to express it.)

For so much of my life, I had repressed myself. When it came to this essential part of who I was, I just let it out. I couldn't help it. I knew who I was and I was not going to let anyone make me deny it or force me to be otherwise.

Dealing with Lee's Family

It was a real struggle with Lee's family, however. They were totally homophobic. Her mother was constantly pushing Lee's ex-husband, whom she didn't like when he and Lee were married, to take the kids away from her. We were living under that constant threat, and it was taking a toll on us. We were both exhausted and stressed out from all the anxiety—when I came up with an idea.

"Look, Lee, you're going to have to scare them," I said. "That's the only way we're going to stop these threats and have a chance to live in peace." I then spelled out the whole plot I had concocted. I told Lee I was counting on her grandmother to make it work—there was something about her grandmother that was very beautiful and my plot depended on her goodness to turn things around. The whole thing involved *high manipulation* on my part.

Early in the evening on the day that we put the plot to work, I called Lee's mother and her ex-husband to say that Lee hadn't come home. I told them I was very worried because Lee had been very depressed, was crying a lot, and had been talking about committing suicide. Everyone was on alert!

A few hours later, when Lee still hadn't come home, her mother and grandmother and ex-husband came over to wait. It was now the middle of the night and I was wailing and crying and putting on an act that could have won an Academy Award! I cried about how upset and depressed Lee had been about the constant threat of having her kids taken away. It was actually an easy act for me to stage because when I envisioned the very real possibility that a mother might lose her children because of our love, hot tears just flowed down my cheeks.

At some point, Lee's grandmother said, "I'm really tired of this." She turned to Lee's mother and ex-husband and said, "Why don't you just leave these girls alone? The kids are better behaved. They look happy. I think you just need to leave these things alone and mind your own business."

Around 1:00 a.m., as we had arranged it, the phone rang and it was Lee. "Baby, come home!!" I wailed into the receiver. "Everyone's here and we've all been so worried! It's okay, it's okay. They promised to leave us alone! *Come home!*"

A short while later, when Lee walked in the door, her grandmother went up and hugged her and everyone was teary. Lee's ex-husband put his arm around her and said, "Don't worry. It's going to be okay." And after her mother and grandmother left, Lee's husband stayed for a while. He told us that he had never wanted to take the kids away. "Who knows, maybe one day we'll all spend Christmas together."

After he left, Lee and I fell back on the couch, exhausted and exhilarated.

Lee's mother never did bother us after this, but the incident left a horrible feeling in me. I had lied all the way through it. I was so ashamed and embarrassed; it took me the longest time to tell Peter. Eventually, I confessed it to him. After I got through the whole story, Peter just looked at me and said, "Zelima, you were fighting for your life."

My guilt went away because that's exactly what I was doing. We were fighting for our lives—and we won.

THE GAY MOVEMENT

One of the reasons I enrolled in San Jose State University was because I read an article in the newspaper about how the student union had voted 100% to accept the Gay Liberation Front as a new student group on campus. It was after Stonewall, and I had this fantasy when I read the article that gay people would be walking around on campus holding hands!

Instead, on my very first day at school, I read an article in the student newspaper announcing that they had to dissolve the Gay Liberation Front. Then-Governor Ronald Reagan had apparently heard about the student union's acceptance of the gay group on campus and wrote a letter saying something to the effect of, "What are you running down there, a cesspool?" Reagan insisted that the Gay Liberation Front be barred from acceptance as a student group; under his pressure the University and student union relented.

Tears flooded my eyes as I read the paper. I felt such a sense of sorrow and hopelessness that I turned around and started to head back home. I was giving up—on school, on everything. But after walking about a block, my grief and desolation gave way to anger. And then the anger grew into a rage and soon I found myself marching to the student union to ask if there was anyone from the Gay Liberation Front I could talk to.

I was given the name of a nice White woman named Patricia who actually was not a student. Patricia was glad to see me when I got in contact with her, but she told me there were only a few people left who had been involved with the group. We met at a church that gave us a place to meet, and that's where we got started. We decided to stay together as a group, and they voted me as chairperson. I was the only student.

In some ways, that marked a new beginning of my life. I became a different person. I was a good leader there for a while. My rage carried me. I was in a rage but it all came out in very positive ways. It was a time when I also learned about strength and courage. It took courage to come out on campus at that time. I was the only openly lesbian woman on campus. Everywhere I went on campus people knew who I was, and I was ridiculed. When students would see me coming, they would point and start to giggle or laugh. I learned to walk with my head and shoulders up, back straight, and limbs strong. I even started doing things like stopping dead in my tracks and walking up to them to look them in the eye until they would stop.

A lot of people from the Bay area started coming to the Gay Liberation Front meetings but most of them weren't in college. The gay students were afraid. It took a while, but slowly the gay students started coming to the meetings as well.

About a year and a half later, I was still walking around campus with my head held high, always expecting someone to make some cutting remark. I remember talking to a friend about how the students looked down on me, when she said, "Zelima, have you checked in lately? People respect you, honey. You are greatly respected on this campus." I had no idea.

What I did know is that the leftist groups on campus were starting to come over to ask about our strategies! We were becoming more and more successful in organizing all kinds of events and activities on campus. During a fair of student groups, we had a room and it was packed. Whenever we went to speak at an event or to a campus meeting, we'd say, "We're here!" The other groups on campus started to pick that up, saying, "We're here!"

I remember one big event we organized. It started because some of the gay students on campus wanted to spend some quiet, introspective time together to find out more about who we were. So they took out an ad in the student paper that said something about gays interested in self exploration, please contact this person. Well, the paper refused to print the ad because of the words "self exploration!" I got really pissed off. I talked to everyone in our group and we ended up creating a leaflet that we distributed all around the University. At the bottom of the leaflet, we wrote: "If the only kind of self exploration they understand is masturbation, it's their problem, not ours." We got so much support, the editor apologized to us!

By this time I had become a U.S. citizen. I had decided to apply for citizenship when I was working at Agfa. I had grown to love this country and the people here. There is oppression against people of color all over the world, but I felt that people here were at least trying to do something about it. I wanted to be able to be part of the struggle to make this a better place without worrying about being deported because of my political activities or because I was homosexual, so I became a citizen.

My political work with the Gay Liberation Front made me feel for the first time in my life that I could say, "I have accomplished something." I started liking myself, thinking I was worthwhile. With Elvie I was being who I thought I had to be, whereas with Lee, I was able to be my lesbian self. I could take hold of myself and say, "Yes, this is who I am." Before this, the homosexuality question hung over me and all I could think was, "I'm sick." The gay movement gave me the opportunity to go out and fight for the right to be who I am. I became proud of who I am. I had so much anger in me, but I did wonderful things with it. I took all that anger and I accomplished something with it.

Even my kids got involved. They were really good when Lee and I told them about being lesbian. They loved Lee and liked us together—and there was a peace in the house, at least at the beginning, that they hadn't felt before. They loved all my friends in the gay movement and joined us in many of the marches. John even spoke for Kid's Liberation at one of them! Our house was the hangout for all their friends.

Lee and I both threw ourselves into the movement and we made great strides together. Lee usually stayed in background except for one memorable moment. The head of the university system, Glen Dumke[11], was coming on campus to give a speech about something and there was going to be time allotted for students to bring requests or grievances to him. All the different factions on campus wanted to talk and everyone expected me to speak for the Gay Liberation Front. I said, "Not this time. Lee, would you do it?" She said "yes," even though she was not the kind to get up and talk, and was really scared.

When the time came, one student group after another got up to speak. Everybody clapped. Then it was Lee's turn. She stood up and said, "I'm Lee and I represent the Gay Liberation Front." As soon as she said, "Gay Liberation Front," the audience started clapping. She then went on to state our grievances. It was so powerful, Lee got a standing ovation from the crowd! It was a great victory. I was so proud of her, scared as she was to do this. We really *earned* our respect.

My days with the Gay Liberation Front at the university came to an end when I started to be resented. I was getting all this credit for the gay rights movement and I was told that I was playing "the heavy." It had been okay for me to play the leadership role when it was dangerous to be out, but as it got safer, people started to become jealous and resentful of my leadership. It was time for me to go, and I was happy to leave my name out during the next election even though many wanted me to run again.

A lot of gay men ended up taking over the Gay Liberation Front, and when I heard some of them talking, it made me sick at heart. Before when we talked, it was always at a gut level: *This is who I am.* We were about letting people see who we were, but they were saying things like, "sexuality is like choosing ice cream. Some people like strawberry, some like chocolate ..."

Well, I ain't no ice cream! Not vanilla, chocolate, or strawberry. I'm a human being. I was glad to be moving on. I also recognized that I hadn't taken a leadership role in the Gay Liberation Front out of selflessness—I did it for myself, as a homosexual person. I wanted to be free, and I was going to do something about it. After a while, I did it for my brothers and sisters, too. But at first I did it for myself and for my love.

When we were done with this work, my friend Arturo told me, "San Jose has changed, honey!" I have the knowledge that we were a big part of it.

PAPI'S WARRIOR DEATH

In the fall of 1972, I got word that Papi was very sick and dying. Steeped as I was in the gay movement, I went there "gay and proud," causing a big commotion! Among other things, I wore *caites,* sandals with leather straps that wrap around your ankles, which scandalized everyone. They said I was in the market hanging around with *cochones y prostitutas* (queers and prostitutes).

Papi never objected or said a word to me about my behavior. His response to others was to say, *"Pues, a mi hija nunca le a importado lo que piensa la sociedad."* (Well, my daughter has never cared much about what society thinks.)

He was good in that way. But then I learned something that made my stomach turn. I had gone with my father's partner, Marta, to the jewelry store one night to help with the inventory. An old *Indio* knocked on the door. He was the night watchman. *"Señora,"* he said to Marta. "I'd like to talk with you." He didn't know who I was; I had never seen him before. And he didn't know that my father was sick and dying. It was the first time he saw Marta alone at the store and he took advantage of the moment to come talk to her.

"Su esposo..." he began. "Your husband brings little girls here in the middle of the night and in the early hours of the morning—little girls as young as six and some as old as twelve. One night he had three little girls."

87

He went on to say, "*Señora*, he stays in here for a long time, for hours with these little girls. I thought you should know."[12]

When he was done, Marta said, "*Bueno, pues, señor. Muchas gracias por decirme.*" (Well, thank you very much for telling me.)

I was numb as I saw her shut the door behind the old *Indio*. My stomach was in a knot. I *knew* what he was talking about. "*Ay, dios mío,*" I half-whispered to Marta.

"*Ay, Zelima,*" Marta said, as if talking to a child. "*Tu sabes como son los hombres. Tu papá es un hombre. Así son los hombres.*" (You know how men are. Your father is a man. That's how men are.) Marta was some seven or eight years younger than I was and only fifteen when my father took her as his girl-friend. She was now in her mid-twenties, and had given birth to two children by my father. Even so, now that he was sick, several times when he tossed and turned and cried out for help, it wasn't Marta he called for but Esmeralda, my mother.

Papi and I had been getting along up to this point. After this, I started having a really hard time with him. I couldn't look at him without thinking about what the *Indio* had said. Marta didn't want him to know, so I found myself getting short-tempered with Papi, picking fights. I had such an explosive mix of feelings, I didn't know what to do. I would feel anger, then compassion. I would feel sick to my stomach about him, then proud. This man who did such unspeakable things was also a seeker, a person who tapped into some essential truths in life as he was dying. And he died like a warrior.

Papi had gotten involved with some kind of guru who believed in reincarnation, and he refused to see medical doctors or take any medication. Papi said he wanted to be *awake* when he died. Every day he would sit and people would come to the house to hear him talk. He offered teachings, saying deep things, and got to be known as a *maestro*.

One day a popular evangelical preacher with a Bible in hand came to see Papi, to convert him on his death bed. The preacher began, "First, there was the Word." My father was ready for him; he closed his eyes and listened to everything the preacher had to say. An hour or so later, when the preacher finally stopped talking, Papi said, "*Bueno, pues.*" He then commenced to go through the preacher's entire speech, piece by piece. "First, there was the Word. Now, what does that mean?"

I really can't remember exactly what my father said. All I know is that it was so profound and deep and true, my mind expanded and I could only grasp it for a minute or two—and then it was lost. I think that's why the preacher got so scared—he recognized that there was truth in what Papi was saying. All I remember is that the preacher started to stutter. He dropped his Bible and his glasses. I was so bowled over by what Papi had said it took me a minute or two to see what was happening with the preacher and help him. He then got up and left, totally shaken.

I had never seen a non-Christian baffle a fanatic before. No matter what you say, they always have an answer. This preacher's mouth just dropped after Papi got through with him; he couldn't come back with anything. Wow! That's my Papi, I thought. And then I sunk deeper into the experience. Here is a man, I thought, who was so violent and abusive. He would have killed me or come close to it when he tried to take me to that abandoned building years ago. Who knows what harm he had done to how many little girls in his lifetime? Yet, at the same time, he was a man who had been searching for something, for truth— and he got it! He reached a profound place of knowing. "Don't judge," were the words that came to me. Spirit was in my heart; I didn't want to go on hating him.

Papi

Papi died right after I left Nicaragua. Before I left he said, "When you see your mother, you tell her for me that we're not through with each other yet. You tell Esmeralda that we will see each other and we will love again."

Breaking Up

Being part of the Gay Liberation Front was wonderful, but it also had its negative side. One of them was that some of the women in the movement were pushing Lee and me to be non-monogamous. We were both very monogamous people, but it got pushed and pushed that we were being politically incorrect by being monogamous. So we tried to be non-monogamous— and didn't survive it.

We had to get separate bedrooms when we became non-monogamous, and we grew further and further apart. I withdrew more and more. There were resentments on both parts. We didn't even know where the resentments were coming from.

Of course, I was crazy, too, and Lee had to deal with that. Even though I had come a long way through my therapy, I hadn't finished dealing with all that what was going on inside me from my childhood. I still had this fear that would grip me and wake me up with anxiety, and I was still dealing with multiple personalities. I also had started using drugs, all kinds of psychedelics as experimentation and bennies to stay awake during exams.

My drug use had actually started with prescriptions for a neck injury when I was married. Some ceiling plaster had fallen on my head and the pain was awful. I was in traction for a while, taking morphine and had become very addicted. Eventually I got over it on my own.

But later, when I was in college, I tried other drugs. Psychedelics were fun. Acid was a beautiful experience that got me in touch with Earth and a lot of things. I took it three times and learned something each time. The fourth time, I didn't learn anything. It was just a trip. The fifth time was the same, so I stopped. I felt I needed to respect the knowledge I had gained. And when the knowledge stopped, I quit.

I tried other psychedelics but stopped eventually because when they wore off, I didn't feel good. But what made me crazy were the bennies. I took them for cramming for exams. Those really harmed me. I became very ill and almost passed out on the street once. They also fueled my violence.

Before I broke up with Lee and while we were non-monogamous, I was going out with a woman named KT. I was on psychedelics and speed when KT called to have a conversation with me. She was trying to be truthful, telling me that she had used me, getting involved with me because she was lonely. "You have so many friends, and I wanted friends," she said. After I hung up, I remember calling my friend, Joyce, to ask if I could borrow her truck, "so I can go beat up KT."

I drove to KT's cabin in the woods and slapped her around. It took me about three days to realize I was wrong. It seemed so right for me to go do that when I was on the drugs. But when the drugs wore off and I came down, I felt awful! I felt I was being like my brother, Hiram, even in the way I was walking. This kind of violence was something I did not believe in, so how could I get so turned around? How was it that it felt so right to beat her up when I was on the drugs? It was the last time I took those kinds of drugs.

Not long after that, and shortly before we graduated from college, Lee moved out. I lost the love of my life.

CHAPTER 6

RE-AWAKENING TO THE SACRED PATH

P eople have asked me how I got to be on my path. In some ways it was by default because nothing else seemed to work for me. I had a very, very deep pain that made a hole in me. The hole went so deep it connected with the Infinite, and became a channel where the energy comes through.

After shaking off the hold of the Catholic Church, I went searching for something to fill the spiritual loss I felt. Then, soon after I started college, I remember lying in bed by myself when I had the urge to open and close my hand, as if I were grasping at something. Sparks started flying out of my hand. Yellow sparks were shooting out. I felt calm and wasn't scared. It felt right. I remember thinking, "Something sacred is happening."

A while later when Lee and I were getting ready to go to sleep, I looked up and was amazed to find that I could see every little bump and speck of paint on the ceiling. "Lee! I'm seeing every little bump on wall, every little speck of gold and silver in the paint, and I don't even have my glasses on. I couldn't see all this even if I was wearing my glasses!" Lee looked at me and said, "How does it feel to be out of your body?"

This time I was terrified! I gasped and started hyperventilating. The ceiling went back to normal.

I started having the urge to go everywhere in my bare feet. Although we lived on a very busy street in a university neighborhood covered with concrete, I walked barefoot to school, drawn to the little bits of Earth exposed wherever trees were planted along the sidewalks. The trees drew me to them and I started to put my hands on their trunks. Three months later, I started to feel a new energy surge in my body. I could feel it coursing through my body and also coming out of my hands.

The healing work began organically. It was nothing that I pre-thought; it just happened. My friends Arturo, Lupita, and María knew something was going on with me. I started touching them, asking if they could feel the energy pouring out of my hands. They'd say, "Yes." Eventually, my friends began saying, "You know, I had a headache before you touched me and now it's gone." Or, "I had a pain here and now I don't feel it anymore." Then I started having my own health problems and when I touched the places that hurt, I could feel something begin to release!

Drawn as I was to the trees, I also started seeing them differently; they had distinct personalities and I could see that they communicated with each other with lines of different colored energy flowing between them. It was so beautiful. I began to have such a sense of the aliveness of trees and of their dignity. The more I got in touch with that energy flow, the more I realized the intensity of the life force. The trees then led me to the stones, the stones led me to the water, the water led me to the winds, and then to the sun and the moon and the stars. I began to have such a sense of the aliveness of Mother Earth. I was guided to open the pores of the soles of my feet and the palms of my hands—even the pores of my eyes—to let the energies of Earth and Sky flow into my body. I started to remember the things Micaela had taught me and the way she taught me, by osmosis, with all the knowledge flowing in through my pores, just as I was now being taught by Mother Earth.

Although this new energy was intense, I never experienced any fear except one time when I looked at the sun too long. I had made contact with the Spirits of different animals, including Eagle who taught me how to gather energy from the sun. I had noticed that Eagle had all this sun energy in him, a sort of electrical energy that I learned he got by looking at the sun in a certain way. One day, while I was waiting for a friend in dancing school, I gathered energy from the sun the way Eagle taught me. A magnitude of energy rushed in that I had never experienced before. I didn't know what in the world to do with it! Luckily, I found a closet at the dance school and went into its darkness. I held my stomach, doing the best I could to handle the energy until it finally calmed down inside me. It was the only time I felt fear in connection with the energy. It taught me respect.

Around this time, I also started to understand the meaning of the visions I had begun to have just a few years earlier. In the late 1960s, I had been having visions of terrible floods and other catastrophic disasters on Earth. At the time, I thought I was looking into the past, into Biblical times.

But now I was beginning to understand that I was seeing into the future. I began to get guidance—guidance from Great Spirit—about the visions. "There is something coming on the Earth that you are being prepared for, something that has never happened before," the guidance said.

I was told about the Path of the Little Sisters; it was a path that would guide us through the intense times that were coming. We would soon experience a time of great destruction and catastrophe; but it also would be a time of creation and miracles. I was told that because we have never been through anything like this, we would not be able to think our way through it. We would only be able to get through it by allowing ourselves to be guided, like babies, each step of the way.

This is the Path of the Little Sisters—a path that requires you to be completely open to guidance and to be free to follow it. I was told that Little Sisters cannot allow themselves to be dominated by anybody or anything. It's not about being rebellious; it's about being free to get guidance directly from Spirit—and to do the work you need to do.

Along with all of this came the drawings. Never in my life did I dream I could draw. It started one day when I was in Arturo's apartment. I picked up a pencil and started doodling. The next thing I knew, I saw a leg taking shape on the paper—a real leg! Something told me to carry on with this doodling. It felt like something had come over me; I just watched my hands making circles, drawing. Later, I took the drawing to school and my psychology professor told me I had drawn a mandala, explaining its significance as a sacred image.[13] This went on for about a year. I was so charged with the new energy in my body, I only slept for about fifteen minutes at a time. I would be talking and then fall asleep. Then I'd get up and draw. I couldn't stop drawing—beautiful things that I couldn't believe were coming out of me.

The drumming started around the same time. It was all of one piece. I was friends with a family of Filipinos, all of whom were musicians. Jick played the flute, guitar, and drums. His sisters, Connie and Alice, gave me a drum and I started playing with them. They said, "Just put your hands on it." I would play and they improvised to make me sound good. They were following me, making me sound great. One day I asked, "How do I follow you?"

Jick said, "Oh, you want to grow?" I said, yes, and they started working with me. Again, something inside told me to do what I was doing with my drawing—to go inside myself and put the feelings out. The first time I played like that, letting the feelings inside flow to my hands and into the beat of the drum, I wrote this poem,

The sound of my
Drum is my soul speaking,
My feelings are released
And flow thru the air –

My soul soars
In tune with
Its own beat

My drum beats
The Rhythm of
     My self

I found the beat
Of my own Rhythm
On my drum –
Only then, could
I join the beat
Of other drums

Only then, could
I join the beat
Of other drums

I had also started writing a lot of poetry at this time. Soon, I was being asked to do poetry readings at various places, including the local TV station.[14]

Sometime in 1973, my friend Arturo came to visit me. I had a little African wooden *osi* drum in front of me, a *maraca* in my left hand, bells on both ankles, and the little *osi* drum beater in my right hand. Arturo picked up my small harp, looked at me and said, "No one would believe you are the mother of two teenage children."

Actually, John wasn't a teenager yet! But I was being a child—my child was coming out. I was making connections with what was deep inside me and bringing it out in drawings and drumming. Something else beyond me was also going on. I could feel the energy in my body. I was following the impulses, letting the energy flow through me, and letting myself be guided.

By this time I was seeing Peter off and on. I remember talking to him about this; he took it all in stride, saying, "Yes, something is happening in you." He told me, "There is something special in you. You could accomplish a lot if you were not so damned afraid of success."

It wasn't just success I was afraid of— I still feared the apparitions that were coming to me. One time, I was sleeping on my mattress, which in those days I just put on the floor, when I felt this intense pain come from below my bellybutton all the way up to my chest and out of my mouth. I rolled over onto the floor and held myself in a tight ball while the pain moved up my body and into my throat where it went, "lick," out of my mouth and up to the ceiling. Suddenly, the pain was gone and an incredible bright yellow light appeared on the ceiling. I could see it beaming down all around me and was so terrified, I did not dare look at it.

The shimmering yellow light stayed on my ceiling for two months, eventually covering the walls, too.

Other people could also see the light, so I didn't have to wonder, "Is this really happening or not?" Friends would come over and say, "Hey, Zelima! You painted your walls yellow." I would say, "No, look closer." They would look closer and see that the walls were still white behind a shimmer of yellow. "Oh, wow," they would say and I knew that whatever it was, it *was* happening. But it was still scary for me. I couldn't look at the light until it had come down into the walls where it wasn't as bright.

I finally lost my fear about this when one of my teachers, Josie, an elder, came to visit for a few of days. While we were talking, I started to feel the shimmering yellow light beaming down from the ceiling again. Getting scared, I said, "Josie, it's happening." She said, "What's happening?"

"That light...." I said, getting shaky and nodding my head upwards.

Josie looked up. "Oh, that's nothing to be afraid of," she said nonchalantly. "This is only God."

I gasped and started hyperventilating, scared to death. Josie repeated, calm as can be, "Honey, it's God." Then she put her hands up toward the light, smiled, and said, so sweetly and with such cheer, "He-llo, God."

I was shaking. I didn't stop shaking until it was over. But afterwards when I thought about how Josie had handled it, I began to be less afraid and started to feel stronger within myself. After that and for the next three years, I had some beautiful apparitions and nothing got to me, nothing. Not that there weren't any obstacles. But before this experience I had always had a fear of obstacles and would resist trying to overcome them. During those three years I just walked right through them. I thought, "This is it. This is the way it is going to be the rest of my life!"

Right.

VOICES & ORACLES

When I consciously accepted my path, the voices started. I would be going about my day, doing things, and I began to hear things like, "Stop. Don't. Not now." Or "Now, do it now." It actually started with a feeling I would get or a light hum that would warn me I was about to get in trouble. As I tuned in, and started paying attention to these warnings, I began to hear words.

I soon came to understand that the voices were my guides, something inside me that would come through in different voices or body feelings that would help me understand what I was to do. Over the years, the voices have been both male and female. A lot of them are African-American voices. They tickle me because they can put me back in balance or set me straight in a way that makes me laugh at myself. I get right back on track.

I also started consulting the Oracle after I got on my path. I would use the Oracle when I wanted to know more or needed greater clarity about something I heard from my voices. One Oracle I started using, the Sacred Path Cards by Jamie Sams, helped me a lot with my healings. After a healing I would ask how my patient is doing. The Oracle would often confirm what I was seeing or give me an idea of the effect that the healing energy was having on a patient. I also learned a lot about myself from the Secret Dakini, and have gotten guidance from the Runes, the I Ching, and the Gong Yee Fot Choy.[15]

But none of these were ever primary. When I hear my voices, I know it's real—a true connection to the Divine. With the Oracles, I might wonder. So I've used them to support or clarify something I already know, and not as guidance I absolutely have to follow—like my voices.

SAN MARTÍN DE PORRES

I fell in love with San Martín de Porres in grammar school when he was Blessed Martin. I saw a statue of him and the first thing that attracted me was that he was Black, dark skinned. I wondered who he was and started asking about him. I found out he was a Dominican brother who was born in Peru in the late 1500s. His mother was a freed African slave and his father a Spaniard, who pretty much abandoned him. When I found out about his love of animals and his kindness to them, I fell in love. He was in my mind a lot when I was a child—and still is.

By the time I started coming into my path and having all these spiritual experiences, San Martín had become my favorite saint. His love of animals, his ability to bilocate, and his gentleness were what made me feel so close to him. I just loved his energy. As I started recognizing that I was walking a sacred path, I decided to create an altar in my home. A lot of different medicine objects had been coming to me. I placed them on the altar and realized I wanted San Martín there, too. So I got a statue of him. I took good care of that altar, cleaning it every day and putting fresh flowers on it.

Later when I was doing prison work, one of the women in jail made me a little blue bracelet. It was so delicate—since they weren't allowed to use strong string—I was afraid to wear it. When I saw the statue of San Martín on the altar, I decided to put the bracelet around his neck. One day my friend Agida came to visit. She went to pay her respects to the altar and when she saw San Martín, she asked, "What are you doing with them blue beads on San Martín's neck?"

I explained, and then she told me a story about San Martín. Agida was very knowledgeable about Orisha[16] and African-based religions. She said that San Martín's mother was a prostitute. Prostitutes in jail practicing Orisha would put blue beads around San Martín's neck whenever they had to go to court because he is known to help prostitutes. I told Agida that a prostitute gave me the bracelet! She said, "That's San Martín's way of saying, 'If you're going to be with prostitutes, dress me up right!'"

99

XOCHIQUETZAL

When I was in college, I stopped using my surname. I just went by
Zelima. I didn't want to use my father's name because I was not wanted by
my family. And my ex-husband's name didn't belong to me either. So I
stopped using any surname. Everyone knew me as Zelima, but people would
ask, "When are you going to get a last name?"

The friends who knew me before, during, and after the energy started
flowing through me started telling me I should choose a *spiritual* name.
Arturo, María, Lupita, Cecilia, Carlos, Pablo, Olga, and Jick and his family
were among the friends who accompanied me through these times when we
had no idea what was going on with me—and they did it like champs. When
the drawings started coming, María and I were working in same office. She'd
finish her work quickly and then tell me to give her mine, saying, "You start
drawing." I would protest, but she insisted. "Something's happening with
you. It's good. Do it." She and the others knew me when I couldn't draw a
thing. All of a sudden, my work was showing up in art exhibits, with people
asking, "Who did this?"

I had never thought about choosing a spiritual name, but these friends
encouraged me and we all agreed it had to have something to do with Earth.
I decided I wanted it to be a Nahuatl name because that's what I have most
in my blood. One day, Arturo and I went to the library. Right away, I chose
the name of the Nahuatl Earth Goddess. But Arturo pulled out another one,
saying he was told to tell me, "This is it. This is the one that fits you—
Xochiquetzal (so-chee-KET-sal), the Flower-Feather Goddess of Art."

I said, "Okay." I didn't know anything about ceremonies at that time.
But Arturo and I did our own little ceremony, getting together to give thanks
for my name. I agreed to let Xochiquetzal come into my being and guide me.

FEELING MOTHER EARTH'S CHANGES

I can date exactly when another one of the strange changes in me
started—it was the fall of 1972 when I was in Managua to be with my dying
father. I had planned to stay with him for about three months, but ended up
leaving earlier—and in a hurry—because I couldn't breathe.

Something was going on with my heart. It felt so tight, so congested. I had these screams inside me that I wanted to let out, but it was hard to find a place where I could do that in Managua. In the college neighborhood where I lived, we could scream all we wanted!

I was also struck by how different the people seemed to be. There was so much vulgarity and profanity on the streets. There had always been some swearing in Nicaragua when I was growing up, but this was different. You couldn't go anywhere without hearing someone hurling out a vulgarity. It was everywhere. I also noticed something in the Native peoples' eyes, the people who had to toil all the time. Their eyes were burning; it called up a poem in me.

Conquered
        Exploited
by worshippers of crosses and lamb's blood.
Strong, brown bodies sweat
            glistening beneath the Nicaraguan sun
Eyes deeply set on faces carved with lines of Oppression
Eyes
        burning
            burning
                burning
with the blend of passions
mañana
    mañana
Will lift the burden
of Now.

I had to get out of there. Even though I knew Papi was dying, I couldn't stay any longer. The pain in my heart was so intense and it was so hard for me to breath, I felt I was going to die. I actually heard a voice tell me that if I didn't get out of there, I *would* die. So I flew back home, thinking my health problems were driving me out of Managua.

The first thing I did when I got back was to get in the shower and start screaming. A neighbor said, "Well, Zelima's back."

Not long after, I heard that Papi had died, sitting up, asking for a pillow. A week or two after that, just after midnight on December 23, 1972, a massive earthquake shook Managua. Three days before the earthquake struck, I wrote a poem about some of the feelings I was having about "HEAVY things" happening all at once and one after another, and everything being up in the air, wondering, "does that mean a heavy rain is going to fall?"

The earthquake leveled five square miles of the city. Ten thousand people died. Eighty percent of all the buildings in the city were flattened, including two of the three main hospitals. Those who didn't die in the earthquake perished in the huge fires that were sparked by aftershocks. Fifty thousand homes were destroyed; 300,000 people were left homeless. Christmas decorations dotted the ruins.

In the horror of what happened in Managua, I realized why I was told I would die if I didn't leave. It wasn't about my health, although my health was related. I realized that the intense pain I felt in my heart was my body picking up the vibration of Mother Earth—the tension, the constriction, the massive pressures that were building up. Other people were picking it up, too, reflected in the tension, the way they were acting with each other.

After this, a pattern started. I would feel a pain in my heart and think it was just me until it would begin to go deep and get really intense. Then I begin to think, "Okay, there is something going on somewhere, something building." The pain would release and then, invariably, I would see in the news that there was a big earthquake somewhere. I now understood that I would start feeling a constriction in my heart and experience short-temperedness in myself and in others whenever a big earthquake was coming in some part of the world.

I soon started to notice that there was a connection between my having a lot of anxiety with something major about to happen with the winds, like a tornado or hurricane. And then I figured out that there was a connection between pressure I would feel in my temples that would give me bad headaches with the coming of major floods. When I started giving workshops and began to talk about this, my students would call me later and say they had started to notice these connections in themselves, too.

Finally, I started seeing things come in cycles. I noticed that a cycle would begin with an increase in things like accidents or car crashes happening locally. Then it would shift to larger things like plane crashes, chemical spills, oil spills. Next would be summer wildfires. I started to realize that the intensity of the wildfire would tell me something about the magnitude of what was coming next—a tornado, hurricane, flood, or earthquake.

When I first started observing this, there would be a long break in between these cycles. Now there are practically no breaks—and when they come, they are very swift. Also, the heartache is greater, the headaches are getting worse, and the anxiety is more intense. But I get my strength from knowing I'm working with the whole. "I'm with you, Mother. I'm with you, Universe. Okay, here we go."

STRUGGLES RAISING MY KIDS

Life wasn't all one big spiritual journey during this time. Far from it! Lee and I split apart in 1973. We both had one more year to go to graduate from college. My heart was broken and I stayed celibate for at least a year, maybe more. I just wanted to be alone, with my kids.

But that, too, was a challenge. We were living in the university neighborhood where a lot of children started being interested in sniffing glue and paint. My son, John, got involved. It was a horror to see my child like that and I didn't know what to do. He was eleven or twelve years old, still in elementary school, and I thought, "Oh boy, my troubles have started."

What broke it up was a crisis. One day, John didn't come home. It got to be midnight, then 1:00 a.m., 1:30 a.m., and my kid hadn't come home! By 2:00 a.m., I was crazed. He finally dragged in at 2:30 a.m., reeking of paint from his nose and mouth.

Before I knew it, I had popped him in the face. His eye swelled up. I wasn't even sorry. Still shaking from the stress, I said, "Stay away from my face," and got into bed. It took a while, but as I finally calmed myself down and started to fall asleep, I heard a knock at the door.

"Mom, can I talk with you for a minute?" It was John. He had sobered up.
"Come in," I said.
"Mom, I just became aware of something."
"What?"
"If I did something bad enough for you to do this," he said, pointing to his black eye, "I have to be doing something wrong."

He then went on to say that if I wanted him to quit sniffing, "we have to move." He explained how friends would hold him down and put a cloth with paint over his face. "We're going to have to move," he said.

"Okay," I said. "We'll move."

The next morning, I went looking for a house and within a week we were out of there. John did stop sniffing paint, but soon he began drinking. Alcoholism runs in the family and John has struggled with it all his life. Years later I learned that, young as he was, John was filled with guilt and remorse about something that had happened to Wanda a year or two earlier that he wished he had done something to stop.

Wanda never talked about it either but I had noticed a change in her and had tried to get her to talk to me about whatever was going on in her life. She insisted nothing was happening. I took both kids to see Peter a couple of times but they clammed up. Both just looked up at the ceiling with arms folded, refusing to say anything. The third time I got ready to take them, they refused to go, saying they were not going to talk to him. By this time, Wanda had become very demanding and controlling, giving orders to her friends— and she started getting into trouble. When she was only eleven, she took an orange van we had and drove it around. I don't know how she did it or how she managed the pedals; I believe I even called the police. But hours later, who shows up behind the wheel of the missing van but my little eleven-year-old daughter.

Later Wanda got into more trouble, ending up in Juvie more than once. They'd call me and I'd go get her. One time she spent the night there because I refused to go get her. By the time she was in junior high school, she was in with some really bad company. She had friends who would come to our house and rob me blind.

We were so close when she was little. I used to call her "sweet baby, sweet baby, sweet baby." She tried to say it back but it came out "babyshoe, babyshoe, babyshoe."

THE JAIL PROJECT

My prison work began soon after my friend Brenda asked if I would join a college group of hers that had decided to go into women's prisons and do workshops on dance and art, and such things. Right away, I said yes. The Jail Project was focused on the Milpitas County Jail, but on special occasions we also went down to Coronado State Prison near Los Angeles.

When we talked to the police about what we wanted to do, they said it was okay but warned us about not getting sucked in. "Don't get fooled! You can't trust these prisoners; they will manipulate you." I found out about trust and respect in a totally different way, working with the women in prison.

The first few times I went to the jail, I brought drums. But the police and some women who taught Bible school complained, so we had to stop drumming even though the women loved it. Then I started doing something else I can't remember right now, except that it, too, was banned. Finally there was nothing left for me to do but use my hands. "Okay, this is how we'll work together," I said. I had the women join me in a circle and, letting myself be guided, I would touch the women and share healing energy.

Not long after this, one of the guards accused me in front of the women of bringing in some pornography they had found. "No, ma'am," I said to the guard. "I don't even look at that stuff." One of the women responded angrily, saying, "You're accusing her because she touches us!" Another said, "What we're doing is sacred." When the guard saw the anger in their eyes, she backed off.

One night the guards let us out into the exercise yard, when the moon was full. The Grandmother was beautiful that night! The women had already learned about being still and opening the pores of the soles of their feet and the palms of their hands to let the Earth's energies flow into them. That night we all did it and one young woman, who really was still just a girl, said, "I think I feel it! It's flowing out!" She extended her arms and all the other women placed their hands under hers to feel it. Sure enough! The energy was trickling at first but then a little stream came pouring out of her hands. The women were elated—it was *real*, they could *feel* it!

When I went back the next week, they told me they couldn't sleep that night. So excited that they had connected with Grandmother Moon and actually felt her energy, they stayed up all night, laughing! The matrons were furious with them because they couldn't get to sleep.

I started bringing in some of my artwork, sculptures I had carved out of soapstone. One of the sergeants loved to see the things I brought, but kept saying, "I'm sorry. You can't take them in." I noticed that she would keep touching the sculptures and was interested in the work even though she would forbid me from showing it to the women. She finally agreed to let some of the work in, when a guard could be there the whole time.

The women all hated this sergeant. So when I started making her a Medicine Necklace, they were furious! My voices had told me to make one for the sergeant. "That bitch!" they said. "What the hell are you doing making her anything?" They were so angry at me I decided to stop making it. But my voices insisted, "Finish it!" So I felt I had no choice but to let it flow.

When I was done, I picked up my Medicine Stick to bless it. I held the Medicine Stick in one hand and the necklace in the other. As I moved the stick in one direction, the necklace moved with it! I moved it another way, and the Medicine Necklace followed! Nothing like this had ever happened before—or has happened since. It was the most powerful Medicine Necklace that ever flowed through me. And it went to a prison sergeant that so many hated.

The women struggled to stay sane in that prison. They had to work really hard not to fall into violence among themselves and with others under the oppression. An African-American prisoner named Sherry told me about a particular day when the women were really feeling the oppression. The tension was building. The women started to argue with one another. Voices were getting louder, women were starting to push each other around, and tempers were rising by the minute.

Feeling things were about to explode into a riot at any minute, landing everyone in lock up, Sherry suddenly found herself hopping onto a table and yelling at the top of her voice, "Hold on, bitches!" Some women stopped and turned to see who was yelling. "Wait a minute!" Sherry hollered, again. "I want to read you something." She started reading. It was a poem I had written to them about the energy work we were doing.

Sisters!
Stronger, stronger
We're getting stronger
Our energy penetrates
through walls
Death
Time
Oppression.

We are here sisters.
We are hearing, gathering,
combining, blending,
concentrating Energy
From earth, sun, wind, moon, universe.

Gathering
Sharing
Life
Energy
which penetrates
through walls
Death
Time
Oppression.

Incredibly, the women all quieted down to listen to the poem—and after that, the tension melted away. Spirit was flowing that day, we had no doubt.

INEZ GARCÍA

Around the same time, I got involved in a prison case involving a woman named Inez García who was jailed for killing one of her assailants in a rape. After being held down by one man and raped by the other, the men left and then called to tell her they were coming back to rape her again. Terrified, Inez got her son's rifle and went out to find them before they found her. She found them, and when one of the men threw a knife at her, she shot and killed him.[17]

I was one among a number of women, mostly lesbians, who had joined in coming to her defense after hearing Inez give a talk about what had happened to her. It was a grassroots effort that several women had begun a few months earlier. We held all kinds of demonstrations to support her after her conviction and imprisonment. We fought for her. We loved her. She's the strongest woman I have ever met in my life—a tiny woman yet so strong, everyone respected her strength.

I saw Inez for the first time the day she was convicted. The women on the Defense Committee were furious when they heard the verdict. Some started throwing things, kicking, and creating a great commotion. The police started arresting them and a crowd of people gathered outside. It was beautiful to see the way the women being arrested walked out with such dignity, some waving at the crowd, as they were led into the paddy wagon parked by the courthouse. I remember screaming at the judge and then at a number of policemen, "You will come down! All pigs will come down!" But they never arrested me because their hands were full with the other protestors. One of the radical papers wrote about my outburst, saying, "This woman stood up and eloquently spoke."

Fortunately, a wonderful lawyer named Susan B. Jordan took Inez's case on appeal and a couple of years later, with the support of all the demonstrations and public visibility brought on by the women on the Defense Committee, Susan succeeded in getting the conviction overturned. I was a member of the Defense Committee but at some point I decided that while the other women were doing a wonderful job, putting their hearts and souls into the effort, I was just another body at these meetings. I had talked with Inez's mother about the ceremonies she did for her daughter anytime she had to go to court. I decided I could contribute more to Inez's cause by doing ceremonies for her than by participating in the meetings. So I created an altar for Inez at home and focused my energies on her behalf in prayer and ceremonies.

I still kept in touch with the women on the Defense Committee, however, and at some point, I learned that many of the lesbian women were starting to drop off, staying away. When I asked around I learned that Roberto Vargas, a Nicaraguan poet and revolutionary (and my first childhood boyfriend!), and Black Panther Angela Davis,[18] who had both just gotten involved in the case, had persuaded Inez that it wasn't the man's fault—the man who had raped her and was out scot-free—it was the system, or "systen," as Inez would say in her Puerto Rican accent. Inez, who wasn't usually easily persuaded about anything, became adamant.

"It's not the man's fault, it's the systen," she started telling the Defense Committee. The women who had been involved in fighting for Inez from the beginning couldn't understand this idea of the man being blameless and raised questions. Inez was firm. "It's the systen." The women who had given their all to defending Inez felt dismissed by her. They were really hurt.

One day Inez called me and said, in her strong Puerto Rican accent, "How come you haven't been to the meetings?"

"Inez, I'm confused." I explained that I didn't really know what I was doing at those meetings, so I was focusing on prayers and ceremonies and, besides, I couldn't understand this idea of the man being blameless. "You confused?" she asked. "I'm going to tell you something and when I get through, you won't be confused." Inez then went on. "You listen. Look what's happening here. The whole problem is the systen. The systen is making the men like this." And she went on in that vein for several minutes.

"Now how you feel?" she asked.

"Inez, I'm confused."

She was quiet for a while and then said, "I gotta go." More silence, then, "*I'm* confused. I call you later."

Inez later called me to ask why the lesbian women weren't coming to the meetings. I told her that they didn't understand all this stuff about the system. But they weren't angry, they were hurt—that's why they were staying away. "Roberto and Angela are with you now," I explained, "but they weren't there when you were in jail. The lesbian women have been with you from the beginning. If you wanted to say something about this it would have been better to do it with gentleness, like this, 'Sisters, I know you're in pain, I know you are hurt. A man did it, but the system also has something to do with it.'"

Inez called a meeting and talked to the women. They *all* came back and continued to fight for her. On March 4, 1977, thanks to their efforts and the work of one exceptional feminist lawyer, Susan B. Jordan, Inez was acquitted in a now-classic case affirming that women have a right to defend themselves against rape.

I recently learned that this strong and gutsy woman, Inez García, died of lung cancer early in May of 2003 at the age of fifty-nine. Susan went to visit her before she died and wrote,

> One of the things Inez said to me was: "Does anyone remember my case?" This question brought tears to my eyes, and I determined right then and there to make sure that those who knew about her case remembered her, and for those who never knew about the case, to bring it into public view again. Her fight to clear her name and bring dignity to rape victims is a timeless story with important lessons for today's world.[19]

Susan hopes to write a book about Inez and her case. I can't think of anyone better to tell the story and share the powerful legacy of Inez García, who is now and forever will be *¡PRESENTE!*

Ball of Light

When Inez was convicted in 1974 my kids and I were living in a rented house in San Jose. One day, it caught fire and burned to the ground. We lost everything, including our little doggie—the only one of us who was in the house at the time. We never found out what caused the fire, although years later a neighbor told my son that one of the boys in the neighborhood had snuck in and was playing with matches. We had to move and start all over— with clothes, furniture, photo albums, drawings, books, appliances, everything gone.

Fortunately, through friends, a great deal came our way. For very cheap rent, we were able to move into a five-bedroom house in San Jose. It even had a backyard. Sometime after we settled in, helped by many friends, I remember being told not to weed or cut the grass in the backyard but just to let the weeds grow. A lot of beautiful plants grew in that backyard!

One day as I was sitting on the ground, meditating among the beautiful weeds in the garden, I suddenly felt this silence come upon me. All the background sounds I had been hearing before—street traffic, insects, birds, people talking—had been silenced. The silence covered everything. At the same time that I became aware of this silence, I also became aware that every blade of grass, every weed in the garden, every insect had also become aware of the silence. We had all awakened to it, they probably before me, and I could feel the blades of grass and the tiniest of flowers opening up to the stillness, the silence.

Then I saw this gold ball coming towards us from the sun. It was moving, vibrating, coming ever so gently and swiftly to me, to us, in the garden. It stopped a few feet away from me, and remained suspended in the air, a little higher than my head. Shimmering rays of metallic gold were shooting out above it, below it, and on either side. An overwhelming feeling of peace enveloped me. I remained keenly aware that everything around me, every plant, every weed, was aware of what was happening. We were all bathing in the beautiful light.

I don't know how long the ball of light stayed there, maybe as long as a half hour. But at some point it went, *fwoom*, flying back instantly to the sun.

I was never the same after this apparition.

How could I be? I had just experienced the aliveness and intelligence of *all* life on Earth. Even the blades of grass opened up when the ball of light came down. They *knew* what was happening. I felt their stillness, their calmness, and the way they were opening themselves up to receive the Creator's energy. We all went through it together, *equally*. And when you realize that a blade of grass knows the Creator just as we do—perhaps better, because they knew the ball of light was coming before I did—it changes you.

I now knew for sure that something strong and powerful was happening in my life, that I had work to do, and that a higher power was guiding me.[20]

HELEN AND THE FIRST "MEDICINE WHEEL"

I started dating Helen just before the fire burned down our house. We ended up living together as partners for five years, until the end of the seventies. Helen was a beautiful Jewish woman who had this incredible Afro. It was huge! "You know where this comes from, don't you?" I liked the way she was proud of the African roots in her Jewish heritage.

Helen taught me a lot about herbs. If she made an herbal medicine and told you it was going to heal you, it would heal you! Helen also was an artist and a very good one. Our five-bedroom home in San Jose was decorated with our art work. We loved the same music, had a similar sense of humor, and laughed a lot. Our home became known as "Medicine Wheel." It was a place where people came for healings and where women experiencing domestic violence or having no place to go after being paroled out of prison came for refuge and transition. We would hold poetry readings and have people over to play music when the women were released from prison. They got a good welcome.

Helen and I were part of a grassroots movement in the Bay area against domestic violence that was led by lesbians. I actually got involved before I graduated from college while I was living with Lee. We would go to women's homes where they were being beaten and get them out. Sometimes the man was there and we had to confront him. The police knew what we were doing and didn't bother us because they didn't want to get involved. We even had a hippy radio station that announced a phone number that women who needed help could call. You'd think that only hippies would call. But no; we got calls from the ghettos, the *barrios*, middle class America, from everywhere.

Our methods were grassroots, too!

When a call came in, the lesbians would drop whatever they were doing and head to the woman's house, a whole column of "dykes" walking down the street together to help the woman. One time there was a woman who did everything she could to keep the man who was beating her from entering the house. No matter what she did, including putting boards on her window, he would get inside and beat her. One night when he broke in, there was this dyke with a sawed off shotgun and a cigar in her mouth, sitting in a chair, just looking at him. That was it. He turned around and never came back!

Another case I remember—this one goes back to when I was living with Lee—involved a pregnant woman with two small children who lived in a heavy-duty ghetto. Her man had been taking her food stamps and spending them on his girlfriend across the way. He hated her little boy, who wasn't his and kept him in a dark room. All the boy ever had to eat was oatmeal. The man treated the boy's younger sister a little better because she was his, but it was still hard. On the day this woman called us, the man had beaten her so bad, her water broke. Ten of us answered the call. It was intense because the houses were so close together, rows and rows of houses. They saw us coming and you could see men running, trying to find the guy to warn him that we were coming after the woman and her children. We were able to get them out safely.

But it was really hard on these women because there were no shelters at that time and most of us didn't have enough space to put them up. So we would take turns taking care of them and they would go from one house to another. It was debilitating for them to go through this and the exhaustion was extreme. Many would finally say, "I think I just want to go home and sleep in my own bed."

That happened with this woman. I remember saying, "Sweetie, please, you'll be sorry if you go back. Look, you've gotten this far, see how far you've got. Just hang in there." But she was desperately exhausted and ready to go back, so we went to Good Shepherd's, a home for unwed mothers. They said they would take her and her little girl, so Lee and I took the little boy. He was the sweetest little kid, but since all he had eaten was oatmeal, he couldn't chew. We fed him rice and beans and things like that. I hated to see him go when the woman's sister came to get him.

In our five-bedroom home, Helen and I had all kinds of women and their children staying with us. Women suffering from domestic violence and women who had been released from prison but had no money and no place to go would stay with us until they could get back on their feet again. I found out that many sisters and brothers were ending up going right back into prison because they were given no welfare or food stamps when they were released and would end up in situations where they'd have to steal to eat. I'll never forget a woman in that situation who stole $4.50 worth of baby food to feed her baby. She was put back in prison and her baby was taken away. She sobbed and sobbed, saying, "They can't take my baby away for $4.50, can they? They can't do that can they?" We had to tell her, yes, they can.

We called our place "Medicine Wheel" because most of the time we had no idea where the money to support all of us was going to come from, where the food would come from. But no one ever went without a meal. We never had any government support but people would always come forward to help. It was not unusual for me to open the mail and find a check for $500 or $1000 to help us. We would use it to give a sister or brother who just got out of prison enough money to cover a month of food and the first and last month of rent on an apartment. Restaurants would send us food and people would come over to help clean the house and fix meals. It was incredible. I was able to focus entirely on doing ceremonies and healings—and, with Helen, to offer needy women refuge.

I Meet Jesus Again for the First Time[21]

To my surprise, not too long after entering my spiritual path, Jesus—the one I had rejected along with everything to do with the Catholic Church in order to free myself from the dogma condemning a person like me to hell— had come back into my life. I began to feel that what I was learning from the trees, the sky, and the Earth was something that Jesus somehow understood deeply. I began to feel that I was just scratching the surface of something that Jesus had actually gone deep into.

I found myself thinking about him a lot. Sometime in the mid-1970s, while I was living with Helen in the Medicine Wheel house, I decided to spend Good Friday with Jesus. I went out into the country and ended up in some kind of barn where I sat meditating on Jesus and feeling close to nature. Suddenly the skies darkened and this huge storm came thundering in. I had never experienced anything like it. The way the storm came, its strength, and the whole feeling I got from it made me think that this was the beginning of the times my voices had been talking about—the times of Earth changes that my visions were foretelling.

As I felt the power of the storm crash around me, visions of the awesome destruction that the times of Earth changes were going to bring flashed before me—and I became terrified! Then, just as quickly as the terror gripped me, a chant came to me—the melody, the words, all as one stream. I remember it clearly:

Don't be afraid. Don't be afraid. Don't be afraid.
Don't be afraid of the rain.
Don't be afraid of the dams breaking.
Don't be afraid of the floods.
Amidst destruction, creation has begun.

Don't be afraid of the drought.
Don't be afraid of the earth quaking.
Don't be afraid of the winds.
Don't be afraid. Don't be afraid.
Amidst destruction, creation has begun.

Let the energy flow. Let your soul shake in awe.
Don't be afraid. Don't be afraid. Don't be afraid.
Amidst destruction, creation has begun.

I sang the chant as it came to me, and as it came, I calmed down, and as I calmed down, I knew, as clearly as I heard the words and the melody, that the chant was a gift from Jesus. He was calming me.

After this experience, I kept thinking even more about Jesus. I had been having all kinds of apparitions with birds and the sun but I kept wondering about Jesus. "He *feels* for real; I wonder if he really is." I found myself asking him to please let me know, let me *know*.

One day Helen was in the living room, sitting by the fire, while I was in the kitchen, cooking Nicaraguan Indian fudge. You have to stand right by it to stir constantly. I was stirring away when all of a sudden, I felt a heaviness come over me. I had the sense to turn off the burner as I felt the heaviness enter me. It was an incredible feeling, but soon I couldn't move. All I could do was just stand there and feel this beautiful, beautiful energy that was coming into me. I knew it was Jesus. His energy had entered me and it was a beautiful feeling. I had been saying, let me know, let me know. And now I knew.

As soon as I could move, I went and shared it with Helen. I said, "Helen, do you want to feel Jesus' energy?" I hadn't bothered her much with my wonderings about Jesus. I knew she had had enough of that growing up Jewish.

But she looked at me in a certain way and said, "Yes." So I touched her. "Do you feel it?" I asked. She smiled and said, "Uh-huh."

Helen went on with her little Jewish self. She liked that Jesus came from her people but that's as far as it went—and I never pushed it further. We respected each other, and I don't have the belief that Jesus wants us all to be Christian.

After I connected with Jesus and started doing healings, Jesus would sometimes come to them. At the beginning, it was always with clients who loved him. If Jesus showed up, I would turn to the person and say, "You really love Jesus, right?" He or she would always answer, "Oh, yes!" And then go on and on about Jesus. When he came, Jesus would often just take over the healings. I had to struggle to get to a chair, I felt so heavy. He would take over, and the room would be penetrated with his energy.

Before Jesus started coming to me, I was very devoted to Ixchen, the Aztec Goddess of Medicine. She taught me a lot. But when Jesus came into my life, I loved him so much I stopped working with Ixchen. After a while, however, Jesus stopped coming to the healings. So I went back to working with Ixchen. Then, Jesus showed up again, so I stopped working with Ixchen. Again, Jesus left. It was a pattern. Each time Jesus would show up, I'd drop Ixchen and anybody else I was working with—and then he would leave. I also noticed that I started having less healing energy when I was working only with Jesus. It took me years to figure out that Jesus didn't want me to drop everybody else—and that the fullness of my healing powers came from working with them all. Jesus was very clear: He wanted me to work with him *and* Ixchen and the others.[22] It was my own Catholic self struggling with this, not Jesus!

MY DEAR TEACHER, MILDRED JACKSON

Helen and I had been hearing about Mildred Jackson for some time. She was an incredible healer and quite famous in the Bay area community. So I never expected to meet her. But I had become very ill, losing a lot of weight, and experiencing high fevers. I finally got over the fevers, but I couldn't regain my strength. I would walk a block and be exhausted.

I didn't want to go to an M.D. because just a few months earlier, Roberto Vargas had given a slide show about the horrors going on in Nicaragua. He talked about long lines of children selling their blood in order to get money to eat. It made such an impression on me that I couldn't go to a doctor. I said, "I'd rather die than take the blood of starving children." That was the image I had in my mind.

I had tried to heal myself with what I knew, still at the beginning of my healing work, but I was way too weak to heal myself. Worried, Helen said, "You're not getting better, you're getting worse." Knowing I was adamant about not going to a doctor, she asked, "Would you consider seeing Mildred Jackson?"

"Yeah!" I said, perking up.

Helen said she would do everything she could to figure out how to find her and get me an appointment. A few minutes later, she came back and said, "Zelima, Mildred Jackson is in the phone book!"

I was about fifteen minutes late for my appointment, feeling bad and panicky about it as I knocked on her door. A tiny little woman in her eighties answered, her head tilted a little to one side. She was so sweet, I instantly felt comfortable.

As I lay on her table, she would touch me ever so gently. With her eyes closed, she would scan my body and then lightly touch whatever spot she felt drawn to. She kept looking for a sign, a scratch, or something on my body. I don't remember the exact words but what she finally told me was, "You're going to be all right. You've got work to do. You're being guided."

I fell in love with Mildred and, from that time on, whenever there was anything the matter with me, I went to her. I had a lot that was the matter with me in those years, including terrible allergies, fluid in my heart that a naturopath said was a congestive heart condition, and problems with my sciatic nerve, among other things.

Mildred taught me a lot about treating the sciatic nerve. When I went to see her, I had no idea what was the matter with me. I couldn't walk, my leg hurt so bad. She looked at me and said, "Sciatic. I know that one very well." I said, "Thank God!" She started at my instep, rubbing up towards the ankle, then up the back of the ankle, a nice and tight rub along the sides and back of the calf to the hip. And that did it.

She had a wonderful sense of humor, along with her gentle sweetness. I remember one time years later when I went to see Mildred. I had gone without sugar and any kind of fish or meat for about ten years but suddenly resumed. It started with some pastry and then some *dulce de leche* I got at this great bakery in the Mission area. As I lay on the massage table, I started confessing. "Mildred, I've been eating sugar."

"Yes, dear," she said, as she gently rubbed me.

"I've had cookies and candy."

"Yes, dear," she said, continuing to rub.

"And ice cream…"

"Yes, dear," she said, the conversation continuing in that vein, while she rubbed and massaged.

When the healing was over, she covered me up with the blanket and said, "Okay, honey. You stay here for a while. And when you're ready to get up, come into the kitchen. I baked cookies!"

She also had a reassuring way of letting you know that all would be well. I would come in thinking I was dying because I was in so much pain. She would look me over and say, "You're going to be all right, dear." The only time I saw her worry was when I had this terrible pain in my leg. I couldn't even lift it to get on the bus. Mildred said it was a blockage, having to do with my circulation, and tried to clear it. But she couldn't, and that's when I saw her worry. What happened next was really weird. Mildred put me on a really strict diet and gave me some herbs to take. I did everything she said until finally one day I couldn't take it anymore. I was so sick of the diet, I got drunk! Lying on the couch, totally relaxed from the effects of the alcohol, I saw something in my leg pinching, blocking things. I actually saw it inside my leg. "Is that what it is?" I slurred to myself. "Well, I'm going to let go of that one!" I moved my leg in some way, and released it! The blockage was gone and my leg was back to normal.

I do not recommend this approach—and I never confessed it to Mildred!

Over the years I knew Mildred, I became more than just a patient—I became a student and friend of hers. Mildred invited me to observe healings she gave and taught me many of her herbal remedies and ways of treating patients. She was a dear friend, a powerful healer, and a wisdom teacher who left behind some of her knowledge in THE HANDBOOK OF ALTERNATIVES TO CHEMICAL MEDICINE, a book I treasure.[23]

Given all the riches of my life in the Bay area, the last thing I wanted to do was move away. But for weeks and months I had been getting messages from Spirit that I would have to move away from California to be near "the heart of Mother Earth." It had to do with the ending of one world and the beginning of another. That's all I could be told.

When I heard someone say that the heart of Mother Earth was near the ancestral lands of the Hopi, I decided to go see. I had no idea where Hopi country was but once I found out, two friends said they would drive me there, to northeastern Arizona. When we got there, I started asking around to see if I could find a Medicine Man. I said, "Spirit is guiding me and I need to counsel with someone."

The first woman I asked just laughed at me.

"Spirit is directing me," I insisted. Still laughing, she said, "Come here. Step into this light." She had a light over her door. "Let me see your eyes, let me see your face," she said.

I stepped into the light. She looked at my face and then looked into my eyes. Stepping back, she said, very matter-of-factly, "All right."

The woman directed me to the Banyacya's house, where I introduced myself to the couple, Thomas and Fermina. I again explained why I was there, that I was being directed by Spirit. Thomas asked me to come closer so he could look at my eyes. Again, I stepped closer and after he peered into my eyes he said, in the same manner as the woman, "All right."

"Why don't you just spend a couple of days here?" Thomas added.

"Yes, thank you," I said, asking if someone could drive me to a bus station when we were through. Thomas said yes, so I told my friends that it was okay for them to go home without me. They left—and my lessons began.

Thomas was a well-known Hopi elder.[24] His wife, Fermina, was an equally powerful teacher and we became good friends while I was there.

One of the first things Thomas told me was that I had been Hopi before. I was wearing a skirt and a top that my mother had made. The top, he told me, was an ancient Hopi design. He asked me to repeat my name and then started to say it over and over to himself, until he came out with: Zu-enima. "That's your name, too," he said, giving it to me. "It means 'She Left To Go Home In A Hurry.'"

I burst out laughing. I had a reputation for doing just that! I would go visit someone and was supposed to stay for hours, days, or even months when all of a sudden I would feel like I had to leave—and would take off *and go home in a hurry.*

Thomas had very peaceful eyes and great intelligence. So much of what he taught me has become a part of my life, I can't remember the details. What I do remember talking about were the visions I had been having of catastrophes and destruction. Thomas told me that these were exactly what the Hopi prophecies foretold and that he was dedicating his life to warning the world about them—a coming destruction brought on by a separation of the human from Mother Earth and all our relations.[25] Thomas also talked to me about the symbols in the Hopi Place of Emergence. He was one of the few who could read them. I just absorbed the information and it became a part of me.

After a day or two, Thomas had to leave. I stayed on for another three days to be with Fermina. When Thomas spoke, you could see his deep intelligence and knowledge. When Fermina spoke, you could feel the truth coming down on you from the ceiling.

One of the most important things Fermina taught me was that every creature on Earth, including the humans, has a job to do with Spirit.

"The job of the human is to pray for every being on Earth," she said. "But the human is not doing that anymore, and it is causing great harm. The human *must* get back to doing the job Spirit gave us—to pray for every being on Earth."

Before I left I asked Fermina about land. "I've been guided to come be near the heart of Mother Earth."

"You can't buy any land that's Indian land," Fermina said. But she pointed in different directions to tell me where I should go to try to find land. I wrote it down to show my friends.

Moving to Arizona

The time to move near the heart of Mother Earth was drawing close, even as my own heart as a mother was aching with my children's struggles. My daughter Wanda was fifteen when she started going out with Norman, a man in his twenties who was abusive with her. Even so, she ran off with him, disappearing somewhere out of the state for a couple of terrifying months.

Wanda tried calling once or twice but we kept getting cut off, so I had no idea where or how she was. Finally, one day, Wanda showed up on our doorstep. She was beaten up so bad that every inch of her body was bruised—even the insides of her ears were black and blue. Norman's sister had helped her get away.

I was in a rage. To see your kid beat up like that, and not for the first time; I was livid. I called some of my dyke friends, including a black belt in karate. Four of them were lined up to go beat him but Norman's sister overheard my phone calls and warned Norman. She was on Wanda's side, but he was her brother after all.

Of course, like the coward that he really was, Norman got scared and called me. "Look ma'am, I think we can talk this over," he said.

"Talk over, shit," I said. "You beat up my daughter and now we're going to beat the shit out of you."

"Look ma'am. I just got crazy."

"You don't have to tell me you're crazy. I *know* you're crazy," I said.

"Yeah…"

I told him what was in my heart and how I was going to love beating the shit out of him so that he would know how it feels to be beaten and never touch my daughter again.

"Look ma'am," he said. "If I see your daughter coming on the side of the street, I'll go to the other side. I will never touch your daughter again."

Finally, I said, "I want to kick the shit out of you, but I will leave it up to my daughter, who will let me know the answer after we talk—and I will try to talk her into it!"

Wanda wanted him to get some of what he gave but she said, "We better not, Mom."

"Aw, shit," I said. Clearly, I was not over my violence! Although I hadn't beaten anyone in years, I, along with my friends, definitely would have beaten Norman.

We soon discovered that Wanda was pregnant. As it turned out, the pregnancy transformed her. She started taking care of herself, even doing yoga! It was beautiful. When she was sixteen, she gave birth to a boy named John who was, as I would say to him, the apple of my eye, the raisin in my pudding. There was something about him that everybody loved. I called him Little Bear.

Before giving birth to Little Bear, Wanda married a man who had two gorgeous little children and had played for the San Francisco 49ers. She named her son after him. But the marriage didn't last long; Wanda left him because he was abusive to her. Wanda was young and had several boyfriends before settling down, some ten years later, with her current husband.

So I spent a lot of time with Little Bear during his early childhood, and that's when I learned how to be a mother. When I had my own kids, I was so confused I didn't even know who I was. I knew myself when I was a baby— I knew my steps, I knew how to crawl, I knew who I was. But by the time I was a mother, I had no idea. To be a mother, I had watched others and imitated them. I had done this with everything.

By the time Little Bear came around, I had gotten in touch with myself and was able to come from who I am. When I would hold Little Bear, it would give me so much energy! I realized that this is the way it's supposed to be—

the mother gives the child energy and the child gives it back. I've always had an image in my house of the *Virgen de Socorro*, Our Lady of Perpetual Help, and now I could see that the little child in her arms was giving her energy. I could see that the baby angels holding up the *Virgen de Guadalupe* were giving her energy. And I could see that this is what was happening with Mother Earth— that the Mother was holding us, giving us energy. However we, her children, were giving nothing back. The same thing was happening with women all over the world—

Delighting in Little Bear

they were giving, giving, giving, but getting no nurturing energy back. The life-giving circle of energy was broken.

I learned these things with my grandson. I used to carry him everywhere and with the energy he gave me, he would actually help me walk. I used to say, "When he was a baby, he carried his own weight!"

About a year after Wanda became a mother, John, my son, became a father. He had just moved to friend's house after I had given him an ultimatum. John had always been so sweet and close to me, "my sunshine," but as he entered his teenage years, he began to refuse to do anything at home. He was a very beautiful young man and took to constantly looking at himself in

121

the mirror and leaving his things strewn all over the house. Then he started taking wrestling lessons. Now when I would ask him to pick up his things and help around the house, he would come toward me with his fists clenched as if to hit me. I finally told him he had to stop doing that or leave. He chose to leave.

Soon after moving to a friend's house, John's girlfriend, Tina, became pregnant. Although he was only fifteen and she thirteen, Tina had begged him, "Give me a baby." They moved into a little apartment after Tina got pregnant and she gave birth to a baby girl they named, Zelima. I tried to help them as much as I could, as did some of my friends after I left the Bay area. I was now a grandmother to two beautiful babies, brought to life by my own beloved children while they themselves were still kids.

I had done my best to get out of my violence and get through my craziness for my children. But sometimes the best you can do just isn't enough, especially when your kids have inherited genes and generations of family insanity, cruelty, and violence. Deep in my heart, I knew that Wanda and John would have to go through some craziness in their lives because it was so embedded in my family. However, I also knew that despite all we had gone through, I had succeeded in giving them two critical things. First, my kids *knew* they were loved. "We have no doubt that you loved us," John told me years later. Second, my kids knew that family patterns *could* be broken. If I made it through my insanity, they could make it, too. No one would ever be able to tell them that they only had a two percent chance of getting through.

But now—without even being halfway through their teenage years— Wanda and John were parents, with children of their own to raise.

All this time, Spirit kept telling me it's time to go, it's time to go. Somehow I felt there was going to be a lot of suffering involved, so I didn't want to move! Despite the challenges with my kids and some struggles that Helen and I had begun to have in our relationship, things were good. Helen did her artwork and helped me with ceremonies; I did my healing work; we both extended our home to women in need—and people in the community really supported us in all this.

But I finally took off one day in 1978 in search of Medicine Wheel land. I was feeling other pressures as well, so I knew it was time to go. A friend named Diane drove with me, along with my grandson, Little Bear. He used to call me "daddy." It was so hard to get him out of that. "No, honey. It's *abuela*," I would say. Knowing that kids had mommies and daddies, Little

Bear figured that since he had a mommy he loved dearly, I had to be the daddy he loved dearly. As we drove to Arizona, I sat with Little Bear's head on my lap. For miles he kept saying, "Oh, daddy, daddy, daddy, daddy, daddy."

Friends in Oregon had told me about a woman named Sue Coleman, who they said lived near the heart of Mother Earth. When we got to Arizona we went to see her. I loved the land immediately. It was high desert, some 5,000 feet above sea level in the White Mountains of Arizona, near the ancestral lands of the Hopi and the heart of Mother Earth. Sue told me that just up the road from her there was some land for sale. She suggested I see a Realtor named Jack Brown in the nearby town of St. Johns.

We went to see Jack Brown and he drove us to an eighty-acre parcel of land that was about two and a half miles up from Sue's. I remember walking on the land, feeling its sacredness. I asked the Creator for guidance in the way Creator taught me. The guidance felt very clear and grounded. "This is the land."

I told Jack Brown that this was the land I was looking for and that I was ready to buy it. He seemed thoughtful but insisted I look at two other parcels. "Fine," I said, "but it's not necessary." Before we drove off with him to look at the other parcels, I tied one of my grandbaby's diapers to a post so that Diane and I could come back and find the land on our own. As we drove around to look at the other parcels Jack Brown wanted me to see, he got lost. He said he had driven these areas hundreds of times before, and could not understand why he had gotten so lost. I told him it was fine. "I already know what Creator wants me to do."

I bought the eighty-acre parcel for $10,000. I had only a fraction of that amount to put down but Jack Brown's company, Apache Title, financed it, so I was able to pay it off gradually over the next three years or so. Before heading back to California, Diane and I stayed on the land for a couple of weeks, living under the trees with Little Bear.

Helen and I ended up moving to Tucson. She was a city girl from New York, so she was anxious about living on the land in a remote part of the country. We moved to Tucson where we could be closer to land, sharing a house with our friends Pat and Marianne, who had also moved there from California. I was able to do healing work and ceremonies but unlike our work in California, it was a struggle. I had to get a job to make ends meet and that was also a struggle. I was often late in making payments to Jack Brown, but he was very patient with me, telling me he did not want me to lose my land— even when I was very late in making payments.

NATIVE AMERICAN MOVEMENT

While we lived in Tucson, I got involved in the Native American Movement and the effort to protect the sacred lands of Big Mountain, or Black Mesa, in northeast Arizona—site of the biggest coal reserves in the country. I participated in pickets and demonstrations in a struggle that pitted Native peoples against corporate mining interests supported by the U.S. government and tribal councils that did not represent the people. In order to continue strip mining the sacred lands of the Hopi and Navajo, the corporate interests and government were forcing the relocation of the people and creating the impression that this was all about an ancient fight between the Hopi and Navajo. It wasn't.[26]

I remember going to Big Mountain for a meeting. Hopi and Navajo people were there together, united in trying to stop the mining and relocation. My friend Fermina also was there. She turned to the Navajo and said, "The government keeps saying we're enemies and that this fight is between us. Look around. We're all here. We are friends."

At one of the meetings an Anglo woman scientist came to speak. I can't remember her name, but the Big Mountain people loved her because she was so sensitive and humble. She had two or three other male scientists with her and said they had discovered something very important.

The woman told the people, "Please don't think we're trying to tell you something you don't already know. We realize you already know this. We took all the things you told us and did some work on it and this is what we came up with."

The people had told the woman scientist that if the mining companies continued to dig at Big Mountain, it would be the end of the world. "You'll know the signs because there will be artificial electrical storms," they said. "The final consequence of the digging will be that, as the world is dying, you'll be able to see your bones through your flesh."

The woman and the other scientists had looked into this, done a study, and found out that Big Mountain has some kind of energetic connection with Tibet. I don't remember the exact words she used but the idea was that these two places are in some kind of magnetic polarity with each other, like male and female poles. Acting together, they generate the energy that flows throughout the world. If you mess with either of those poles, you're messing with the energy.

I remember the scientists saying that they were going to take the results of their study to the United Nations. I don't know what came of it. What I do know is that 12,000 Navajo have been removed from their sacred lands—and the digging into Mother Earth at Big Mountain continues. [27]

Praying the Sweat Lodge

When I got involved in the Native American Movement, I met a Native brother named George, who invited me to a sweat lodge he ran in Tucson. I had never participated in a sweat before so I went, even though I was being treated for heart congestion problems. There was definitely a part of me that was saying, "Don't you dare go in!" But I felt so drawn to it I didn't tell George about my condition; I entered the darkness of the small round dome—the "womb of Mother Earth."

There are four rounds to traditional sweat lodges; each one gets hotter as more and more stones are brought in to the small enclosure. Water is poured over them to create an enveloping hot steam. It wasn't long into the very first round before I found myself gasping for air. I could hardly breathe as the steam heat from the red-hot rocks built up. The heat was suffocating. I had made a terrible mistake! I thought my heart would burst and that I would die. If I hadn't been with a knowledgeable sweat leader, I just might have died. But George took charge, saying, "Open up your heart! Open your heart! That's the only way you're going to get through this. Open up your heart!" I tried to focus on opening my heart. As I did, I began to feel my chest and heart muscles relax. As my heart relaxed, my breathing got easier and I was able to focus on further relaxing and opening my heart.

It turned out to be the best thing I could do for my heart—on more than one count. It took only one experience of the sweat lodge for me to know that this was how I wanted to pray—in the womb of Mother Earth.

Years before I had ever seen a sweat lodge or knew much about them, I had a dream that I was in a dark place with a fire in the middle of it. A Native brother was in there doing some kind of ceremony with a group of people, among them a Catholic nun. He was doing the ceremony when he took a cup of water, drank it, and looked up. Fire came out of his mouth. Then he looked at me and gave me the cup to drink. I drank it and fire came out of my mouth. He continued with the ceremony and right before it finished the Catholic nun said, "I'm so sorry, I must leave. But I want you to know that I am very aware of the presence of God here. The presence of the Creator is here, and I thank you." She left and the dream ended soon after.

I started going to George's sweat lodges every week. The sweat was the highlight of my week. After going to a few of them, and without my asking, George started teaching me how to lead a sweat lodge. "I'm teaching you this because you're a warrior woman," he told me. George did warrior sweats, which means he ran intensely hot sweat lodges. He wanted me to be a warrior sweat lodge leader.

George started teaching me the songs and the prayers, everything about the sweat lodge in the traditional Indian way. I tried so hard to learn the prayers and the songs, but they would just go right out of my head. No matter how hard I tried, I couldn't remember them! I went to George's sweat lodges every week for several months. I kept going, kept trying to learn, because my inner voices told me I was supposed to be a sweat lodge leader.

But at some point, I heard, "Yes, you are supposed to be a sweat lodge leader, but of a different kind of sweat lodge." I learned that I was to lead a "Little Sisters" sweat lodge. In Little Sisters sweat lodges, unlike traditional sweat lodges, women in their moons would be welcome. Wombs bleed, I was told, and the womb of Mother Earth needs the blood.

In time, I started leading Little Sisters sweat lodges and was told always to say that this was a Little Sisters sweat lodge, not a traditional one. The prayers and songs developed, coming to me as we went along. I was told that the Little Sisters sweats would be about preparing for the times of changes that were coming on Mother Earth—the times we are in right now.

MOVING TO THE LAND

During this time, Helen and I had drifted further and further apart from each other. We broke up soon after another woman, Adrian, moved into the house with her young daughter, whom I still love dearly. Helen and I had been together for five years. Although the last two were challenging, the first three years with Helen were absolutely wonderful.

I'm not really sure what the partnership with Adrian was about; we were together for only a year or so. But it was with Adrian that I moved to the land—to the eighty acres I had bought near the heart of Mother Earth. I had gotten a call from some women of color gypsies in Arkansas who said a sister from Tucson they called "Somoa" had gone crazy and that the White women there wanted to put her in a mental institution and "throw away the key." The gypsies wanted to protect her by bringing her to me for healing. So they drove all the way from Arkansas in a long van smelling of incense; then we all drove to the land together. Somoa ended up living with me for about three years, traveling wherever I went, and healed beautifully.

Adrian and I had bought a trailer and a friend loaned us a bigger trailer, which housed four women who came to live there, including Somoa, whom I was treating, and Alma Luz, the sister of my friend Rita, a Nicaraguan lesbian I had met in San Francisco.

One morning in the fall of 1979, I woke up and started packing my clothes. "Where are you going?" Adrian asked.

"I don't know but I'm going someplace."

"How long are you going to be gone?" she asked. "From the way you're packing, it looks like you're going to be gone for months."

"I don't know, Adrian," I said. "I don't know what I'm doing but I'm going someplace."

The other women living with us on the land came around. "What's happening?" they asked.

"I don't know!!" I said, frustrated because I really didn't know what was happening. I only knew that I couldn't stop until I was done packing. Adrian was really good about it. She said, "I don't know what's happening with you, but why don't we just take a ride. Let's take a ride into St. Johns." I said okay, leaving my packed suitcase in the trailer.

We drove into town and stopped by the post office. A letter from my mother was waiting for me in the mailbox. I opened it and read, "Come immediately. Lotus, your beautiful sister, is dead in an airplane accident."

LOTUS

My mother stopped hitting Lotus at some point after I got married and had moved out. I think it had to do with my mental breakdown—not wanting the same thing to happen to Lotus. But it also had to do with the fact that Lotus was starting to fight back. Instead of beating Lotus, Mami started giving her anything she wanted—and Lotus just got wild. She got so wild that Mami couldn't control her, so she sent her to my brother, Hiram.

Although Lotus eventually did go insane, she had a sweetness to her that never left her. Years later when I was visiting her, Lotus started telling me about what had happened when she lived with Hiram—and how scared she was of him because he would beat her. She told me about one incident when Hiram was chasing after her, to whip her. She ran into her room, locked the door, and put the chest and other heavy furniture against it, but Hiram managed to break in. He beat her senseless with the buckle of his belt. She showed me the scars where the flesh had been torn from that cruel beating.

I lost it! The violence in me surged and I instinctively got up, put on my boots, and started out for Hiram's house. "Don't!" Lotus pleaded.

"I have to," I said.

"No, you don't," she said.

"After what you just told me, what the fuck do you expect me to do?" I demanded.

"Forgive him," she said. "I have."

Lotus also forgave my mother, but she couldn't work out the insanity that my mother's cruelty had caused her—even though she didn't remember it. Lotus was in her twenties, talking to me one day about how confused she felt about her life, wondering why she was so crazy when I said, "Honey, you've gone through so much." Looking completely innocent, Lotus asked, "What do you mean? What happened to me?" I started to tell her some of the things that happened to her when she was a small child but she cut me off. "No, no, that didn't happen," she said, quickly changing the subject.

The next time I saw her, Lotus said, "Zelima, do me a favor, make me a promise."

I said, "What, baby?"

"Before you tell me anything, stop and think," she said. "Is that going to hurt me? If you think telling me is going to hurt me, please don't tell me."

I was seeing Peter at the time and when I told him about this conversation, he said, "That's not fair. You don't have to hold on to all that." I understood that I didn't need to comply with what Lotus asked of me—but I never told her anything more.

Lotus *was* crazy, and part of it was being very much into sex. "Where can I meet a lesbian?" she once asked me. "I want to know what it's about." After she figured out we had Black ancestors, she decided to become a prostitute because she wanted to feel her Blackness, the oppression suffered by our ancestors—and you couldn't get more oppressed than by working as a prostitute. "Well, I've got a pimp and I'm making a lot of money," she told me. "But my pimp's driving me crazy! He's in love with me and he keeps calling me in the middle of the night, saying, 'Baby, this is your man. This is your man, baby, this is your man. I'm your man and you're my woman.'

"So it's not going too good," she concluded.

Then there were the drugs. Lotus was trying all kinds of drugs, like a lot of us did at that time. But Lotus got hooked on cocaine. She wanted me to try it. I did and it made me feel numb. Lotus insisted I try it again. The same thing happened, so I said, "No, thanks." I didn't like feeling numb. In hindsight, I think that's precisely why Lotus liked cocaine—it numbed her.

By the time I was with Helen, Lotus was addicted to cocaine and had started dealing it, although I didn't know it at the time. She was making a lot of money and would disappear for several weeks at a time, which had me sick with fear and anxiety. One time, after she had been gone for a few months, she called to say she had been in Guatemala, living with an archaeologist who wanted her to have his baby. Lotus was very beautiful. The archeologist had offered her a lot of money to have his child and asked her to think about it. She did and decided it wouldn't be right, which is why she was back in California.

Sometime after that Lotus was involved with a guy who ended up in jail. When she went to visit him, she was stoned. The police noticed, searched her car, found drugs, and she ended up in jail. When a college friend of mine learned about it, she posted bail for Lotus. It was incredible! My friend actually took out a loan on her house to come up with the bail money. Lotus never skipped and eventually got off the charges. She was lucky that time. But then she disappeared again.

Weeks went by. Again, I was worried sick. One day I got a call from the Mexican consulate. Lotus was in Mexico—in jail! They had found cocaine stitched into her suitcase. At first I thought we were talking about a small amount of cocaine, but when I asked, they said they found a *huge* amount of cocaine hidden in her suitcase. I was stunned. Lotus had asked the Mexican authorities to call me to let me know where she was but had pleaded for me not to tell the family.

So I didn't. But Mami kept calling me, saying, "Where's Lotus? You haven't heard from her?"

"No, Mami. I haven't," I lied.

Then one morning my mother called. Her voice was dead level with the accusation: "Zelima, you *know* where Lotus is!"

"Mami, I don't know what you're talking about," I said.

"Oh, yes, you know exactly what I'm talking about. You know where Lotus is. I *dreamed* it. Lotus is in jail!" she said.

"No, I don't know. How do you know?" I fumbled.

"*¡Lo soñe! ¡Jodido! ¡Lo soñe!*" (I dreamed it! Dammit it to hell! I dreamed it!) she yelled into the phone. I kept trying to deny it. Her last words before she hung up on me were, "I *know* you know."

They may have taken away Mami's visions when she was a child but they didn't take away her dreams. Her dreams were dead on.

I wrote my sister a letter. "What do I tell Mami? She knows. She dreamt it."

Soon after, I got a call from the consulate. Lotus said it was okay for me to tell Mami, but Lotus had other news for me: she was pregnant. Her boyfriend, who had gotten her into this mess in the first place, was also in jail. He had lied to the Mexican authorities, telling them they were married, so they had been given conjugal rights.

"Don't tell anybody," Lotus again pressed me.

Mami called the next day. "Lotus is pregnant and you know it," she said, not even giving me a chance to deny it. She had dreamt it. There was nothing you could do when Mami dreamt it.

In the fall of 1979, we learned that Lotus was going to be transferred from Mexico to a prison in Los Angeles as a result of a prisoner exchange treaty signed between the U.S. and Mexico. We were all so happy! When I was doing prison work in Milpitas, I had gone down to Los Angeles on a few big occasions to do workshops at the very prison where Lotus was going to be sent. I wrote to my friend Sherry, who had been imprisoned at Milpitas and had been transferred to the L.A. prison, letting her know my little sister was coming and asking if she would take Lotus under her wing. Sherry wrote back, "Certainly, I will."

So we were all set—I thought.

On October 27, Lotus was at the airport waiting with the other prisoners to fly to the States in a commercial airplane. My sister Zela was also there. Zela had gone to Mexico to help bring back Lotus's baby daughter, Ursula. A little government-owned twin-propeller plane pulled onto the tarmac and the authorities put out a call, asking if anyone wanted to leave for the States right now. Ever impulsive, Lotus said, "yes," boarding the plane with one or two other prisoners, their guards, and the pilots.

En route to California, the pilots learned that there was a thick fog and diminishing visibility at their destination. They asked permission to land at the airport in Tijuana, Mexico. However, visibility at the Tijuana Airport was also limited and the Tijuana radar and instrument landing systems were not operating that day. So the Tijuana air controllers asked their counterparts in San Diego to radio the data necessary for the small plane to make an instrument landing. In a tragic comedy of errors, neither the pilots nor the San Diego air controllers were bilingual, so communications went from tower to tower to pilots. In the translation, the pilot failed to maintain the proper altitude as he approached the runway. He struck a telephone pole and crash landed three-quarters of a mile inside the U.S. border and two and a half miles away from the Tijuana runway.

Everyone on board was killed.

When I read Mami's letter, I went hysterical. My beloved baby sister was dead!

That's what the packing had been about. But as it turned out, even though I was packed and ready to go, I didn't make it to California in time for the funeral because we had car trouble on the way. When Adrian and I finally arrived at my mother's house, a member of my family answered the door. I went into the bedroom where Mami was sitting alone.

"Mami?"

"¡Ay, Zelima!" she cried, distraught. "Your poor baby sister. *Desde que nació* (since she was born) …" But Mami never finished the sentence, too overwhelmed with grief, guilt, and remorse.

SOMOZA'S DIPLOMAT

When my friend Rita found out that I was in the Bay area for Lotus's funeral, she called me at my mother's house. "Zelima, I really need you to come," Rita said. "My father's here. He's dying. He has cancer real bad. Could you come? Maybe you could prolong his life or at least make him feel better…."

Rita's father had been a Somozista, a high-level diplomat serving the regime. That's what I knew about him. He had fled after the Revolution and he and his wife were living in California with his sister. A lot of upper class children fought for the revolution, including children of officers in the Somoza regime, like Rita and Alma. But the fathers never lost the love for their children nor their children the love for their fathers.

He was not *my* father, however! I loved Rita and her sister, Alma, but *this*…. There was no way I could do healing work on someone who served the murderous Somoza regime in that way! As I was getting ready to tell Rita that I was very sorry but I could not help, I heard my voices say, "Go!"

It was absolutely clear. No question about it. *"Go."*

I told Rita I would help. It was no simple matter, however. We didn't know how long I would be working on her father, so Rita drove Adrian and me all the way back to Medicine Wheel to help us bring our things to California. We moved in with Rita, and then I went to work.

The first time I saw Rita's father, I was shaking. When I touched him, my hands were ice cold. I was so confused. I thought I would see a man exuding hatred. Instead, I just saw a dying man.

My voices said, "Be calm. You *need* to do this."

I worked on him a while, and then I told him that he was very ill and that he was going to have to change all kinds of things about what he ate and how he behaved if he was to get any better.

He liked me. But he said, "I'll have to think about it." A few days later, he said, "I can't change." We continued with the healings, working to relieve his cancer pain and keep him comfortable.

Meanwhile, a bishop and priest came every day, treating him like royalty. They wanted to be there when he died.

At some point, after I had been going to work on him every day for a few weeks, my voices said, "Don't come back until we tell you." So I stayed away for a while. On the day I was told to go back, he seemed to be in pain so I started working on him. His wife and cousin went out, leaving me alone with him for a while, so it was just the two of us.

He soon started having problems breathing. I helped him as he struggled for breath, at first, gasping. Then the breaths became very gentle, pants of released breath. I was aware as I was working with him to ease his breathing that something very sacred was happening. I could feel the sacredness of the life around us. It wasn't until later that I realized I was engaged in a death ritual, performing the rites of passage. I had never experienced anything like this before.

Right before he died I heard the words, "Father, into thy hands I commend my spirit." I heard those words as he let out a last breath, a long exhalation that released the life in him. It took *my* breath away. My gaze was drawn up to his third eye. I will never forget it. In my trance, I could see that as this diplomat in the service of the murderous Somoza died, his third-eye chakra opened wide![28] His face was serene; he had no pain.

This man, who served Somoza, died in my arms with no pain and with his third-eye chakra wide open. A feeling of perplexity crossed my face. Then, clear as day, I heard a voice say two words.

"Don't judge."[29]

Chapter 7

Medicine Wheel

After Rita's father died, Adrian and I got a place of our own and stayed in the Bay area for about a year. I started working at one of the first alternatives to mental hospitals, in geriatrics, with the elderly mentally ill. Rita was working there and had told them about me, saying I was a *curandera* and that the Latinos in the community were already seeing me. I actually got hired to be a *curandera*, working under a psychiatrist! It was quite an experience.

I remember working with one of the patients who was on so many drugs he couldn't get up out of bed in the morning without slowly rolling over, setting one foot down, rolling some more, then setting down the other. I gave him healing baths with salt rubs, massages, and other treatments and soon he told his psychiatrist, "I don't want these drugs anymore." They took him off the drugs. I kept working with him so he didn't experience any withdrawal symptoms and before I left the place, he was happily taking dancing lessons!

Much of what happened during this year is lost to me. I was in such grief over the loss of my sister. I can't even remember the name of the place where I worked. My daughter and Little Bear came and stayed with us for a while. Wanda said I used to scream at night in my sleep.

Mami Walks Proudly

At some point before the year was out, Adrian and I broke up. A friend came to get me and I moved back to Arizona, living with my friends Pat and Marianne for a while in Tucson. But I ended up going back to California soon after when I learned that my mother had gotten sick. I found out she had been in bed for a month!

Mami was living in a neighborhood with a lot of Latina friends, in an apartment that Zela and her husband owned. Her friends told me what she'd been through with my siblings. "They don't love her. They treat her terribly," they said. Also, Zela's husband didn't like Latinos and didn't like it when they visited Mami.

Mami and I, sometime in the 1980s

Mami was deeply ashamed of the way her children treated her. She was now living through the long time of being on the receiving end of what she had done to my siblings when they were kids. Her life was such a misery, I felt so sorry for her. To heal her body and get her out of bed, I gave Mami salt baths, massages, and herbal treatments. But I also felt drawn to do whatever I could to ease Mami's misery and shame. I wanted my mother to save face with her friends; I wanted them to know she had a child who really loved her. So when her friends came over, I would give them foot massages, rub their shoulders, and make them teas like a humble and dutiful daughter doing her mother's bidding.

Mami really lit up when she was finally well enough to walk to the store. I would go with her, walking a step or two behind, with my head bowed, rolling the cart, like a good daughter. Her friends would be talking on the sidewalk and I could tell that they loved to see that! My mother held her head high, so proud, walking to the store with her daughter following, respectfully, a few steps behind.

ON TO MEDICINE WHEEL

When I got back to Arizona, I lived briefly at a women's community in the Tucson area. That's where I met Ocean. She had so many girlfriends. They all went crazy over her—and she wanted me, too.

I said, "No, honey. I'm a monogamous person. I'm not into casual sex." Ocean ended up changing. She started to become celibate and soon made herself indispensable. I found myself liking her and, in time, I fell in love.

Ocean had a motorcycle and a very homey van called "Ali-om," which had two beds and a little stove. She sold the motorcycle and we used the money to go to Medicine Wheel.

We lived in Ali-om until we met some neighbors, Bill and Edie, who had a trailer park. They offered to have us stay in a two-bedroom trailer that needed to be cleaned up. It was a mess, but we got it spick and span and then lived in the trailer park rent-free in exchange for helping to take care of the place. Meanwhile, lots of people had already started to come to Medicine Wheel, so we began making building plans.

I wanted a house and healing center with round rooms. Bill, a master builder, built the shell of the first and largest circular room. He taught Ocean, who was an amazing builder herself, how to create this kind of structure. Ocean picked it right up. Years earlier, she had built a little place of her own—cutting the wood, milling the lumber, and all.

So after Bill created the shell of what became our living/dining room, Ocean finished it off with her beautiful woodwork, using weathered planks

Medicine Wheel

and other materials she salvaged. She then took charge of building two similar but smaller circular rooms on either side of the central room. Friends helped us build, and we all took our orders from Ocean.

When it was finished, people would remark, over and over again, on

what a beautiful and unusual place Medicine Wheel was. The central room, our living/dining room, was an octagon twenty-five feet in diameter. It was sunk, hobbit-like, into a small hill. The front door opened to an entrance hallway that led down into the room. A woodstove was tucked on one side near kitchen cabinets and a din-.

Looking out the ground-level picture window

ing room table; bookshelves and a couch and chairs filled the other side; colorful carpets covered the Earth floor. Skylights let in lots of light between the wood beams above and two big picture windows on either side of the entrance let in even more light. They also gave you an insect's view of the world! The windows were waist high inside, like regular windows, but because they were at ground level outside, looking out you would see things from the perspective of the soil and the grasses and brush that grew out of it.

The central room had doorways on either side leading to two round bedrooms, each fifteen feet in diameter. And behind the central room, there was a ten-foot-square healing room with walls that angled up to a point some twenty feet above, creating a pyramid.

This was Medicine Wheel.

Connecting More Deeply with Mother Earth

When I first came to the land in 1978, I had camped on it with my friend and grandson for about two weeks—as long as our food lasted. I had already been feeling and experiencing Earth's energy for several years, but as I lay on the land for those two weeks, it was an experience of a whole new order of magnitude of energy. When we finally went into the little town of St. Johns,

Diane said something about it being "Saturday." I thought she was talking about something to eat! That's how disorienting—or re-orienting—it was.

As Medicine Wheel opened into its fullness, I felt my body, spirit, and mind being released to the land and gave myself over to experiencing the deepening connection with Mother Earth.[30] I was awakening to the fullness of the life on the land, becoming conscious of even the tiniest insects, seeing the beautiful artwork on the miniature wings of a little bug that flew into my hand. I was so impressed, overwhelmed with the beauty and complexity of Creation. And I awakened to even deeper awareness of the consciousness in all life.

One day I encountered a tiny seed. I was getting ready to do a workshop out of state. Usually, I would start preparing for the workshops about two weeks ahead of time by going out to the land to ask the trees, the sky, the stones: what am I to tell the human people? They would give me an idea of something to think about and then, when I got to the actual location of the workshop, I would go to the land there and again ask the question.

This time I felt called to go out to the land *three months* ahead of the workshop. So I went out and asked, "What do I tell the people?" All I heard was the word "communication." I listened further, but nothing else came. A few days later I went out for a second time and asked the same question. Again, the word "communication" came to me—and nothing else. The third time I went out to prepare myself for the workshop, I got the same answer—"communication."

I finally got it. I was being asked to meditate on communication. So after that I would sit outside, looking at everything in the natural world around me, and say, "I'm here. I'm listening."

I started hearing the message. It had to do with the way humans see the natural world around them. I was told that the human did not really know much about the trees and plants and natural life around them. My voices said that humans see trees and plants in certain ways and *think* they know them, but they really don't. They don't know the *real* trees or plants. There is so much fear of the human on Earth that the natural world conceals its true essence from the human and other animal people. This is what I was to communicate to the people.

I had this message in my heart as I later went on a Medicine Walk, walking barefoot on Mother Earth, taking each step as a prayer. When the White Buffalo Woman brought the people the sacred pipe to use to send their voices to Great Spirit, she said, according to Black Elk, "With this sacred pipe you will walk upon the Earth; for the Earth is your Grandmother and Mother, and She is sacred. Every step that is taken upon Her should be as a prayer. The bowl of this pipe is of red stone; it is the Earth."

So that's what I was doing on my Medicine Walk, taking each step as a prayer with the message for the people in my heart, when I saw a tiny little seed with shiny, fuzzy tendrils. It looked like a little spec of tumbleweed. I was in a trance-like state. So when I saw it rolling along the ground, I slowly reached down and caught it in the palm of my hand. I put my other hand over the delicate seed so it wouldn't blow away, and I then looked in on it through the opening between my hands.

Because I was in a trance, the little seed didn't feel me. So when I looked into the opening between my hands, I *saw* her—I saw her as she *was*. When the little seed realized what had happened, she freaked out! She pulled her little fuzzy tendrils together, moved to find the opening between my hands, and then flew out in the opposite direction of the wind. She had been moving in the direction of the wind when I found her. Now I could see that she was not just drifting with the wind; she was moving on her volition!

I continued my Medicine Walk, going just a little bit further before turning around to begin the mindful walk back home. As I walked, I suddenly felt guided to go to the other side of the road. Drawn to a little hole in the sand, I bent down and looked in. Tucked inside were several of those little seeds, all huddled in a circle, their fuzzy tendrils linked like arms over shoulders. They were talking! I could sense one of them saying something like, "I blew it! They found out our secret!"

Suddenly the little seeds sensed my presence and stopped talking. I could see them beginning to push their tendrils together as if getting ready to jump into the wind and flee. I placed the palms of my hands over the hole, and released all the love and healing energy I had. Feeling them relax, I said, gently, "I love you," and left. [31]

COYOTES & SNAKES

I had always been terribly afraid of snakes, but when my path started I began experiencing snakes in Spirit. I found I wasn't scared of them, even though they looked so real. Snake and Bird were the first who came to me in the Spirit realm. I was told that they would be my totems—all snakes and all birds.

When we first moved to Medicine Wheel, I was a little anxious that I wouldn't be able to tell the difference between a real snake and a spirit snake. It was never a problem. I became friends with the real snakes on the land.

The friendship started with drumming. When we first moved there I would drum every day to the snakes and coyotes and all the life on the land. I wanted them to know that we had no intention of hurting them, that we respected them. Soon, snakes started coming around. I didn't mess with them but I would say, "I'm your friend. You can smell me, feel my vibration." They would go along their way.

After a time, they started coming closer. They knew we weren't there to hurt them. That was clear in the drum beat and in the way I interacted with them. Animals understand. The closer I am with animals, the more I understand how they are in tune with spiritual vibration. When I start to do a healing with animals, they usually look at me sideways and then look up over my head to see how high the energy field goes. Once they see my aura, it's total trust. They know who that energy is. It's the same with snakes. They can see my energy.

We came to the same understanding with coyotes. I would put meat out on the hillsides for the coyotes. We could see them come get it. For years Medicine Wheel had this energy that surrounded and protected us. We had chickens without a coop. The chickens would run free all day long, and roost in trees or in a little hut we had. With all the coyotes around, we never had a problem—until later when the energy shifted.

HEALINGS

During the years that we lived there, people came from all over the place for healings and ceremonies—and to hang out. Everyone liked the energy. I would get mail from people who had heard about me and after exchanging letters, they would want to come. People came from out of state and even from out of the country. After we got the sweat lodge ceremonies going, people would travel long distances just to come to them.

I was also invited to give workshops, mostly in Arizona and California, so I would meet more people who would be interested in coming. With the workshop income, contributions I would receive for healings, and a small amount of money Ocean had coming in every month, we were able to make it. I even got the dog food free from a local butcher. He would give me meat that was too old to sell. I was so grateful, I started making him special dishes, and then he really got generous with his meat! Our dogs were thrilled.

We also had children living with us off and on. Little Bear spent quite a bit of time with us. Whenever Wanda was having financial problems or troubles with men, she would let him come. He used to love it, and went to the first grade there.

Adrian's daughter, Tina, also came and lived with us for about a year. Tina was in elementary school and had been getting into so much trouble she fell behind a year in school. Tina actually asked her mother if she could come live with me. Adrian told her daughter, "You know Zelima will beat your ass if you do with her what you've been doing with me, don't you?"

Tina said, "Yes, I know." So Adrian brought her to Medicine Wheel. During the months she stayed with us, I *was* real strict with her. But it seems that's just what she needed. By the time she went back to her mother, she was getting straight A's and had caught up with her grade level.

The other child living with us for a time was David, the twelve-year-old son of a woman named Emma who was dying of cancer. When Emma first came to Medicine Wheel, she was very sick with cancer. I worked with her every day for about two weeks. Emma started feeling so much better, she ran around saying, "I'm healing! I'm healing!"

At that point, she told me she had to go back and take care of business. I pleaded with Emma not to go back. I said she was still very sick and that if she went back right now I was not sure I could help her later.

But Emma left—to go home and take care of business.

Months later, Emma returned with her son, David. She was nothing but skin and bones. I did my best to work with her but it was too late. She was too sick and only survived a few months, dying at Medicine Wheel.

Emma didn't want her mother or any member of her family to know that she was dying. She had some really hard feelings towards them. I kept urging her to give me her mother's phone number so I could call her. "What you're doing isn't right," I said. But she refused.

Finally, after one of these conversations I remember feeling so frustrated I reached down and shook her. "You're dying!" I said. "I have to call your mother. What you're doing isn't right. You don't want this on your soul."

Emma looked at me, shocked—and then gave me her mother's phone number. I called her mother and she came to Medicine Wheel. They made up. Emma later said, "I'm so glad. I don't know how I missed seeing how beautiful my mama is." Emma's mother came to Medicine Wheel from New Mexico and was right there with Emma when she died.

CEREMONIES

Every year for nine years, from 1981 through 1989, we held a ceremony at Medicine Wheel to pray for Mother Earth.

I was guided to use the Secret Dakini Oracle to create the seven-day ceremonies. The Dakini Oracle is an ancient, left-handed Tantric system, originating from a temple in India that has stone carvings of sixty-four Dakinis, which represent the female principles of intuitive wisdom. The Dakinis serve as a mirror of your mind and have helped me so much over the years to understand myself.[32]

One of the cards that was especially helpful to me was the Number Five card, which has an image of the elephant-headed Hindu God, Ganesh, sitting inside a spider's web. Ganesh is the Remover of Obstacles and I kept pulling this card over and over again. It teaches you to confront your inner obstacles to get through something. Every time I came up against an obstacle, I would just cry. That didn't help! After drawing this card, I started saying, I'll confront the obstacle. I used the Dakini card as a visualization, seeing myself in the spider's web—sitting in it, but not caught in it. The Dakini Oracle made a big change in my life.

Before the ceremonies, I would consult the Dakini Oracle to help me focus on the teachings for each of the seven days or to determine when in July we should have the ceremony. We always held them in July when the rains came because it was the coolest month of the summer.

As people arrived for the seven-day ceremony, I would ask them to leave their troubles, resentments, angers in the "burden basket." If they wanted them back after the ceremony, they could pick them up. But to pray for Mother Earth, we all needed to free ourselves of these kinds of burdens. I also asked everyone who came not to use drugs, cameras, or tape recorders. When you photograph a ceremony, you take away from the spirit of it because the important thing in ceremony is the intention and the energy we each bring to it. Taking photographs draws away from the intention and takes the energy elsewhere.

At this time I also kept getting strong messages not to allow any tape recordings or videotaping of my teachings or workshops. It was related to a message I kept getting that "You must mature undisturbed." I got that message over and over again, so I thought it would be this way forever. But now they're saying, "Get the teachings out however you can."

Each day of the ceremony included a Little Sisters sweat lodge, teachings, and a workshop. The first sweat lodge of the seven-day ceremony was usually held at night. Night sweats are to get rid of

One of the bedrooms in Medicine Wheel

old stuff. Actually all sweat lodges are about that, but the night sweats are especially focused on cleansing. After the first day, the sweats would be held in the morning to help everyone get centered and ready for the day.

We had an outdoor kitchen and everyone brought food and water to share. We would make breakfast together after the morning sweat lodge. Then, the teachings would take place. If I felt called to talk about certain things, it would influence me in terms of what days to pick for the ceremony. For example, if I felt guided to talk about the power of love in the spiritual realm, I would make sure to have the ceremony fall on July 11, since 11 is the self-creative card in the Dakini. We would actually begin the day by dedicating it to the power of love in the spiritual realm.

July 12, corresponding to the 12 card, would be dedicated to going beyond the eagle—letting go of obstacles that leave you in bondage. July 13 would be dedicated to issues of death and rebirth, and so on. I would use the Dakini cards for each day as a take-off point for the teachings I felt guided to bring forth.

144

Later in the day we would have a workshop. They were all healing workshops of one kind or another. Sometimes the workshops focused on healing demonstrations. Sometimes we talked about food. I remember one time we did a workshop on cancer and the foods that help to get rid of cancer cells. A lot of people loved that one because it left them with a feeling of hope—that there was something you could do to help get rid of cancer cells just as you could do certain things to help get rid of a cold. We also gave workshops on creating Medicine Necklaces, Medicine Drawings, and other things I felt called to teach.

A couple of weeks before each ceremony, I would go on "vacation," camping somewhere so I could relax and let Spirit guide me about the upcoming ceremony. I would spend the time praying about what I should say to the people who came.

One of the workshops we put on every year because people just loved it involved having everyone dress up to reveal a part of themselves they didn't usually express. During the year, I would collect bags of all kinds of clothes and accessories from thrift shops and places like that. The participants would go through the bags, creating costumes that somehow brought forth a part of themselves that they hadn't expressed. Then we would drum and dance these parts of ourselves.

Sometimes the parts of themselves that people would express were so funny, we would just laugh hilariously. Other times people got so caught up in bringing forth these new aspects of themselves that we were all moved to another plane. One time, for example, we were dancing these hidden parts of ourselves and it started raining. No one stopped. Everyone just kept dancing as the rain poured down. All of a sudden, there was a roll of thunder so powerful and profound it literally shook the Earth. We were all so caught up in the dancing nobody was scared—even though the ground shook! We were all just struck with awe and excitement.[33]

At night, people would gather to talk informally and then sleep in the camping gear they brought. There were usually around thirty people there, sometimes many more, plus whatever pets they brought with them. Many of the same people came year after year, but there were always some new people. Men were welcome but it was mostly women who participated. The guys who came were pretty tough! I admired them because they had to be pretty secure to experience and appreciate the power of women. I remember when a Native brother came. He was so impressed with the power of women he

145

witnessed, he said, "The brothers are always talking about the power of women, giving it lip service. They ought to come here and experience it!"

On the seventh day, we ended the ceremony with a great big feast. I had two big cauldrons that we would put over the open fire, cooking a wonderful meal. When the food was cooked, we would first serve it to the animals, then serve ourselves, and we would all eat together.

I had this old man of a dog named Barney. He was really old when I got him, abandoned, full of worms, and lonely. But he lived five more years after I brought him to Medicine Wheel. He was so loved, he couldn't believe it. During each of the ceremonies, he would be wandering all over the place. But he always knew the exact time the food would be ready on the last day. He was right there waiting to be fed. Barney was also a dancer; he would dance to the drums. If someone was drumming off beat, he would knock their hands off the drum with his nose!

BACK INTO VIOLENCE AND ABUSE

Despite—or right alongside of—all these beautiful things I was experiencing at Medicine Wheel, I found myself back in my childhood, locked into an abusive relationship. The violence I saw inflicted on my daughter by her various male partners was now being inflicted on me by my own partner! I used to say that I would never let anything like that happen to me; I would never allow anyone to abuse me. Yet, here it was, happening. I never intended to lose my strength. I couldn't even imagine it. But I did—and through it I learned, very painfully, just how women can slide into abusive relationships and become trapped in them.

It happened, in part, because of my feelings of empathy for what Ocean had gone through in her childhood. All my partners, except two, had difficult childhoods. My heart just went out to women who had tough childhoods. I would feel all this empathy and want life to be better for them. I realized later that I was really just dealing with my own childhood issues through theirs.

Ocean came from a very violent home. Her mother was an alcoholic who was constantly beaten by her boyfriends. The boyfriends would also beat Ocean. This happened as far back as she could remember, to a time when she was so young she couldn't talk. As Ocean got older, there were times when her mother wouldn't come home. She learned of several places to go looking for her. One was a hotel where she once found her beaten black and blue. The last time Ocean's mother failed to come home she was found on the street, her head face-down on the sidewalk. She had been beaten to death.

Ocean would recall these horrible incidents and I knew what was coming. I started to see a pattern: within a day or two after recalling these stories, Ocean would get violent with me. One time she pulled my hair out so bad I had a bald spot. She was much stronger than I was, so I lived in fear of her.

When I tried to pull away, Ocean would say she had a mental illness and that she was trying to change and needed my help. "You take care of me when there's something wrong with my body, why not when there's something wrong with my head?"

"Yes, but you're hurting me," I said, urging her to go into therapy. She promised she would but never did. Mine was a slow descent into dependence and helplessness. I used to drive myself everywhere, for example, but because Ocean wanted to be the one to drive, I stopped. Eventually, I actually got scared to drive! I became more and more insecure, losing my self confidence. It got so I ended up thinking that Ocean could do everything and I could do nothing. I *know* what women go through, how easy it is to slide into being a victim and how hard it is to break out.

I finally did find my way and put a stop to it. It was triggered after I got one of her beatings. When I started to say something to her, she put her hand in my mouth and started to pull my tongue out. I clamped down my teeth and bit her! She started screaming. I could have kept on biting but I didn't. I let go, and soon after I left Medicine Wheel to go to a workshop in Tucson. While I was gone, with the help and support of friends, I got enough courage to say it's over.

Ocean wanted us to stay together. We did for a while, and she never beat me after that. But her temper would still rise up, and even though she wouldn't hit me, there was a control issue. It all came to a head when Ocean and I got into a big argument when we were on the camping trip just before the July ceremony in 1985. A friend of hers had come with us and things got erratic. She set Ocean off. We got into an argument and I felt her come at me as if to beat me. By this time, I'd had enough rest from her abuse that I said, "Okay, let's fight."

I started dancing circles around her. She tried to hit me, but she kept missing, telling me to stay put. Another time she tried to hit me, I popped her in the eye. She was stunned. I was into it. All this rage came out in me. I said, "Come on!" But she walked away. I said, "That's it, Ocean. That's it."

Ocean left right before the seven-day ceremony. She knew that during ceremony I needed my space. Letters came from her saying she still loved me and wanted me back. I didn't read any of them until after the ceremony was over. Later, when her friends came, I told them it was over. "I'm through." The love was real, and it was really hard breaking off with Ocean because she had so much beauty, intelligence, and goodness. But I had to stay true to my path; I had to break it off.

CHILLING NEWS

Before Ocean and I broke up, some tax assessors from Apache County came by one day in the summer of 1985 for a routine check to see if any improvements had been made to the land that would need assessing. As they reviewed their land surveys, they came to an astonishing conclusion.

"You're on the wrong land."

"What??"

"You're on the wrong land," one of the assessors said, repeating the chilling news. "This is terrible," he said. "I feel bad having to be the one to tell you, but this is not your land. You can't stay here."

He showed us the survey plats, pointing out our location west of Route 191, in areas 12 and 13 of Witch Well Ranches.

"The land you own is over here," he said, pointing to a spot on the exact opposite side of Route 191, located in what were also termed areas 12 and 13 of Witch Well Ranches.

I was stunned. The land they said I legally owned was some five or six

miles away—land I had never seen. The land we had built Medicine Wheel on was the land where I tied my grandson's diaper in 1978.

We went straight into town to see Jack Brown. Ocean brought the survey plats with her to show him. When Jack

The cabin Joan built at Medicine Wheel, now in disrepair

heard the story and saw the plat, he was deeply concerned. But he told us not to worry that he would straighten things out. His words felt so true, we stopped worrying.

A couple of weeks later, Jack Brown told us he had checked things out and learned that Medicine Wheel's eighty acres actually consisted of two forty-acre parcels belonging to two different parties. "But don't worry," he reassured us. "You're not going to lose it."

By this time, we not only had the original Medicine Wheel structures on the eighty acres but also a cabin and trailer. The trailer belonged to Emma,

In the kitchen of Medicine Wheel

who had lived there when she was so sick with cancer. Before she died, Emma told me she wanted me to keep it. The cabin was built by a woman named Joan who had muscular sclerosis and had come for treatments. She asked if she could build a cabin to live in and give as a gift to Medicine Wheel. The builders she hired constructed a cabin with two large round rooms, each twenty feet in diameter, and a screened-in porch. As it turned out, the cabin was on one of the forty-acre parcels while my home was on the other.

Jack Brown and I talked a few times after this and he continued to reassure me that all would be fine. At some point he said it looked like he might be able to obtain one of the forty-acre parcels but not the other. I urged him to keep trying to get both, since the land was ceremonially connected—plus, we had a house on one parcel and a cabin on the other.

I continued to live at Medicine Wheel, expecting that sooner or later Jack Brown would fix the problem. I would check in with him from time to time, and he would reassure me that he was still working on it. A year went by. Before the annual seven-day ceremony, Joan and I went camping so I could get ready for it. When we got back I found that two of my beloved roosters were dead, as was a guinea hen—killed by coyotes. The energy on the land had shifted.

We went ahead with our annual seven-day ceremony and then, as fall came, more things started to shift and feel less certain. My mother had to move out of her house and into an apartment, so my friend Carolina and I went to California to help her. It took longer than we expected, causing problems between Carolina and her girlfriend, both of whom had been living at Medicine Wheel in the trailer Emma had left me. By the time we got back, Carolina's girlfriend was gone. A short while after that, Carolina decided to leave.

Joan and I stayed for another couple of months. I was feeling so alone and bewildered about what to do. Jack Brown was still saying that he was going to take care of things, but now I wasn't so sure. "Am I going to have to accept that I'm really losing this?" I kept thinking.

None of my friends were able to help—they had no idea how to advise me. I think they were as paralyzed as I was at the thought that we might lose Medicine Wheel. No one wanted to believe it. Of course, since then, lots of people have told me things I could have done, but at the time I had no advisors, no money, no lawyers.

Winter was approaching and things felt like they were falling apart. I was sick with anxiety about what to do. Jack Brown wasn't making any progress straightening things out. The county assessors had said I couldn't stay there. I had no money—and with life being so uncertain at Medicine Wheel, I couldn't encourage more people to come to the land. At the end of November 1986, I decided I had to leave my beloved Medicine Wheel. I gave Jack Brown the phone number of a friend where I could be reached in Tucson, and drove off.

The heartache was unbearable.

CHAPTER 8

MEDICINE JOURNEY

S everal months before I knew I was going to have to leave Medicine Wheel, I did a Medicine Drawing—an intuitive way of drawing I learned from Spirit that brings out what's going on within. In the drawing I was dressed in beautiful embroidered clothes with a full peasant skirt. I had high Indian boots on my feet and a Medicine Hat on top of my head. Dressed for winter, I was standing on the roof of my house at Medicine Wheel, getting ready to fly.

"What in the world is this?" I said. "It looks like I'm going on a Medicine Journey."

A Medicine Journey is a journey of transformation. By the time you get to your destination, you will be different. It involves discovery, learning something new—and sometimes having to go through obstacles. I thought it was going to be a nice journey; I looked so happy in all my beautiful clothes.

Little did I know what lay ahead. When I lost Medicine Wheel, I lost *everything*—my home, my job, my workplace. I had to start all over again, from scratch. And with no money because most people who came to me for healings had very little to donate, and the animals I treated had no money. So I usually had very little money, just enough to get by. But that was enough as long as I had Medicine Wheel—a place to live and do healings. Now I had neither. Struggling through one disappointment after another, I often wondered, "What did I do wrong to deserve this?"

The only thing that kept me going was my path, knowing there was something I had to do that involved Mother Earth and healing. I knew I had a path because I was still able to do healings. I could feel disasters before they happened. I was being taught new things. If I didn't have a path, none of this would happen. That's what I kept telling myself.

When things got really tough, I would say to myself, "They're making me tough for the hard times to come. I probably wouldn't be able to go into hard times from easy times. That's why I'm being toughened up."

WANDERING, HOMELESS

When I left Medicine Wheel, I drove to a friend's house in Tucson and stayed on her couch for a few weeks. I found some odd jobs and as soon as I had earned $500, I rented an apartment. But since regular jobs were hard to find in Tucson, and finding new clients for healing takes time, I soon had to leave the apartment; I couldn't make the rent. So I spent most of the rest of the year homeless, staying here and there with friends in Tucson—and a lot of time in my car.

It was a scary time, driving from one place to another, fearful that someone would break into my car at night.

In time, the Bahai let me have some space where I could teach classes on healing, and at some point I got a job working in a group home with developmentally disabled adults. Slowly, I started to get back on my feet.

GIGA, MY LAST PARTNER

I think I first met Giga, a beautiful Puerto Rican woman, at a benefit for Medicine Wheel that friends held before I left the land. She did a poetry reading. But I didn't start to get to know her until I got to Tucson. I ended up falling for her like no one else. I was completely out of control. We spent about three tumultuous years together.

Giga could insult me just like my mother, and would leave me at the drop of a hat over things most people wouldn't even argue about. We actually got married, having an ancient Lakota ceremony for women that some Native sisters performed. Before we had the ceremony, making a lifetime commitment to each other, I asked Giga, "Are you sure you want to do this? We could just make it for five years...." Giga said, "I want it forever."

The first time she wanted to leave me we were only married three days! She left three weeks later. It was on again, off again the whole time we were together. I had to pray to get over my obsession with her—and finally did, sometime before my mother died in 1992. Yet there is a part of Giga that is so intelligent, filled with a deep wisdom, very psychic and perceptive that I will always remember with love.

During this fifteen-year period, everything is so hazy; all I can remember is whether something happened before Mami died in 1992 or after. I have a very hard time remembering dates anyway—part of my dyslexia. But I did my best to piece things together for this book by working around the few dates I do remember, like when my sister died or my children were born, and then working with dates that friends remembered or with major news events of things happening around the world. This fifteen-year period, though, was the most challenging to try to figure out.

After Giga and I broke up I realized that what I wanted for my own personal life more than anything was a peaceful heart and mind. I hadn't found it in any relationship, so I decided to be celibate for a year or two. After a couple of years of celibacy, I decided I had what I wanted—peace of mind and peace of heart. So that's what I've remained, a celibate woman.

LAST CEREMONY, LAST HOPE

I went back to Medicine Wheel three times after leaving at the end of 1986 to hold ceremonies for Mother Earth. I would always check in with Jack Brown to see where things stood. During this last ceremony, in the summer of 1989, I had again left word with him that I would be at the land.

On the last day of the last ceremony, Jack Brown drove out to see me. The ceremony was over but there were still a number of people hanging around. A double rainbow arced over the land. Jack told me this was very unusual, especially because of its location. He said he thought it was a sign of the power of the Creator blessing our ceremony. We thought that, too. He then told me that he thought I would be able to have the land we were on, *plus* the land that was legally mine.

I remember turning to everyone who was still there, saying, "Jack Brown says he thinks we'll be able to keep Medicine Wheel *and* the other land!" Everyone cheered and celebrated.

From the time I had bought the land until I paid it off a few years later, I struggled hard to make the payments on the land—and was late a lot, sometimes *very* late. But Jack Brown was always so patient with me. I believed in him.

However, after I returned to Tucson from Medicine Wheel, there was no word from Jack Brown. I called several times, unable to reach him. When I finally got him on the phone, I asked, "What's happening? Why haven't you gotten in touch with me as you promised?" He shrugged me off, saying, "I've been in Alaska!" It was a completely different tone of voice. The hope and expectation that he would fix the mistake drained out of me. I did not hear from him again after that.

Eventually, I went to a lawyer who sent him a letter. Jack's son responded. There were no more promises of correcting the mistake or restoring my land. Instead, there was an offer of $5,000 to compensate me for my loss. I couldn't even begin to rebuild Medicine Wheel with that amount of money! I was broke and had no money to pay lawyers to sue for just compensation. Later, another lawyer, working pro bono, sent him a second letter. But he never even responded to that one.

As the years went by, I lost track of Jack Brown, but I never let go of Medicine Wheel. It was always in the back of my mind. I kept missing the land, and couldn't understand why I was guided there if nothing was going to happen. I would agonize over it, knowing I had no money or power to bring it back to life. If something was going to happen with Medicine Wheel, it had to come from Spirit—because I wasn't doing it. All I could do was pray.

JESUS, DIVINE MASTER OF HUMILITY

In time I found some steadier employment in Tucson, including working at Job Corps, helping high school dropouts. I always tried to find part-time work to support me because I needed to be able to continue doing my healings. To stay on my path I *had* to continue my healings, even if it meant rarely having more than it took to pay the bills each month—and too often not even that much.

One night, sometime in the late 1980s, I went to bed and fell asleep. I didn't drift off to sleep; I just remember being awake one moment and sound asleep the next. I was alone. It was one of the many times Giga and I had broken up.

The next thing I knew, I awakened to a powerful and vivid experience that I would describe as a dream, except it didn't feel like a dream; it felt *real*.[34]

I was in the doorway of what looked like an ancient space. The doorway was very low and I can't remember if the door was already open or if I opened it. It was dark inside, lit only by some torches in holders on the walls. As I walked in, I felt this deep, deep feeling of respect. This ancient space held this beautiful, deep feeling of total respect that penetrated right through me, entering every cell of my body. I kept walking deeper into this ancient, dark place with this beautiful feeling of respect.

I saw two people leave. I could barely make out the one who exited on my left; the other, a woman, left through an exit on my right. There were other people leaving, too, but I couldn't see them because it was so dark, and I'm not sure if they saw me. All I could see or feel was their deep respect.

Finally, I came upon a cot with a person lying on his side on it. I was at his feet, but didn't pay too much attention to them. Instead, I started moving up the cot on the right side of his body. Halfway up, I saw a ball of bloody flesh on his side. My gaze went up to his face. I was stopped still by his eyes, which locked onto mine. Those eyes, all I remember were those eyes. Even though it was dark in the room, I could see that his eyes were dark and completely at peace, despite the intense pain he must have been in.

He spoke—and I knew who it was.

The knowing was deep in me as I looked into those eyes. The next thing I remember was being at his feet, sitting on a chair. He was still lying on his side, looking at me, talking to me. I don't remember everything he said but I do remember feeling his *humility*. I have never seen or felt such humility. It was not something he was trying to be but something he is. I was perfectly aware of his divinity, but when he spoke to me, it was as if he were speaking to an equal. That was how great his humility was—he spoke to me as if I were an equal, even though I was perfectly aware of his divinity. I have never experienced anything like this feeling in my life, ever.

He was speaking to me and I was calm, feeling a calmness I have never known before. At one point I asked him, "Do you want me to be a Christian?" He lifted his right arm where the wound was as if to stop me. And then he said the only words I still remember. "I want you to be as you are. There is a reason why you are the way you are. There is work to do."

He told me a few other things and then closed his eyes. I got up again. I was trying to help him. I knew he had to die. But if possible, I wanted to release the pain. I started working on him, touching his feet, the wounds on his feet. I felt him shaking and then go into convulsions. I made myself very calm and lay behind him on the cot, putting my arm around him. I got myself as peaceful and calm as I could and let that energy go into him. He stopped shaking. Very gently, I got up and went to work on his feet again. He had convulsions again. So I did the same thing again, lying behind him until the convulsions stopped. I went back to his feet, and then I felt his Spirit leave. When I looked into his eyes, they were just as peaceful as before—except they didn't have the energy behind them.

I put the sheet over him and then, I woke up, calm as could be. "Phew," I said. My mind went blank after that. Sometime later, I came to again. It was still dark. Again, I said, "Phew." Then I went to sleep.

My life changed after that encounter. I now *knew* that I didn't have to worry about any dogma. When I looked into Jesus' eyes, I saw Truth. I learned that there *is* Truth, but it is not dogma. What I saw in his eyes was Truth, which just *is*.

I knew that there was no need to worry about being condemned if you weren't a believer or if you were a homosexual. Jesus is not about dogma and condemnation. He lifted his arm with that awful wound and said, "I want you to be as you are. There is a reason why you are the way you are. There is work to do."

What is my work? I now knew that it had to do with being homosexual—being a homosexual with Spirit flowing through me. As strong as this energy flows through me sometimes, which people can feel and experience in healings and workshops, it's flowing through a *lesbian* woman, an ordinary person with lots of challenges, and not really highly educated.

It made me think back to Mr. Heller and the time he told his assistant that he was starting to doubt the Catholic Church because he couldn't believe the gates of heaven wouldn't be open to me. I think that's what Jesus was talking about: "Oh, yes! God loves this homosexual."

When I woke up, I remembered everything Jesus said, but then I forgot. I believe I retain the memory of what he said somewhere—and that it will come back to me someday when it's needed.

MAMI'S DEMONS

Sometime in 1991 or early 1992, Mami had a stroke. I dropped everything to go be with her. My daughter, Wanda, told me she wanted to see me and her grandmother, so Wanda and her husband drove from Albuquerque, where they were living, to Tucson and, together, we drove on to California. After Mami got out of the hospital, I stayed with her for several months in her little apartment, taking care of her. I got a check from her insurance for my caretaking, so I was able to continue paying rent on my place in Tucson. Friends took care of the animals.

I did a healing on Mami as soon as we brought her back to her apartment from the hospital. At some point during the healing, I realized that Mami couldn't move—she was paralyzed. But the energy, Spirit, was so strong, I didn't get scared and, somehow, Mami wasn't scared either. I kept doing the healing, my eyes closed as I moved with the energy, until suddenly I opened them and saw what was happening to my mother's mouth. It was contorted in that Planet-of-the-Apes way that it would contort sometimes when she beat me as a child. I have no idea how she managed to contort her mouth in that awful way. But I started to make the connections.

Spirit was so strong, with the energy flowing, that I just kept doing the healing despite the ugly face. By the time I was done, Mami's face had gone back to normal. She was still unable to move for a little while. But when her muscles came back to life, she spoke as I helped her get up.

"*¿Se me salió, verdad?*" (It came out of me, right?)

"*¿Qué, Mami?*" (What, Mami?)

"*Eso malo.*" (That bad thing.)

"*Si, Mami.*"

Sighing with relief, she said, "*'Ta bueno.*" (That's good.)

That was how it went the first time. The same thing happened every time I did a healing on her after that—and Mami understood exactly what was going on. I started noticing that after each of these sessions, her face was getting softer and softer.

After one intense healing that left her terribly weak, I tried to explain that she was feeling the way she was because so much had come out of her, adding "*pero se va a mejorar.*" (But you will get better.)

"*Si, si. Yo sé lo que está pasando.*" (Yes, yes. I know what's happening.) "*Se me está saliendo todo eso malo. Está bueno.*" (All that bad stuff is coming out of me. That's good.)

Mami suffered another stroke and was back in the hospital. Drooling, incontinent, and eighty-one years of age, there was no way she could go back to her little apartment and ever take care of herself again. So we went to my sister's house after Mami got out of the hospital, staying together in the same

157

room. It was a sweet time with my mother but after three months, I had to leave. I felt like I was a kid again in Zela's house. I'd go take a shower and someone would say, "I need to take a shower. Get out, please." I could never finish a shower. I was constantly reminded that I didn't live there—it wasn't my house. It brought back so many bad memories I finally said I had to go home. I did not want to leave my mother—that was very painful for me. But I couldn't stay, either.

My brother Hiram pleaded with me to stay. He and his wife, Wanda, really supported me and the way I took care of Mami. We had been having some good talks. Hiram offered to pay me $800 a month on top of the insurance payments if I stayed. He had gotten to really love my mom and didn't want me to go. I saw him sit next to Mami, holding her hand while she was sleeping, saying, "¡Ay, qué mamita más linda, esta!" (Oh, what a beautiful little mother she is!)

The last healing I did before I went back to Arizona was the hardest. Mami got paralyzed as usual, but the paralysis went deeper. She could only move her neck a tiny little bit—and her eyes. They were filled with hatred! As I worked on her, she followed me with her eyes, staring at me with this incredible hatred.

"Mami, usted sabe lo que esta pasando. Le va a salir lo malo." I reminded her that she knew what was happening. That the bad things were going to be coming out.

But she just kept pouring the hatred out of her eyes, following me as I continued to work on her. "Mami, es parte del tratamiento." It's part of the treatment, I tried to tell her. More hatred.

Finally, I said, "Okay, Mami." My voices had said to leave the scene. I had planned to bake some pastelitos for her, the Nicaraguan pastry she loved so much. My voices said to leave the room. I was guided in my speech.

Very deliberately, I told Mami that I was leaving and that I would be in the kitchen making her the pastries she loved.

She didn't say anything. Pure hatred came out of her eyes! Before I left the room, I lit some sage and when it started smoking, I went up and down her body, enveloping her in the cleansing, purifying smoke and then I did the same thing to cleanse myself. When I finally was able to walk out of the room and get to the kitchen, I saged myself all over again!

I started making the pastelitos. Mami must have stayed put for a long time because I already had the filling made and was starting to shape and roll the little *pastelitos* when she walked into the kitchen. Mami had this expression on her face that I only saw once in a great while when I was growing up—it was the sweetest face with the most innocent smile.

In a sweet and gentle voice, she asked, *"¿Qué estás haciendo?"*

Mami didn't have to say she was sorry; I knew it from the way she asked me what I was doing.

"Los pastelitos, Mami."

"A ver. Te ayudo." (I'll help you.) She sat down at the table, took a ball of dough, and started rolling it out. We rolled *pastelitos* together.

I came back to see Mami a few times before she died. The last time I saw her, Mami sat next to me and touched my face so tenderly. She had never done that before. Smiling, she looked at me with loving eyes and said, *"¡Qué linda!"*

Soon after that visit, Zela put Mami in a nursing home. Mami wanted to die and had stopped eating. When they would bring her a tray of food, she would throw it away. She didn't want to live, but she was scared of dying—worrying about what was ahead of her. Mami and I had talked about this when I was taking care of her. She was aware of the evil that had been inside her and was afraid that she was going to go to hell.

"¿Quién sabe? Quizás Dios me va a castigar más." (Who knows? Maybe God is going to punish me more.)

I would try to reassure her. *"Ya sufristes, Mami. No vas a sufrir más."* (You have already suffered. You're not going to suffer more.)

But she kept wondering if God was going to punish her more.

So as Mami was dying, she kept fighting death even though she didn't want to live anymore. Zela told me later that she came up with an idea to help Mami cross over. Zela thought that if she could make Mami think Lotus was there, Mami would let go and allow herself to die.

"Mamita, aquí está Lotus. Te vino a traer." (Lotus is here. She came to get you.)

Mami lifted her head and looked around, but seeing nothing, fell back onto the pillow.

Then something happened that my sister hadn't planned. Zela heard my father's voice. Papi said, "Tell her that Humberto is here."

"Mami, aquí está Humberto," Zela said. Mami turned and looked. A peaceful look came over her face, her eyes closed, and she was gone.

COMADRE ANITA

The day after Mami died, I called Anita, a very Catholic woman in Tucson that everyone called *Comadre* Anita, who would come to me for healings. I can't remember why I called her; I didn't call her a lot.

"How are you doing?" she asked. "Not too good," I said. "My mama just died and she was afraid of going to hell. She died with that fear."

"Oh, my God, I dreamed about your mother!" Comadre Anita said. "That's who it was! That's what the dream I just had was about—your mother!" Comadre Anita then told me about her dream.

She and a friend were at a ranch, sitting in the front yard when this lady came towards them riding on horseback. The lady riding the horse was very little (like Mami was before she died), with black hair. "All of a sudden I realized that the lady was someone I knew who had died," Comadre Anita said. "We got real scared, seeing this dead lady coming towards us. So we ran into the house. But the dead lady kept coming toward us, riding to the front door!

"As we were running out the back door, away from the dead lady, here comes Jesus!" Anita said.

"Who are you running from?" Jesus asked her in the dream.

"A dead woman!" Comadre Anita answered.

"I *know* she's dead. I sent her to you," Jesus said. "She needs your help. She's not ready to see me and I sent her to you so you could get her ready. I want her to come to me."

When she finished telling me the dream, Comadre Anita said, "I know why you called; you needed to call. That dream was about your mother. Your mother's all right. She's going to Jesus."

IVAN DIES

When Mami was sick, I called Ivan's wife to ask why he hadn't been around to see her. "Ivan's not well," she said, They lived an hour or more away. "There's no way he can make that trip very often," his wife said.

Ivan came over before I left and I noticed he had a little belly. He had always been thin and fit. I wondered if he had cancer.

When I came back to California for Mami's funeral, Hiram told me that Ivan had pancreatic cancer. He was too sick to make it to the funeral. Before

I left California, I went to see Ivan. The first thing he asked was, "Did you see mom? How did she look? Devastated?"

I said, "No. She looked okay, but it didn't really look like her either."

Ivan was wondering how she looked dead. We talked. "Have you heard that it's terminal?" he asked.

"Yeah."

"What do you think?" he asked.

"Well, Ivan. You've always been brave." His wife looked at me, smiled and nodded. Ivan always had been brave. He was never afraid to face a gang even if he knew he was going to get whipped.

He reminded me, "I came close to dying twice before."

Ivan was wild. He wasn't out of high school when he was thrown in juvenile jail for beating up a homosexual man. Before this, he and Hiram had robbed a church. His first wife was only fifteen when he married her and he was very oppressive. He was also as racist as can be. As far back as I can remember, people called him "*El Negro*," an endearing term in Nicaragua. In the States, they called him "nigger" and "jungle bunny"—so he hated Black people. I never understood why he would hate Black people because White people would call him names that were insulting to African-Americans. Despite all this, Ivan was very handsome, extremely intelligent, and had a dashing personality that just drew people to him—especially women.

He was in his late twenties the first time he got shot for messing with another man's woman. Ivan used to say that he had spread his seed all over, and had more children than he knew. When Ivan was shot, he was in a coma and nearly died. The first time he saw death he knew he was going someplace not good. He remembers being in a really dark place. He fought like crazy to come back, but he kept going into the darkness walkingthrough what felt like walking through cobwebs. He got really scared. Ivan had never been scared before. He said he was shaking, saying, "Please! Give me another chance. Please!"

He pulled through. He was good for a while, going back to his wife who took care of him until he got well, and then he left her again. Eventually he got hooked up with another woman and was beating her. She tried to leave him and started seeing another guy, who went after Ivan and shot him. The second time he got shot, his spleen was gone and part of his liver. Again, he faced death and fought to come back.

Ivan had dropped out of high school and gone into construction and then into the trailer-home business. For a while, he had done well enough to own two airplanes. But he lost his business because he was spending so much time in the planes.

Eventually, Ivan did get through his insanity. We talked about it that last time I saw him.

After he lost his spleen and part of his liver, Ivan again promised to be good. He was living with my mother and staying away from situations with women that had gotten him into trouble. But he was being bad with my mother.

My mother had broken her leg and was upstairs, resting. Ivan had a friend over and when the friend left, he got furious at Mami because she hadn't served him and his friend coffee or anything. At this time Ivan was really crazy, going around saying things like, "There is only *me*. I am it." He was menacing and abusive with Mami.

I had seen a psychic who told me that my mother had broken her leg and was praying the rosary. She was exactly right. When I went to visit Mami, she told me what happened with Ivan, how he was treating her. I tried to stay calm. But when my brother came home later, I went into his room.

It's the one and only time I used my power in this way.

Ivan was lying down on his bed when I walked in. He was probably on something the way he greeted me. I stood firm and began, "Mami said …" I launched into what Mami had said Ivan had done, how he had behaved, and how abusive he had been.

"Yeah," Ivan replied, like so what?

"Don't you ever treat my Mami like that again," I said.

He looked at me with a face that said, "Who do you think you are?"

I got closer to him and said, "Don't you ever, don't you ever disrespect my mother again."

He hurled some abuse at me. I forget what we said. It went back and forth. But I was not afraid. I stood firm. I kept my intention. My voice was dead level and clear. At one point, Ivan got up as if to hit me. I went right up to him and just kept saying what I was saying, level and firm, right in his face. I wanted him to look into my eyes so that the power would come through me. I never insulted him. I was just very clear and very firm in my voice and my intention.

At some point, I said, "Lie down!"

Ivan got on his bed, looked at me, and said, "Don't you do any witch-craft on me."

When I left his room, I *knew* Ivan was scared. I also knew that I must not do this often—or maybe *ever* again.

"When you came to me, you scared the shit out of me!" Ivan confessed, as he and I were talking one time. "But it was good. I was so big and here's my little baby sister, scaring the shit out of me."

Soon after that showdown between us, Ivan had an accident. He was in his car when something fell off a dump truck onto his car, crushing the car and then his stomach. He was shaking all the time after this and his doctors prescribed therapy. Ivan came to know a lot about himself through the psychotherapy and a biofeedback machine that the therapist used. He became a really fine gentleman, lost all that racism, and opened to love. He thanked me for that day we had it out. It was the beginning of the turn, he said.

I remember him telling me, sometime after his therapy, "I want to be good. I don't care about going to heaven like Hiram. I just want to know what it feels like to be good." He said he felt sorry for his kids. "It's too late for them, but I sure wish I had another. I'd spoil that kid."

Well, Ivan had four more kids with his last wife. She was a strong woman, unlike the others, and he loved her. He had never been true to any woman but he was true to her and good with his kids. Not long after he married her, someone who knew him from the old days asked, "How many girl-friends do you have now, Ivan?"

"I have one wife and two girlfriends," he said. "I have a wife who is the mother of my two girlfriends."

Ivan was fifty-four when he died of pancreatic cancer—two weeks after Mami died.

GOLDEN DAWN

One of the bright times during these challenging years was when I started working at a wonderful place called Golden Dawn. My friend Ken, who worked with me at Job Corps, had told me about it after he started counseling there.

It was my dream job. I loved every minute I worked there. Bill and Becky, who founded and ran Golden Dawn, were into growth therapy. They really cared about kids and had all kinds of things going on for their benefit.

163

I was able to use my artwork, drumming, and other things with the kids, and they were healing! I worked with some wonderful counselors, including Bob, Kirsten, Lori, and others. Golden Dawn got voted by clients to be the best counseling place in Tucson.

I was there for two years, working part time so I could do my healing work, and I lived in a nice little house in a beautiful Black neighborhood where people helped each other out. I had a Conure parrot named Totzl who would fly all over the neighborhood. She had her favorite tree and places to visit. Neighbors would watch out for her, calling me to say, "You're baby's here, honey. I'll call you when she goes."

It was the first time in a long time that I was feeling self reliant, confident.

One night I dreamed that I had asked my supervisor at Golden Dawn about my hours. He said my job was gone; there were no more hours there. I woke up very upset and consulted my Oracle. The Oracle said Golden Dawn would be going out of business. I asked my friend Joel if he would do an I Ching reading. He was a master at the I Ching; he knew so much he was invited to China. Joel's reading said everything would be fine—it looked like Golden Dawn would have government contracts, lots of new income.

But it didn't turn out to be fine. The money did come and Golden Dawn expanded to include a clinic for pregnant women, a nursery for babies, a hall for juveniles to get tested for drugs. But the money wasn't there for the kind of work we were doing. With the government money came managed care and the requirement for more traditional, drug-reliant therapies.

It hadn't fallen apart when I left the first time.

I had been working at Golden Dawn for about two years. I had been living in my beautiful neighborhood for even longer. I was teaching healing classes at the Open University in Tucson. My classes were among the most well-attended.[35] I was doing healings. I could pay my bills without sweating it.

But Wanda had been calling me for some time, asking me to move to Albuquerque. She had a young daughter, Sonia, by her second husband, and was now having trouble with her marriage. She and her husband had talked about coming to Tucson, but I knew the job situation. There weren't many jobs and Arizona was a right-to-work state. You could be fired at any time with no severance. "I'm just one person. This is a family," I thought. I finally gave in one day when Wanda called, crying. "*Please*, mom. I really need you. I'm so lonely!"

"All right, honey. I'll come," I said. Soon after, I left my beautiful neighborhood and wonderful job, and moved to Albuquerque.

It was a mistake.

By the time I got to Albuquerque, my daughter and her husband had separated. I realized that what Wanda really wanted was a babysitter. She wanted me to be with Sonia the way I had been with Little Bear. But things were different. Sonia had a mother and a father; my grandson didn't have a father. And Wanda was now a grown woman in her early thirties, not a teenage mother.

I moved out three months later, when I got a job in the neighboring town of Socorro, working at a very dysfunctional shelter for women. I was there for about a year, got in trouble with my supervisor by speaking out over the way one of the women was being treated, and quit before I was fired. A friend who had been urging me to come back to Tucson happened to call right at this time. She said she would come get me, saying her husband couldn't wait to meet me. We left with my two dogs, Starfire and Sheba, and my bird, Totzl.

OUT OF THE FRYING PAN AND INTO THE FIRE

My friend hadn't told me her husband was a racist. Everyday I was there, as he was reading the morning paper, he would ask me, angrily, why are minorities doing this and that? Starfire was just a puppy, but he would go out and kick her. He would abuse his wife's dog, too, but she wouldn't say anything. With the little bit of money I had left from my job in Socorro, I quickly moved to a place next to a trailer park. But I couldn't take it for long. The house didn't have screens and it was full of flies and bugs from the stable next door.

From there I moved to the women's community where I had stayed briefly in the 1970s. But this time, the stay turned into a nightmare. My little family now included three dogs because Sheba had a puppy, Beloved. I was told I had to keep my dogs fenced in, even though I noticed that the dogs belonging to White women were allowed to run free. There was one woman in particular who hated my dogs. I did fence them in but she'd cuss at them as she went by, so they would bark at her.

I had started working at Golden Dawn again and had only been there a few months when Kirsten, now a supervisor, got in touch with me while I was doing a home visit and said, "You've got to go home! Someone called the pound on your dogs!" One of my neighbors had called Golden Dawn to have them warn me. The woman who hated my dogs said they had gotten loose and attacked her and that's why she called the pound. The neighbor who called to warn me said the woman was never attacked. The dogs *had* gotten out but all they did was bark at her. I ran home, got my dogs, and drove to my friend Ellen's house in Arivaca.

Before this, Ellen and I had been talking about my moving to Arivaca. Things at Golden Dawn just weren't the same. My friends and coworkers there were still wonderful but all the changes meant that there were tons of forms to fill out, less pay, and less flexibility with how you could work with clients.

Ellen had a bus that she and her former husband had lived in for a while, which she was offering me. I moved in with my dogs and bird. It was parked on top of a hill. However, as soon as the desert summer sun hit it, the bus turned into an oven. It was so hot one of my drums burst. So I moved into a tent under a tree, where I learned about the insect people.

It started with the grasshoppers. I was spending a lot of time watching them and then began hearing voices—not quite like my voices. They had a sort of high hum sound. What I heard from the insect people in general was that insects were the closest people to the Earth and were very needed. They worked with Mother Earth and the soil, helping her. They were the closest people to Mother Earth and they wanted me to tell the human people about that. So I did. About a year later, someone invited me to see a movie called something like "Bug World." It was all about insects. I thought, "All right! They made it to the movies!" They're putting something out there that's creating awareness. I was really happy that they were in the movies.

I made friends with one grasshopper who was having a hard time because he was missing a leg. I made a little house for him and put it to one side of the sink in Ellen's kitchen. Ellen told me they like tomato leaves so I picked some from her garden and as I was putting them in his house, I noticed that he had left and gone to the other side of the sink. I moved the little house over there. He liked it and started eating the tomato leaves. The grasshopper lived in that little house until he died. He'd hang out there while we washed dishes and everything. When he died, Ellen put him outside on ground. Within a day or two, he was covered with insects. They were eating him, completing the cycle and circle of life.

I spent the winter in the tent and then someone offered me a little cabin, which I moved into. I had no money and just went hungry when the contributions from healings weren't enough to feed us. I didn't want to keep burdening my friends, so I didn't tell anyone. There was a place where they gave away bread. That's what my dogs and I ate when there was no money. I lost a bunch of weight, but at least I had the little space in the cabin. It was owned by a woman whose mother was a fanatic Christian and I stayed there for about three or four months until the woman was put in jail for growing marijuana. Her boyfriend was also put in jail. The mother told me she didn't want me there. She said I was a witch and I had less than a week to get out.

HOMELESS AGAIN

This time I really lived in my car—driving around to different places in Tucson every day for several months, trying to find places to park where I would feel safe spending the night. I had four dogs and a bird. During the day we would hang out in the parks unless I had a healing. I would go to my clients' homes and got enough money doing healings to feed myself and the doggies.

It was such a hard time, so scary and dangerous. I felt such despair. How did I get into this mess? How do I get out of it? I remember crying to Great Spirit, "I don't understand what I've done! Why am I being punished like this? If I'm not doing what I should be doing, please tell me what it is that you want me to do!"

I was in my car with the window open, despairing like this and feeling so alone and forsaken when a tiny little seed flew into the front seat. It was the kind of seed with the tiny fuzzy tendrils I had encountered once at Medicine Wheel. The beautiful seed stayed there for a while, suspended in the air, shimmering, and then left, going back out the window.

An overwhelming feeling came over me. I felt Spirit was saying, "Look. Look at this!" as a way of telling me that there is a bigger story going on here. I was not being punished. It was just something I had to go through.

It soothed my soul but it didn't make the daily struggle to survive any easier.

A friend had been urging me to come and stay with her but I hadn't wanted to take her up on her offer because I knew her partner didn't like me. I didn't want to cause trouble. But one day when she came to see me in the park, I was feeling dizzy. And when she said, "Please come home with me," I got the clear guidance to "seize it."

I stayed with her for a little while, and did some healings while I lived there. My friend did acupuncture and said I could use her room. But things didn't work out with her partner. I left after we got into an argument over spilled crumbs, and ended up spending the night with a neighbor of a friend whose sick cat I had healed. She was the sweetest woman, but kind of crazy. Her house was a mess; you could hardly stand the smell of cat pee when you opened the door. The next morning she said, "Let's go to a hotel! I've got money." It turned out she was selling her house.

We stayed in a hotel for about two weeks. Then another friend, Coyote, talked to a friend of hers who owned apartment buildings. She happened to have a duplex apartment vacant, and said I could have it with no references. At the same time, Wanda somehow found out what condition I was in. My daughter sent enough money for me to pay for the first and last month's rent.

NICARAGUA, DEVASTATED

It was now 1998. I know because I was in that duplex apartment when Hurricane Mitch devastated my beautiful Nicaragua. I saw it on the news. In my journal, I wrote, as I was experiencing the devastation:

Much of the country is under water, volcanic eruptions, mud slides. They said on the news that it wasn't the winds that brought about most of the destruction. It was the water, rising over.

Nicaragua. Nicaragua. All the people. The sadness goes so deep inside me. Sinking within me.

"They chose to leave this way," I am told. "They made a contract." I accept the possibility.

The sadness goes deep inside me, sinking within me. Letting myself feel dazed while reaching in to align with the God presence within me. *The God presence is within me. The God presence is within me.* Great Spirit, how am I to do my work? I am already falling apart, feeling lonely and old. Yet, I wish so much to be your instrument, oh, Great One.

Since 1972, I have not seen Nicaragua. What kept me away was financial poverty. Family crises and responsibilities, too, but mostly financial poverty. Although many times I have felt sadness and resentment over this, somehow, I also felt Spirit was at work. And now, remembering how much I wanted to live in Nicaragua, I believe Great Spirit put insurmountable obstacles in front of my wish so I could survive. I still have work to do.

Nicaragua, *te lo prometo.* I promise you: To use and contribute of my life's energy to the best of my ability. To continue inner healing and development and pray to be a finely tuned instrument of Spirit's energy and healing power. For the betterment and joy of the whole.

BACK ON MY FEET

With the duplex my friend Coyote helped me get and Wanda's support in covering the down payment for rent, I had the jumpstart I needed to get back on my feet.

I found a job working as a telephone pollster on political issues. It's a terrible job because people hate you when you call! But there were some really interesting people I worked with—street people, teachers, counselors, psychologists—all out of work and needing to take whatever job they could. It was a part-time job that helped pay the bills, and the work stayed at work, so it was fine. I had learned long ago that I had to work around my path. Anytime I worked fulltime or was consumed fulltime by work and was not able to do healings, I'd get sick. Eventually, the telephone calling job got to me and I found work taking care of elders. That's how I met my friend Marion and her beautiful mother, Dollie. I loved it. I could really put my heart in it.

So I had a job, a place to live, and I started doing healings. Soon after, I also started giving classes and workshops again. My friend Ken from Job Corps and Golden Dawn days had become a priest in the Independent Catholic Church. Years earlier, he had been a Roman Catholic priest. He was living in Indiana and had invited me to come give some workshops there. I remember the feeling I had the first time I went to South Bend of being greeted by the beautiful tall trees by the river near Ken's house. I felt they had been calling me.

In the spring of 2000, I got invited to give a workshop in southern California by a friend of Ken's. A couple of weeks after that workshop, I found a small hand-written note tucked in a side pocket of my suitcase. It was written by Elise, one of the participants in the workshop who was on retreat at the small center where I stayed and later drove down the mountain to the airport with me on the day I left. The note said, "If you ever decide to write the story of your life, I'd be glad to help in any way I can."

In fact, I had started writing my life's story when I moved into the duplex. My first reaction was, "Yeah!" I didn't even think about whether to do it or not, even though other people had wanted to write my story before and I had said, "No." One woman even came to Arizona. We spent some time together but she didn't have a clue as to what I was about. But with Elise, even though I only knew her briefly, I trusted her. Her eyes tell a lot and it's real easy to see who she is. So I packed up what I had written and sent it to her.

Later, as we started working on the book, my voices told me that we were sisters. We had been blood sisters in a past life. Elise was told the same thing by a psychic. I believe that's the only way we could have done this work together. And it's the only thing that explains how Elise would sometimes write things that I hadn't even told her. A poem came to me about it.

Sisters
Caring, sharing
Blood runs deep
In the river
Which flows through many lifetimes
To merge once again
With the ocean of the
Oneness
And the Eternal Now.

ANT PEOPLE

It was while living in this duplex that I really got to know the Ant People. When I first got there and went out to my little backyard to hang my clothes, the ants would crawl up my pant's leg and bite me. The ants were all over the place and everyone in the neighborhood was getting poison to kill them. My neighbor asked me if I needed help spraying since there were ants all over my walls—and soon they would spread over to his again. "I can't do that," I said. "If people spray, it's not just the ants but all insects that will get killed." He said, "I'll just put the poison in the ant hole."

I didn't want to kill the ants, but what was I going to do? I didn't want problems with my neighbors. So I started praying to San Martín. This message came to me: "Instead of putting poison in the hole, put food around their home."[36]

It was so beautiful. During four years I lived there, I really got to know the Ant People. I got to know what they liked to eat because when they really liked something, they'd shimmy and vibrate! I'd get them more.

One little ant hill had been causing all the problems. By the time we had made friends, I swear they had built condominiums! But they stayed in the yard. I'd go out barefoot to hang my clothes. I'd be careful, but they were aware of me, and I never got bit. My friends would come over to see what was happening—the latest ant construction project! It was fascinating.

Some little ants kept coming into the house and I finally had to put some poison out. But I just put it up as a barrier around my space. I was told that it was okay to do that, but only around my space.

One time I made the mistake of giving them a raw egg to eat. They got caught in the goo and a few ants were dead by the time I went back and saw what was happening. There was one ant left alive in the egg, so I put a little stick in the goo to get it out. The Ant Person completely trusted me. I took him in the house and turned on the faucet. Using little drops of water on my finger, I washed off the egg. The Ant Person stayed on the stick until I got it back home, and then stepped off.

The Ant People told me that they were important to Mother Earth, but that most of their food has been taken away and they were starving. Sometimes all they had to eat was dog poop. They were asking the humans for help. "Just give us your leftovers," they said. "That will help."

Before I left, I did a ceremony for the Ant People. A few friends came. We did a good ceremony to pray for them.

ORDAINED A PRIEST

My friend Ken and I were on the phone one day. He was talking about the small seminary he had established to ordain priests in the Independent Catholic Church and, as we were talking, he said something about my healing work being my "ministry." I laughed. He said, "Yes, you have a ministry.

Your healing work is a ministry." Then I heard myself asking, "Can I be ordained in that church?" Ken said, yes, he thought so.

I couldn't believe I had asked the question! What was going on? Why would I ask for such a thing? As I thought about it, I decided it must be because it would give me protection to do my work. "That's good enough," I thought.

But about a week after Ken and I talked, I started to experience ecstasy. I would think about Jesus and feel this peace inside me. I thought I was being chosen. I was so excited about becoming a priest for Jesus, although I had told Ken that I didn't want to call myself "Christian."

"Jesus came so humble and Christianity has gotten to be so proud," I said. The thing that impressed me most about Jesus was his humility. That's an integral part of his being. So I told Ken that I didn't want to be called a Christian, just a "follower of Jesus." That I do with great love.

One night, about a month before my ordination, something very strange happened. I had very noisy alcoholic neighbors in the duplex where I lived who often kept me up, playing loud music at night. This night, I was awakened by very loud music, although it was a strange kind of music, not like what they usually played. It was so loud I got up and went over to their side of the duplex to ask them to turn it down.

On my way there, I realized the sound wasn't coming out of their apartment. It was coming out of me! Usually when I hear my voices, I hear them inside myself. But this sound I was hearing outside of myself. I realized it was an auditory hallucination. Feeling anxious, I went back into my apartment and after I had centered myself, I connected with Spirit.

"I'm having auditory hallucinations," I said. "What am I to do?"

A voice said, "Listen."

So I did. I really focused on listening, until I finally got what I was hearing. It was ancient Catholic chanting. I knew that's what it was. It sounded like monks. Then female voices came into the chant, which I thought must be nuns. It was beautiful.

After the female voices, Native voices came into the chant. It was a deep hai, hai, yaa yaa, hai, hai, yaa yaa. The chant became a beautiful blending of these three. I'll never forget it, because I heard it outside of myself. It was so powerful.

It got me thinking about how, for some reason, I was born Catholic. When I let it go years ago, I would get so angry when people would say,

"Once a Catholic, always a Catholic." I said, "I will never be Catholic again." And I was so proud of my father, because even when he was dying and a priest friend came to see him, asking, "Humberto, do you want to confess and have the last rites?" My father said, "How silly you are—of course not!" I was proud of him for that.

But it's different now. There's something about the Catholic Church. I don't know what it is, but it's been coming to me that there is a reason why I was born Catholic. That night, after hearing the beautiful and powerful chanting, I heard a voice say, "You and the people you are working with are going through a Catholic evolution. You are part of a Catholic evolution." I know there is something in the Catholic Church that is worth saving. It is evolving.

I was ordained at a ceremony in Indiana. It was outside under the trees at a retreat center where I had given a workshop. It was the most beautiful experience I have ever had besides having babies. The trees were speaking. They were hamming it up! The birds came in—they are one of my totems. At the deepest moment, the birds started being heard. The trees would swish when something important was happening. I felt Jesus was there and that Nature loved Jesus because Nature was there, intensely, with him.

There were around twenty or thirty people there, including Elise. She said she had never been to Indiana before in her life but it so happened that she and Sister Carol, with whom she lived and worked, were going to be in Indiana at exactly that time, doing site visits for Carol's alternative loan fund. They both came to the ceremony and Elise was one of the three witnesses, along with the bishop and Ken, who signed my ordination papers. I was the first person to be ordained as a priest in the Native American branch of the Independent Catholic Church.[37]

HIRAM DIES

Not long after I was ordained my brother, Hiram, died. He and his wife, Wanda, had become born-again Christians. Hiram had gotten totally into it. For him, it was all about the Bible and right and wrong. This was the same man who was so violent with his children when they were young that his daughter once jumped out of a second-story window rather than face him when he was coming after her.

173

But we shared some closeness when Mami was dying. Hiram acted very humble, coming over every day to be with Mami, treating her with love. In the meantime, his own daughter didn't want to have anything to do with him. His heart gave out on him when he was sixty-six; he died of congestive heart failure.

ON TO ALBUQUERQUE

My daughter, Wanda, and I had been in close contact during this time. She was very loving and would tell me beautiful things the way she did when she was a kid. "My mom, the love of my life," she would say.

Wanda had some health problems and underwent a very serious operation without telling me until a couple of days before she had it, too late for me to do anything about it. I came home a few days after her operation and found a desperate message from her on my answering machine. "Mom! I'm in so much pain! Please call me!" She was in a motel with her sister-in-law after the operation. When I called back, Wanda told me what was happening. Her doctor had accidentally prescribed a *double* dose of the pain prescription—a *lethal* dose. Fortunately, the pharmacist caught the mistake. They tried to get a hold of the doctor to redo the prescription but it couldn't be called in; the doctor had to write it and he was out of town. Meanwhile, Wanda was in extreme pain.

I got a friend to take care of my animals and took a plane to be with her. By the time I got there, she had the prescription but was still in a lot of pain. I got in bed with Wanda and started to work on her. Within a half hour, she was laughing so hard I had to leave the room so she could stop, since laughing hurt her.

After that incident Wanda kept calling, asking me to come to Albuquerque. She said people kept asking her about me, asking when was I going to come because they wanted healings. She left me all these beautiful messages—and sent flowers, candy, all kinds of gifts, and money.

I was still struggling financially, but I had clients and a little job; I was getting my bills paid. It actually felt like things would be getting better. I didn't want to move. What finally pushed me into moving was worry. Wanda wasn't recovering well from the surgery, which had taken place some six months earlier. She wasn't feeling well, and I was worried.

My son, John, also happened to be in Albuquerque. He had moved there a number of years earlier, after leaving Tina. In Albuquerque, he married and had two more daughters, Nicole and Amanda, but that marriage, too, ended in divorce. John was later involved with a woman who gave birth to his son, Jesse. She subsequently left him, and he was now living with a girlfriend. Although John never finished high school, he had always been able to find work in construction. He was a very good worker and managed to keep his jobs even though he was constantly battling alcoholism.

So I moved to Albuquerque sometime in the summer in 2002. Three months later, I was taken to the emergency room, doubled over in pain. The doctors told me I had a "devastating" illness. Tests indicated I had pancreatic cancer that had progressed to the liver.

CHAPTER 9

SHAMANIC DEATH

I had been having terrible pains in my stomach and back for several weeks. At first, the pain came and went. I thought it was an ulcer or a serious gastric problem, but nothing I did seemed to make it any better. I was losing weight and the pain kept increasing so that by the time I went to the emergency room on December 6, 2002, I had lost thirty pounds and was in constant and severe pain. I knew there was something seriously wrong with me.

I must have been put on some kind of morphine. The painkiller knocked me out and I don't remember much except that they ran test after test, including one where they gave me some awful substance to drink. As I drifted in and out of consciousness, I heard someone say, "You're in the hospital. Don't worry. We're taking care of you." Another person, with a very sweet, gentle voice, said, "We're concerned about you. We're taking care of you; we really care."

The same sweet voice at some point told me, "Zelima, they found cancer. We're going to have to admit you. But please don't worry. We have the best cancer team here in the state." All I could say in response was, "I knew there was something very wrong."

The next morning, two or three doctors came into my room. Two nurses were already there. One of the doctors started to speak. "We've come to talk to you about the tests results. They show you have a terminal illness."

The doctor went on to say something else about my illness, but I didn't hear another word. As soon as he said the words, "terminal illness," I felt this beautiful Light go on within me and an even brighter Light lit the room. A feeling of such joy flashed through me—a deep gladness that despite everything I had been through in my life I had stayed true to my path, and the thought, *I am going to see the Creator!*

Then, I heard a little voice inside me say, "Well, you might heal."

The doctor's voice came through. "Do you understand what I'm saying," he said. "You have a terminal illness."

I had a big smile on my face. "What are you feeling?" he asked.

"I feel joy," I said.

The doctors looked bewildered.

"The way I see it," I explained, "it's a win-win situation. I'm either going to see the Creator or I'm going to heal. If I see the Creator, well—*I see the Creator*. And if I heal, I'll have learned something."

I overheard one nurse say to the other, "With that attitude, she's probably going to heal."

The doctors were pleased with my attitude, but kind of confused as to whether I was in denial or not. They didn't hold on to that for very long. It was pretty clear I wasn't in denial. They told me I had pancreatic cancer, and that it had progressed to the liver.

Later that day, one of the doctors said that one of my options was chemotherapy. "I don't want chemo," I said. I had heard that chemotherapy has healed people but I didn't want it for myself. First, they weren't saying that it was going to cure me and I just knew I didn't want to take in those toxic chemicals and then bring them to Mother Earth. I love Mother Earth and I want to be good food for her when I die. It makes me happy to think that someday I'm going to be eaten, that my body is going to nourish Mother Earth and all who dwell in her in the great cycle of life. I didn't want to bring those poisons to her.

The doctor also said something about having an operation to remove the cancer. "What would that do?" The doctor said, "It will give you a little time." When my son, John, asked one of the doctors, "Does my mother have a year?" All he said in reply was, "I'm sorry."

"You mean there's no hope?" John asked. "There's *always* hope," the doctor said.

I thought it was ridiculous to go through surgery and all that for a little more time when I could see Spirit, I could go to the Creator. Besides, a nurse told me, I would have to be on a bunch of pills all the time after the surgery to keep me alive.

At some point later that day or the next, a doctor from India told me he wanted to do another test. He said he wanted to do a certain kind of biopsy with a small incision and needle. It sounded reasonable so I said, all right. But a woman doctor came to see me soon after and said she didn't think I should do that. "In your condition, as weak as you are, you could get an infection," she said. "That would be very painful. I don't think you would want to endure that kind of pain."

When I told the Indian doctor that I had changed my mind, he said, "Well, if you don't take the test, I won't feel qualified to answer questions about your case. I won't have sufficient information." I decided to go ahead with the biopsy.

From the moment the Light appeared sometime on Saturday morning when I heard the words "terminal illness," it stayed with me the whole time I was in the hospital. With everything that was happening, all the decisions I was being asked to make, I needed to think straight—but I couldn't, as drugged up as I was. So I started meditating and going to the Light. By doing this, I found that I was able to control the pain, taking fewer pills than they were prescribing and being less foggy. Two days after working with the Light like this, I had the biopsy.

The results showed no malignancy! The diagnosis was "severe chronic pancreatitis." I was released a day or two after the biopsy, with an appointment to come back and talk to a specialist. But I don't remember being told the results of the biopsy until some time after I was released. I learned about them from a Tucson friend when we talked sometime after I left the hospital. He had been worried because he couldn't reach me. When he called the hospital to ask what was wrong with me, they told him the biopsy was negative.[38]

When I went to see the specialist at the University Cancer Research and Treatment Center, the Indian doctor was also there. They both seemed happy for me about the biopsy results, saying there was not a trace of cancer. I asked why everyone had been so sure that I had pancreatic cancer that had spread to the liver, saying my illness was terminal and telling my son I didn't even have a year to live. "Anyone who saw the initial test results would have come to the same conclusion," the specialist said.

In fact, the specialist said, there was some controversy about the results of the biopsy. While he and the Indian doctor thought that the mass did not appear to be pancreatic cancer, others believed there was a sampling error with the biopsy and that the original test results showing pancreatic cancer that had metastasized to the liver were right. They said there is still a chance I have cancer, even though they didn't think so, and that there was another test I could take that would go deeper into me, with a tube going down my throat. I said, "Forget it! I cannot handle more pain." The specialist assured me it would not hurt; I would be under sedation. But I said, no. I was satisfied with their diagnosis.

Early in January, I got a call from another doctor at the Cancer Research and Treatment Center who said he wanted to see me, that it was important. When I got there, he looked me in the eye and said, "I think you have cancer. We need to take more tests because the results of the biopsy are too dubious." He told me about the test with the tube going down my throat, guaranteeing I wouldn't feel any pain as I would be sedated. I told him that I did not want to take the test. He said if you want to take a chance, fine, but you're taking a big chance.

I don't know why, but he scared me. I agreed to the test.

During the weeks before this test I had been working with the Light to let Spirit heal me—and I felt much better. I wasn't taking any pain pills or other medication. But every time I took another test, it seemed to set me back. I would be exhausted and stressed, as the question of whether I had cancer or not kept coming back up.

The test with the tube down my throat didn't show any malignancy but it showed there was an obstruction, a blockage, in my pancreas that the doctors said needed to be operated on immediately. The doctor wanted to schedule me for surgery, and another pre-operation test. I told him I did not want to undergo any surgery. He said, "You have a very dangerous condition." We went back and forth about this until I finally said I was going to do my own thing first. If that didn't work, I would think about it.

"All right, if that's what you want," he said. "But it's against my better judgment. You have a very dangerous condition," he repeated.

A few days later, I had the test he prescribed, which also showed no evidence of malignancy.

When we met again after this test, the doctor asked me how I was feeling. I told him I was feeling better. I felt like I was healing. "Good," he said. "But you've got that blockage we need to address," he said. "I feel like that's healing, too," I said.

"Oh?" he said. "Well, we'll see about that," as he ordered another test.

I had been working with the beautiful Light for over two months now, beginning soon after it first came to me in the hospital. At first, I stayed connected with the Light because it was so soothing and felt so good. It helped relieve my pain and I was able to reduce the number of painkillers I took, stopping them altogether about four days after I left the hospital.

I also changed my diet to carrot juice once I got home. I drank plain carrot juice, carrot and celery juice, carrot and beet juice. I would eat organic salads, and slowly I started feeling the life force coming back into my body. When I asked my voices if the carrot juice diet was making a difference, I was told, "It will help you, but don't expect too much from it. What you really need to do is go within, work with the Light."

At the beginning, I didn't know if the Light was coming to heal me or to take me to the other side. The first or second night I was back home, I was sitting up in bed when all of a sudden the Light turned brilliant inside me. It filled the room! I was sure this was it—I was going. "Oh, my gosh! I'm crossing over!"

But, of course, I didn't—instead, the Light stayed with me and I started to learn things. I realized I was seeing both the Light of crossing over and the Light of healing. At the beginning I couldn't tell them apart; they felt the same. Then I realized it *was* the same Light, except that the Light of crossing over was brighter, more intense. Later I came to understand that I was in between two worlds. Maybe I was being given a choice. I don't know.

One night after I had been talking to my son on the phone and was getting ready to go to bed, I felt Jesus' energy come into me, through the top of my head all the way down to my toes. We had been talking about Jesus. My son is a born-again Christian with very black-and-white ideas. I was dying and he was worried about my soul. "Jesus is the only way," he said. "This is the way it is, Mom. The end is coming, and those who don't believe will be punished and go to hell. You'll go to hell if you don't believe, and I don't want you to go to hell, Mom."

As we talked I heard a voice say, "Jesus would never talk like that. All Jesus would have to do is enter a room and everyone would be transformed by his mere presence. No one would mind transforming because they are just going to be more of who they really are."

This is what I was thinking when I felt Jesus' presence. I'd had a connection with Jesus for a long time and I have no doubt that he is the Christ, but I do not believe that everyone has to believe in him and that this is even something he wants. That night, as I felt his energy enter me from the top of my head all the way down to my feet, I heard him say, "Use the Light to heal yourself."

The Light started coming in stronger and he began to instruct me. "Go inside yourself and confront the pain. Confront the dark place in there, confront the tightness. Just look at it, at what is there. And then say to that place of dis-ease, "The Light is within you. The Light is within you. The Light is within you. The Light is within you." Keep saying it until you can feel the vibration and see it light up.

I tried it. It gave me such a beautiful feeling, I kept doing it, going to all the places in my body that felt dis-ease.

One or two nights later, Jesus came back and told me what to do next. After the first part—going to the place of dis-ease and repeating the words, "the Light is within you"—I was to go *inside* the place of dis-ease. I was to move into the dis-ease and acknowledge that it is not separate from me but a part of me. Once I could feel myself becoming one with the dis-ease, I was to repeat the words: "The Light is within me. The Light is within me. The Light is within me. The Light is within me." I was to keep saying it until I could see or feel the place of dis-ease light up from inside.

I did this night after night. Sometimes I would wake up in middle of night, glad to have awakened so I could do this exercise because it made me feel so serene. But I realized that it also was making me feel better! I would feel as if something had gotten released inside, there was less pain, I could breathe easier.

Then I would be called in for further evaluation, with all the questions about whether I did or didn't have cancer and whether I should or shouldn't agree to yet another test or procedure. Every time I underwent another test, it would wear me out, often causing me pain. I would start feeling sick again!

After the last test, I *really* felt sick. They injected some kind of dye in my vein that burned and gave me a weird feeling all through my body. They said it would give me a funny feeling, like I would have to pee, which it did. A day or two later all my veins popped out—in my arms and legs, everywhere. I had varicose veins like I have never had before, and they still haven't gotten back to normal.

I had always gotten the results of my tests right away, but this time I didn't. I called several times for the results but no one seemed to be able to find them. When I went in for an appointment with a couple of doctors and a surgeon, all they talked about was surgery. I asked them about the results of the last test. They said they didn't know anything about it and the question got lost as they continued to discuss the need for surgery. I didn't know whether they were talking about surgery to clear the blockage or exploratory surgery to look for cancer. I just kept saying, "I don't want surgery."

While I was there, during a break, a friendly woman doctor stopped to ask how I was doing. "I'm angry," I said. "I feel like I'm being pushed into surgery." She was sympathetic, saying, "That's not good. It shouldn't happen." I then told her that I still hadn't gotten the results of the last test about the blockage and that it was very important to me. "I've been calling and asking for it and no one can find it." She told me she would go look it up on the computer—but never came back. When I ran into her again, a little while later, she told me she couldn't find the test results.

Finally, sometime in March I got a message from a secretary saying I had an appointment at such and such a time with four doctors she named. I called back and said, "What for? I'm sick of this!" They told her it was for an evaluation. "What do they want to know?" I asked. She didn't know.

I finally agreed to go since I was still waiting to hear the results of the last test. When I went for my appointment, the secretary said they had to reschedule because not all the doctors who wanted to meet with me were available. I told her it took me over an hour to get to the hospital by bus, I was exhausted, and I would not come back again. One of the doctors came out to see me. His first words, besides hello and how are you were, "Before we send you off to surgery, we have to do one more test."

"Wait a minute," I said. "I haven't agreed to any surgery!"

"You haven't?"

"No, I haven't," I said. "I haven't even gotten the results of the last test."

"What test?" he asked.

"The one you did about the blockage," I said. He was actually the doctor who administered the test.

"Oh, I don't remember the results."

"Well, I'd like to know."

"All right, I'll go check."

He left and was gone for about a half hour. When he came back, he resumed the conversation, saying, "Now, about the operation..."

"Wait a minute," I said. "I would like to know something. Have I made any progress? Has my condition improved?"

"Yes," he said. "But that happens with pancreatic cancer. Sometimes there's improvement, things seem all right, and then they get worse."

"Doctor, how many tests have you taken now? Four? Five? They all came out negative. What is this?"

"If we could find where it is ..." He was talking about exploratory surgery!

"Look, what did the last test show about the blockage?" I asked.

He paused. "It didn't show up. The blockage is not there."

"Thank you," I said. "That's all I can handle right now." I left—and never went back.

GOING TO THE LAND TO HEAL OR DIE

Wanda was in no shape to take care of me. She was still having health problems of her own while trying to raise her daughter, having just separated from her husband. John was living at a girlfriend's apartment, with no place of his own and struggling to make ends meet.

I was so weak and depressed. I spent most of the time in my room, trying to stay with the Light and keep my hopes up. There was no going back to the doctors and the hospital. What was I going to do? I couldn't stay with my daughter—it was a burden she couldn't handle, creating huge stress and tension for both of us. But I had run out of money and now I was too sick and weak to work.

My friend Ken had bought some land in Arizona, right outside of St. Johns, about forty miles from Medicine Wheel. He was planning to use it as a base to build the Native American branch of the Independent Catholic Church and had driven a camper there. But he didn't stay long, going on an assignment to Latin America. The camper was still there and since he wasn't using it, he said I could stay in it if I wanted. A friend drove me down to look at it, but the camper was so small—just a loft bed, stove top, counter, and bench table—there was no way I could move there with all my animals.

As the weeks passed, I became more and more desperate. I couldn't believe I was being exposed to the power and beauty of the Light at the same time that I had to live in such a stressful and oppressive situation. I was too

MEDICAL HISTORY OF ZELIMA'S ILLNESS

Following are the medical facts available from records and reports written by physicians attending to Zelima from December 2002 to March 2003.

Zelima Xochiquetzal was a 63-year-old woman who presented to the emergency room at the University of New Mexico Health Sciences Center on December 6, 2003 because of worsening abdominal pain. She related a history of about a year of upper quadrant and epigastric abdominal pain that had been progressively worsening. There was also a weight loss over a three-month period, as well as four days of nausea and diarrhea without vomiting.

Her family history was significant for a brother who died of pancreatic cancer. Zelima herself was a light smoker with only social alcohol. Emergency room evaluation showed normal labs including white blood count, liver, kidney, and pancreas tests. Abdominal ultra sound showed a heterogeneous mass in the pancreatic tail, as well as two hypoechoic liver masses. Zelima was admitted for presumed pancreatic cancer metastatic to the liver. Her hospitalization tests included abdominal CT with IV contrast which showed enlargement of the pancreatic tail (3cm x 9cm mass) and multiple cysts in the liver. A CT guided needle biopsy showed only chronic pancreatitis.

Two more markers, including CEA and CA19-9 (tumor marker for pancreatic cancer), were normal. An oncologist was consulted who deemed that there was "no cancer." There were no GI (gastroenterology) consultation notes available.

Subsequently, as an outpatient, Zelima was seen by a gastroenterologist on January 14, 2003, who recommended an ERCP (endoscopic retrograde cholangiopancreatography). Zelima subsequently underwent this test, which showed a pancreatic duct stricture. On February 21, 2003, she underwent an endoscopic ultrasound with a fine needle aspirant of the tail of the pancreas. This showed very few cells, which included necrotic debris, red blood cells, hystiocytes, and fiberblasts. There were no malignant cells identified.

This is the end of the available data.

[Note: A physician consulted to review the medical records noted that if a doctor suspects a malignancy but the tests keep coming back normal, the protocol is to keep looking for cancer, including exploratory surgery.]

weak to deal with it and had no resources to move on. I pleaded with the Creator. "Please, I can't take this anymore. If I am to do your work I need your help!" But help wasn't coming and I just couldn't see any way out. So I stopped trying to heal myself.

Then, I stopped trying to live. I didn't eat for a couple of days and then I added not drinking. I tested it to see how it would feel. It wasn't hard at all. I kept wetting my lips. I didn't want to suffer if I didn't have to, and I wasn't suffering.

I had asked a friend to promise she would do her very best to make sure my animals got to a good place if anything happened to me. That was my only concern. My friend didn't know that I had stopped eating, only that I might die of cancer sometime soon, given what the doctors said.

I was very clear headed. I felt I had no choice and, in good conscience, could stop trying to live. I kept wetting my lips, getting weaker and weaker.

But at some point, I went into a rage with God. I told the Creator that I was not happy with the way I was leaving this life. I did not feel I deserved to leave in this way, and I did not understand why I had to have so many struggles, especially financial struggles. I worked so hard, why didn't I get to taste the fruits of my labor? I loved doing healings and got great enjoyment from helping others, but I needed something for myself, too. Why was that being denied me? "You never give me the whole thing, I'm only thrown crumbs. Or else I'm given something for a little while only to have it taken away from me. I know I'm just a little thing and you're real big. But this little thing is telling you how this little body feels." I said it all—and I was glad I said it.

Less than two hours later, I got a call from the friend who had promised to take care of the animals. She said she had come into some unexpected money with the death of a relative. She had seen some information about large dome tents that people have converted into homes, including one twenty feet in diameter that cost around $7,000, which was the amount she had. She said she would use the money to get it for me, if I thought I could live on Ken's land. The dome was portable, and I could eventually move it to my own land, if things worked out, she said.

Suddenly I knew what it felt like to be a little bug drowning in a cup of water until someone unexpectedly comes along and pulls it out. From the time I was little, I did this—pull drowning bugs out of water, making sure they were okay after I scooped them out. I often wondered how it felt to be rescued like that. Now, I knew.

I started eating again—and making arrangements to move. I had no idea if it was going to work out. All I knew was that I desperately needed to be on Mother Earth—to touch the trees, look at the sun and moon and stars, and gather the healing energies if I was going to live. And if I was going to die, I wanted to die on the Earth, looking up at the sky.

So I went to the land to heal or die on Mother Earth, putting myself completely in the hands of the Creator.

BURNING HOT SUMMERS, FREEZING WINTERS

Friends made it possible for me to move back to Arizona, to Ken's land in the White Mountains. It was the beginning of June 2003. I was so weak, I couldn't even carry a flower pot, dropping it. A couple of friends came from Tucson to pack up my things in a U-Haul and drive me and my animals to St. Johns. As we got closer and I saw the landscape change as we drove into the high desert, I started chanting. I hadn't chanted in I don't know how long, and I felt a new energy come into me.

Other friends were planning to get there a day or two earlier to assemble the dome so it would be ready for me to move into when I arrived. But there was no sign of them! Here we were, in the middle of the high desert, with a U-Haul full of stuff, plus seven cats, three dogs, five birds, and a rabbit—and just this tiny little camper. My friend, Tim, had been only an hour's

My home on Ken's land in Arizona

drive outside of Tucson when his engine blew. He wasn't able to get there until several days later.

That night as I fell asleep, the sky was the roof over my head. The Earth was sending me energy up through my feet, and I could see the four directions—the sky and the four directions. I was so glad to be there, even as more things went wrong.

The cat walk that my friend, Linda, had built with a friend of hers to protect the kitties from coyotes (until I could get the communication going with them) was blown apart by the strong desert winds soon after they drove off in the U-Haul. The cell phone that another friend had gotten for me couldn't get a signal on the land or in St. Johns, so the only way for people to reach me was if I went into town to use a pay phone. My friend, Tim, who was so beautiful doing his best to put the dome together, ended up putting the skin on inside out. I found out the first day we had strong summer rains. Water came pouring in all over my bed, clothes, and furniture!

But Spirit was giving me signs I recognized. When the dome was put on inside out, it was a reversal—what Micaela used to do when she wore her clothes inside out. It was a sign to me that things are as they are supposed to be, even if they are hard. Then the ravens came by the side of the dome. Okay, magic is afoot.

A few days later, I was talking to my friend, the wind. In that part of Arizona, the winds can get very heavy. Death was on my mind a lot and I remember wondering whether I would end up dying of cancer or of some natural catastrophe out there in the desert. I said, "You know, Wind. If I were

 to die in a catastrophe, I wish it could be with you because you would be gentle."

Two or three days later, this incredible gust of wind came blowing across the desert. It swept under the four-by-four beams that were anchored into the ground, holding the dome in place, and lifted the whole thing up! The wind lifted up the dome and then dropped it down very gently. I was inside at the time but didn't get hurt. In less than an hour, I had a surprise visit from Ken who came from out of state with a friend, Kevin, who happened to have a box of tools and could fix the twisted beams. Later my friend Sharon's husband, Vernon, came down from the Navajo Res. He anchored the dome with iron pegs and heavy-duty cable.

So I knew magic was afoot, even as it got harder and harder to live there. It was well over 100 degrees every day during the summer. In the hot desert sun, the metal frame of the dome under the canvas skin would heat up. I had to keep going into town to get ice to cool down the bird cages. When I was finally able to get one of the big cages out of the dome and under the shade of a brush cedar tree—the only shade around—my Amazon parrot, Shalu, said, "That's good."

A neighbor's dogs kept coming over, fighting with my dogs. Four of them would come over to beat up Starfire, who was getting up in years. By the end of the summer all four of those dogs were living with me, starting with Onyx, a large black Labrador-type dog.

It was a hot day in the middle of July when it began. I kept getting the feeling I should go over to my neighbor's place, so I drove over and found Onyx unconscious and near-dead; his water bowl bone dry. He had been tied up and the chain was wrapped around his neck, choking him. I don't know how I managed to lift him into my car, as heavy as he was, but I brought him home and started trying to revive him. He had suffered so much and looked so pitiful, Starfire came over to lie down next to him, and give him some of her energy. It took Onyx over a week to recover and during that time he and Starfire became really close. He grew to love her so much in that short time that when his companions, Tigger, Boots, and Reno, came over to beat up Starfire, Onyx would try to go after them. But I had tied him up until he healed, so all he could do was bark. I later asked my neighbors if I could keep Onyx, and they agreed.

I had gone from a size eighteen to a size three during my illness. That summer I dropped down to a size two. I had no electricity, so there was no carrot juice diet. The little grocery store in St. Johns didn't have any organic anything and it was so hard to cook in the little camper, I often found myself eating canned foods. Even so, I was slowly regaining strength. To keep the wind from blowing into the dome through the cracks around the beams, I walked around the land, picking up large rocks to put around the perimeter. There was a well on the land but the water was non-potable, so I could only use it for cleaning, pulling on a rope to draw up a two-gallon cylinder of water. I had to go into town to get drinking water for myself and all the animals. I hauled bags and cases of dog food, cat food, and bird food, and heavy propane tanks for the little stove-top burner in the camper. I'm not sure how I managed, as weak as I was when I arrived, but by the time the summer was over, I was lifting five-gallon jugs of drinking water.

I was also meeting some nice people in St. Johns. One day as I was walking out of the bank, I ran into a woman with gray-blond hair. She had such a sweet smile on her face, I said hello. We started talking and I found out that she loved animals as much as I did and was using her retirement money to take care of 300 dogs! Mary and I became friends.

Later that summer when Tigger, Boots, and Reno had basically moved in with me, along with Onyx, I came to understand that Tigger's violence was connected to having had her children taken away from her each time she got pregnant. Her violence against other dogs—always females—was from her own self-hatred as a female. I made a promise to her that she wouldn't have to give up the puppies she was carrying. But I had no idea how I was going to do it, when Tigger gave birth to six puppies. All I had to live on was my social security check of $450 a month and $78 of that went for car insurance and $29 for drinking water. I often had to wait before going into town for mail or water until I knew the monthly check had been deposited because I didn't have enough gas in my car to get back home.

When I told my friend Mary what I had learned from Tigger about herself, she told me she would help with the cost of the dog food and getting the puppies spayed and neutered if I kept them. She also sent one of the men who worked with her to put up a little fence to keep the puppies penned in. My little family of animals suddenly increased from three dogs to thirteen.

STONE PEOPLE

All that summer, I found myself being drawn to stones on the land. I felt this urge to gather them. I had been drawn to the Stone People before but this was intense. I would get called here and there to pick up this stone and that. I had piles of stones lying around everywhere—around the dome, the camper, on tables, and kept feeling drawn to gather more. I had no idea why; I just knew I had to do it.

One day I picked up a blue stone. As I held it, I could feel it healing me and I became aware that the Stone People were connecting with me. Tuning in, I heard that I was to gather as many of the blue stones as possible. They said, "There is a deep longing in just about everyone. People don't even know what they're longing for but when this stone is held with the left hand, it sends healing energy." I understood from them that there is something physical in people that causes this emotional longing—and not the other way around. The blue stones penetrate that physical place with healing energies and the emotions improve, they said, telling me to gather and keep gathering.

I began to feel like I was collecting precious gems. Images started coming to my mind of taking one of these sacred stones and making it the center piece of a Medicine Necklace,[39] placing other stones on each side. I wondered how I would polish the stones since I didn't have a stone polisher—or electricity to run one! I heard a voice say the stones were not to be polished. They were to be left as they were. Images of people wearing the Medicine Necklaces came to my mind and I saw the way the stones would guide the wearer and provide him or her with a deep connection to Mother Earth. I saw the stones vibrating healing energy out to the world.

So I started making Medicine Necklaces for friends; a few people bought some. In the past, my voices had always warned against photographing or videotaping medicine objects or ceremonies. Now I was being told that "this Medicine needs to get out. Even if people just see a picture of the stones and the Medicine Necklaces, it will make a difference."

In time, I began to feel that certain stones wanted me to have them by my bedside. One of these was a stone that felt really good in my hand. It was the color of Earth, just an ordinary rock as large as my hand, the kind you see all over the place. One day, as I was holding this stone, I felt an outpouring of love coming from it. I had never thought of stones as affectionate! I had experienced their intelligence, the knowledge they gave me, but not affection. I felt an intense love coming from this one. It was magnetic, going so deep within me, it scared me.

"Don't be afraid," I heard. More images came into my mind. I could see the stone had endless love to send and receive, without becoming attached. All I had to do was open up and let it in. So I did, feeling the love pour into me.

Right after that, I went to go get my neighbors' pregnant dog, Tigger. I had asked them to let me work with her for a few days because she was causing so many problems, coming over each day to attack my dogs. That first night I told her, "You are here for a healing, Tigger. You and Starfire *must* become friends." I reached out to hold her, and she let me. I held her close that night and I could feel all the love that the Stone Person had given me pour into that dog. The love kept flowing out and she kept receiving it, nestled in my arms. At one point she had tears in her eyes! I had never seen that before in a dog. It was so beautiful. I understood that the Stone Person had prepared me for healing Tigger.

Another day, when I was holding this same Stone Person, I started moving my thumb around. I had been using tools to work with some of the other stones, a needle to get out dirt, a knife to clear away some debris. As I was rubbing her softly with my thumb, I heard the words, "See what happens when you softly, gently, and tenderly touch a stone." I was rubbing the stone softly, but not soft enough. I kept hearing, "See what happens when you softly, gently, and tenderly touch a stone." Every time I heard those words, I understood I was to work the stone even more softly, more gently, more tenderly. I lightened up on my touch and all at once I saw a different color appear. The stone went from brown to a purple color. Wow!

I kept caressing the stone, softly, gently, tenderly. Then an eye appeared! An awareness came to me that the stone was female. I got a knife to try to get more of that purple-blue color out of the stone and was guided to "do a little bit but that's it." I saw what looked like a place where there could be another eye and went to carve it. "We are not humans!" I heard. "We do not look like humans. Don't try to make us look like humans!"

Okay. I stopped trying to carve another eye and started to work the eye that had revealed itself. "Don't touch the eye!" I heard. A couple of times as I got close to the eye, I heard, "Don't touch!"

Then, again came the words, "See what happens when you softly, gently, and tenderly touch a stone." So I put down the knife and went back to the gentle caressing. When I stopped, I saw why I was warned away from the eye—there was a face in the pupil!

As I worked with more and more stones, I saw that they all had faces, first noticing their nostrils and noses. Later I was told that I was shown their noses first because the Stone People wanted me to know that they breathe. They warned me against looking for human-like noses in their faces. Their noses might be on the back of the head and might not look at all like a human nose. The important thing was to know that all stones breathe, they told me.

The Stone People revealed themselves to me as I softly, gently, and tenderly touched them. Many of the faces had mouths with teeth. Some of the faces were pretty or bold looking; some were what people might consider to be grotesque. "We want to present ourselves as we are," I heard, learning that the contorted "grotesque" faces were honored by Stone People—it was a sign of how many changes, transformations they had undergone. Their faces reflect the work they have done to transform the things that come into the Earth.

I noticed that I could always see the faces better at night when I was working in the dim light of a candle or flashlight. When I asked why, they said it was because "we work with darkness and light in sacred unity." When the energy of light and darkness came together, they became alive, more whole. I also noticed that each stone usually had many faces. I was told that they have a multidimensional existence—all those aspects of themselves are contained in one body. I came to understand that they are masters of transformation—constantly changing, moving from mountain to sand and sand to mountain.[40] I could feel their ancientness and started calling them the Ancient Ones.

As I continued working with the Stone People, I learned that each time a person is drawn to a stone, picks it up, and begins to softly, gently, and tenderly touch it, an energy is released that is sent into the Earth and out into the universe. I learned that just as they are calling me, they're calling other people.

I was tired but I kept collecting stones. My back was hurting from bending down so much and I wondered, "Do I need to keep doing this? I don't know what to do with them all."

The words came: "You are working with a large army of magnificent warriors. We have been preparing for this moment for thousands and thousands of years." We want to speak with the human, they said.

Sometime later, I was talking to my friend, Fern, telling her about the Stone People. "The Ancient Ones want to connect with the human," I said, explaining how I was getting all these messages. "Oh, you've always had that in you," Fern said. "Remember that poem you wrote about when the Ancient Ones will speak?"

In 1976, a poem came to me. I can't claim I wrote it; my hand just moved. It was a prophecy that came through me about the times of Earth changes I had been envisioning for some time, the times of great chaos—of both destruction and creation that were ahead. The poem talked about a time when the ancients would speak. "When it is time, the ancients will speak and you will hear what you are not expecting, and also what you know."

It would be a time when the grandfathers would return and the grandmothers would rise! The Great Mother would ask her daughters to rise and sons with gentle hearts would be called.

Give me your hands.
A circle has been made.
The ancient and new are one.
Energy will flow and there will be creation.

I always thought the Ancient Ones in the poem were humans from the past—prophets returning at the time of Earth changes. I never dreamed the Ancient Ones in the prophecy were Stone People, even though I had always called the stones we used in sweat lodges, "Ancient Ones."

After that phone conversation it all came together. The Ancient Ones are speaking. That means we are *now* in the time of Earth changes that so many of us had been foreseeing. The Stone People want to communicate with the human in order to help us, help the whole, through this time of Earth changes. They are a band of mighty warriors coming not to fight but to transform. They are, after all, the masters of transformation. Everything on Earth eventually goes to the ground, they said, including feelings and emotions. They can transform all kinds of things, including negativity. The work they've done shows in their faces—and they have been preparing for this for thousands of years.

I knew my work with the Stone People was part of my sacred path, the Path of the Little Sisters, when they told me that in order to work with them, I would have to obey, following their instructions. The Path of the Little Sisters is about being open to guidance and allowing yourself to be led through a time of Earth changes when we would not know how to respond, so we would need guidance.

The Stone People gave me such a feeling of joy. Some nights when I was exhausted and depressed about my situation, I would connect with them and experience a deep sense of joy just knowing they are here to help us through the changes with Mother Earth.

As I continued to work with the Stone People, I awakened to the power of the healing vibration that was being released each time I would "softly, gently, and tenderly" touch a stone. It made me think about all the pain in the world, all the killing. I thought of terrorists who have so much pain they commit suicide in order to blow everybody else up. I thought of people in this country who ask the government to execute people, kill them in cold blood, in order to "bring closure" after the murder of a loved one. I thought of how everyone's answer seems to be "kill, kill, kill."

I found it incredible to think that the Stone People were here with another answer. All we had to do was work with them, softly, gently, and tenderly, to activate a healing transformative energy. I was told to tell all the people who have been praying for a higher vibration on Mother Earth, and all who live and dwell upon her, that their prayers were being answered—and that they should continue praying for this. The movement has started in that direction, the Stone People said. We're moving towards something very beautiful, even with all the destruction that's going on.

FALL INTO WINTER

That fall, Elise came to visit. It was clear there was no way I could continue to write my life story. It took all I had just to stay alive! Elise came with a tape recorder and for three nights we sat by the fire in the dome and I told her the story of my life. During the day, she helped with chores around the campsite.[41]

I was living like an animal. I had been close to animals for a long time, but now it was different. I was living with them as an equal. I had always believed that all life is equal; I never thought one life form was superior to another. Now I was living what I believed.

Whatever little I had, my animal family and I shared equally. Some of my friends kept urging me to get rid of the animals so I could get out of there and save myself. They said there were lots of places I could stay, with them or with others, if I didn't have all those animals. I tried to explain, but they didn't understand. It was impossible for me to think about my own survival without thinking about my animals' survival. I couldn't survive at their expense—and I didn't want to live without them.

Living so close to them, all of us sharing in the struggle to stay alive, I came to understand that we were co-evolving together. All species on Earth are co-evolving. I was being given the privilege of really seeing and experiencing the co-evolution. I could see, in a whole new way, their deep spirituality and what wonderful beings these animals were. We were in this mess together—in this little part of the desert and on Earth.

Winter came. The temperatures dropped below freezing, as low as eight degrees. All day I would be outside gathering dead branches for kindling and chopping firewood for the wood stove. Still, I couldn't sleep at night. As the night temperatures remained in the teens and below, I had to get up every hour to feed the fire to keep the dome warm enough so the birds wouldn't freeze.[42] Even with layers and layers of blankets over their cages, if I didn't keep the fire going all night long, the water in their bowls would freeze. The Conure parrots had each other to huddle for warmth, but no matter how many blankets I put over Shalu's cage, I couldn't keep him warm; I almost lost him that winter.

I couldn't keep myself warm either. I moved the bed right next to the wood stove and friends sent me wool blankets and comforters. My body ached under the weight of all the blankets, but still I would be chilled. Before my illness, I was never one to get cold easily. But after losing all that weight, I would get cold even when the temperatures were mild. I was now down to a size one.

One night in December, I thought I was freezing to death. It's hard to explain but I was so cold, my bones felt like they were going to crack. My chest was so heavy, my lungs and breathing so tight. It was a cold that went beyond cold. I prayed that my animals would be okay, closed my eyes, and said, "Okay, this is it. I won't survive this night."

For some reason, after a few minutes, I opened my eyes again and saw a light at the foot of the bed. It wasn't a bright light, but it was very soothing. I looked at it and it calmed me. "Thank you, Creator," I said, recognizing the Light. As I continued looking at it, I started getting warmer. The warmth went deep into my bones, feeling so good. I kept getting warmer and warmer until I actually started to perspire! Here it was snowing outside and freezing inside—there was nothing but a canvas skin separating me from the outdoors—and I was sweating! All I could say was, "Thank you, thank you, thank you. Gratitude, gratitude, gratitude." I said it over and over again, until I fell asleep, warm in my bed—hot actually.

A few days later, cold again as I was trying to fall asleep, I started to have chest pains. I felt an intense pain radiating from my chest down my right arm, which went completely numb. I remembered hearing that this was a classic sign of a heart attack.[43] I closed my eyes and started praying. The

Light came. I didn't ask for it, but it just came—and in ten minutes, the pain in my chest was gone and the feeling came back in my arm.

The same thing happened again a few days later. The Light kept coming—keeping me alive through the winter.[44]

WINTER INTO SPRING

In February we really got going on the book. The three tapes we recorded in November just created an outline. Now Elise was calling me to get the details, tape recording long conversations over the phone. Every time a plane would fly over or the wind would kick up, my cell phone would disconnect and we'd have to reconnect.[45] Lots of times, I would go on talking, thinking we were still connected when I had lost the signal minutes ago. We'd have to go over it all over again, which at certain times was especially hard.

As I talked at length about my life, reliving very painful memories from my childhood, I started to feel sick and my mind would go hazy. I don't know how many times we went over things to try to sort out what happened and when. Often, several weeks after we talked about a certain period of my childhood, a memory of something horrible that I had forgotten would come up, like vomit. It was so painful sometimes I could hardly say the words and when I did they would leave me feeling sick and vulnerable.[46]

After several weeks of this, I got so confused. I felt I was lost in my childhood and started getting nervous. In the middle of this, I lost one of my puppies! Almost overnight, Gordito got sick and died. I still have no idea what happened to him; it was so sudden. Every day, when I would feed the puppies their snacks, training them to get along with each other, Gordito would outshine the rest. Whoever was "good"—whoever would just wait patiently and not try to grab the snacks out of my hands or snatch them away from somebody else—would get the treat first. Gordito was the Number One good boy. Now he was gone.

With the painful loss of my Gordito and so much anxiety growing inside me, I began wondering why I was writing this book, what use was there in telling all these awful stories. It was making me sick; it would sicken others.

Then my true intention came to me—I was reminded of it. I called Elise right away to tell her I had something very important to say. "Going back into my childhood is necessary for what we're trying to say," I said. "I'm grateful you've been able to guide me through it and not let me go crazy. But my *true* intention with this book is to bring people closer to Mother Earth—to share how to gather energy from Earth and Sky, to teach the Dance of the Soul, and to bring people to the Stone People for knowledge and guidance through these times of Earth changes. That's it. This is my true intention."

There were still more horror stories from my childhood to tell. My body began to ache. I had a hard time releasing the pain—nothing seemed to work. I was in such pain, it made my daily chores of feeding the animals, chopping wood, getting water even more difficult. I got lost in the stories again and my daily struggles made it worse. I started to feel deserted by God, San Martín, Jesus, everyone. *Why have you abandoned me?*

Walking with this question aching in my heart, I heard an answer. It came slowly. I started to remember that when I was eleven and couldn't handle hurtful words, I would tighten something inside me until the words wouldn't hurt me anymore. I began to realize that it wasn't my intestines I had squeezed, but my pancreas. This was the cause of my illness, I thought. I started going inside the pain, confronting it, until I could feel the grip on my pancreas begin to release and the Light appear. I was not being abandoned by the Divine; I was to turn to the Divine within me, to the Light within me, to release the pain.

Soon after this, a nightmare began when a crazy neighbor started shooting dogs. One of his victims was my beloved Felicidad! I found her lying dead with a bullet between her eyes. She was the sweetest dog in the world. Who could do such a thing to this beautiful innocent being? Felicidad went everywhere with me, slept on the bed with me, befriended all the other cats and dogs in our family and was a real leader even though she was one of the smallest dogs in the tribe. She had this way of showing up that reminded me of Liza Minnelli coming on stage, full of herself and raring to go! I screamed from the pain of losing her. Some of my neighbors wanted to kill the guy. Feelings of violence welled up in me, too; I was so angry and filled with grief. But I prayed. I prayed, instead, for his healing—and asked my friends to do the same. "If someone shoots him," I said, "he'll just be one more fool that bit the dust. But if he has a change of heart that would be a huge shift, a huge shift for Mother Earth."

I kept getting warning signs that my other dogs were in danger, too, so I started tying them up to keep them from wandering off and getting shot. They would get loose and I would have to tighten their collars. It drove us all crazy.

About a week before he shot Felicidad, the same guy killed one of my neighbors' dogs and badly wounded Sassy, a black Labrador. I had gone over to borrow their phone and found them huddled around Sassy, who lay there in agony. A bullet had ripped through her thigh bone, pulverizing it. Below her knee, the leg was broken so it just dangled, held by the skin. My neighbors were trying to figure out whether to put her to sleep or see if the vet could save her by cutting off the leg. It was a four-generation family and the great-grandmother, Juanita, was a nurse. She was still practicing after fifty years of nursing. After feeling the thigh bone, she said, "It feels like sand."

I got down on the ground and started working on Sassy. I gave her healing energy for an hour or two to relieve the pain and get her calm enough so I could begin to work on the wound. I sprinkled golden seal and myrrh on the wound and created a cast with a type of bandage used for horses.

For the next three or four weeks, I would work on Sassy every day, usually in the morning and sometimes in the evening. I would go over to my neighbors' or do it from home with absent healing. I had started doing absent healings during the winter with my friend Fern, when she had knee replacement surgery.

In about two months, Sassy was out running with the other dogs. Juanita said she had never seen anything like it. "The crushed bone all of a sudden just got cured. It was like all the crushed pieces came back together," she said.

Weeks before this, one of Sassy's puppies had wandered over to my place. She was just a little thing but somehow managed to make her way through the desert. There was something about her eyes and her looks—even the cries she would make at night as she slept and the wild hiccups she got—that reminded me so much of myself as a child. I was just going through the hardest parts of my childhood for the book when this little puppy showed up. I felt that she had come to help me work my way through it. Zelimita was what I ended up calling her.

BACK TO JACK

Life was hard, one challenge following another, but I had made it through the winter. I was alive! And I was aware of the power of the new healing energies flowing through me, as well as the incredible knowledge I was gaining from the Stone People and from working with the Light. I felt an urgency to teach what I knew. This knowledge was for the times of Earth changes, and the signs were absolutely clear—the times of Earth changes were here and now, they had begun.

I decided to get back in touch with Jack Brown. On May 10, 2003, I sent him a sixteen-page handwritten letter, telling him about my life and what had happened since we last had been in touch. I found out he was now Senate Minority Leader of the Arizona State Legislature and a member of the ethics committee. In the letter I reminded him of the ways he had been so patient with me when I was late in making payments and of the promise he made when he discovered the terrible mistake he had made. I wrote about all the ways I had tried to get him to fulfill that promise and how I finally had to turn to lawyers but couldn't afford to hire them after the initial letters they wrote to him went nowhere. I said,

I am asking you to keep your promise to me, and take responsibility for your mistake. I am not asking you to take pity for the suffering your mistake caused in my life, nor am I asking for charity. I am asking for what is rightfully and in all conscience due to me.

With the help of friends who knew about banking and building, I figured he owed me $46,270.[47] Of course, I feared I had no legal claim—whatever statute of limitations there might be had probably long run out. I just hoped (and prayed) that he might respond out of a sense of honoring his word.

I got no response. A month later, when I called his office, Jack's secretary, Denise, told me the Senator did not recall seeing the letter. I went into town and faxed it, calling Denise to ensure it had arrived. Denise said she had my letter in hand and was "printing it out now" to put on the Senator's desk. She said she would make sure he saw it in the morning

Several phone calls later, Jack agreed to meet me to talk about the land. On July 3, 2004, he met me in the parking lot of the supermarket in St. Johns. I got into his car and we talked. He offered me $10,000 to compensate for the mistake, which is what I paid in 1978 for the eighty acres, saying land values hadn't increased that much in St. Johns. As an alternative, he offered to buy me some land that had electricity accessible—and then drove me to a couple of places around town that looked like trailer parks.

I told him I was not interested in a trailer park lot or in money for land. I had land. What I needed was a home, a structure in which to live and out of which to do my healing work. That's what I lost when the county discovered his mistake. Jack responded, "You didn't have a home, you had a tent."

Our conversation ended soon after this when he said that I was asking him to pay for my own failures. He also said that back in 1986 he told me he could get forty of the eighty acres I lived on, but that I had rejected that offer.[48]

A couple of weeks later, I wrote back, repeating what he had said, especially about my living in a tent, writing, "A tent is what I have now and it's unbearable to live in." I wrote that I was not asking him to compensate me

The dining room of Medicine Wheel

for all the suffering his mistake caused me, just to restore what I lost in 1986 when we discovered his mistake. I enclosed copies of photographs of Medicine Wheel that Elise and her friend, María, had taken just a couple of months earlier, at the end of May.

Elise had come back to visit, bringing María. They had been at a conference together in Albuquerque and drove over, staying for a couple of days. Elise knew that I had met a woman named Tammi who was now living in Medicine Wheel. She and María said they wanted to meet her and go see the place.

I had met Tammi one day when I ran into my friend Mary in St. Johns. Mary introduced me to her, saying she lived in the most beautiful and unusual home just down the road from her. When she started describing the house, I knew it was Medicine Wheel. Tammi got tears in her eyes when she realized I was "*that* Zelima." She had been praying to meet me, she said, explaining that when she first moved to the place, she found a red trunk full of letters from people thanking me for healings.[49]

Tammi wanted me to come over to see Medicine Wheel, but there was no way I could. It was too painful. So Elise and María went and took photos. I enclosed copies of those photos in my letter to Jack and told him that someone lived there now who "just loves it."[50]

I wrote, "Although land values may not have increased that much, building costs have increased a lot. If you think it's fairer to figure out what you owe me based on what it would cost today to build my house and cabin

201

that would be fine with me." I also said I needed to be able to access the land I legally owned, saying, "As I wrote in my first letter to you, I haven't even been able to find it. I ask that you or someone who works with you take me to the land to show me exactly where it is and how I will be able to access it. Accessible land is what I paid for back in 1978."

Jack ended up referring the matter to his son, attorney Doug Brown. But when he and I talked, Doug said my home was "worthless" and that all they would offer was to exchange the eighty acres I legally own, which is inaccessible until a road is built to get into it, with another eighty-acre parcel—putting me right back where I was twenty-seven years ago, before building and losing my home as a result of Jack Brown's flawed real estate transaction.

My last communication was on February 7, 2005, when I wrote to Doug, sending a copy to Jack. I said their offer was "inadequate to my loss and unacceptable. It is neither just nor fair. I have no other recourse but to take the next steps available to me."

On February 9, 2005, again with the help of friends, I filed a complaint with the Arizona Department of Real Estate, seeking an investigation of the matter. I had heard that there was no statute of limitations on these investigations, but that turned out to be wrong. They soon sent me a notice saying there was nothing they could do.

Sometime after that, friends began to organize "Arizonans for Justice." They created a website and petition drive, calling on Jack Brown "to compensate Zelima Xochiquetzal fairly and equitably for the loss she suffered 20 years ago from your devastatingly flawed real estate transaction which resulted in her building a home and healing center on land that belonged to others. While there may be a statute of limitations on legal actions, there is no statute of limitations on ethics and right-doing. As an elected public official, you have a special duty and responsibility to act honorably and justly and with integrity."[51] More than two hundred people signed the petition.

But Jack was not moved.[52]

SUMMER, THE DEVIL, AND THE ALL GOOD

As the summer wore on and there was no sign of movement on Jack Brown's part, the heat and the dust, the daily challenge of living in a camp, the exhaustion, the constant worry about running out of money before the next social security check came, started to get to me.

One morning, after I had done all the morning chores, feeding the animals, watering them, I thought, "Now I should take a rest." I went to lie down in the camper and that's when the fear started building. "What am I going to do? How am I going to survive this?" As I felt the anxiety building, I said, "No, enough!" I went inside myself and started looking at the fear. I went into this dark place, confronted the fear, and began to pray. Soon the Light came in, and it felt good.

I was beginning to calm down when the birds started screaming. It wasn't their usual, "Come—gimme, gimme, gimme." They were in fear! I got up and hurried over to the dome to check on them. As I rushed over there, the dogs were watching me. They knew I wasn't angry but concerned. I could see that they shared my concern.

The birds were freaking out! The heat of the day was starting to build up. I had been getting ice everyday to put on the cages to keep them from roasting. But they were all screaming, including Shalu. "We can't take this anymore!" I started petting each one of them, saying, "We need to pray. We are all in a real mess. We are all suffering."

I picked up one of my drums. "Creator, Great Spirit, I need to speak with you." I didn't try to make the drum sound pretty. I just tried to let the birds' and my own feelings of pain and suffering flow through me. The birds soon found that I was in rhythm with them. They started screeching with intention. We were all in harmony. We put out our pain to Creator. We cried that the whole world is in pain and that we want to do our part. But we can't do it when we're all in so much pain.

I could see out the flap of the dome that the doggies were by the fence and very much with us. This went on for more than an hour. The birds even started taking their little steps. They were used to dancing but they hadn't done it since I left Tucson. So they were doing their little steps, beginning to think about dancing, too. We all felt better after that.[53]

But I had been in a real struggle, in real pain, for several days—days of desperation.

The girlfriend of one of my neighbors had gone crazy. They had about a dozen dogs—two females with puppies among others—and they were starving, sick and hungry. They said they could only afford one bag of food for all of them. The dogs had worms, their eyes oozed, and their ribs stuck out. The woman couldn't handle it anymore. One day when her boyfriend wasn't around, she got someone to come kill them all. It was a massacre. All the dogs were dead, including my Onyx who had been going over there to be with a starving female and her puppies, which weren't even his. Reno had been there but managed to escape, one whole side of him covered in the others' blood.

I could hardly take in the news. Right before this, I had felt an oppressive evil energy sweep through the desert where we lived, infecting us all. It was something I had experienced twice before in my life—and I had learned how to guard against it. But my neighbor's girlfriend didn't know how to protect herself and she just went crazy. My animals had felt the evil energy, too, especially the puppies. For three days, they howled and kept doing everything they could to try get out of their pen. Another puppy, one from the same neighbor, actually found his way to me right before it happened. I called him *Buena Suerte*—Good Luck.

Now, another beloved member of my family was gone.

It started with the killings—this feeling of desperation. It was just too much for me, way too much. I kept remembering my doggy and his incredible loyalty, how Onyx faced starvation and death to be with his loved one. What a beautiful being, now dead. I was suffering, and surrounded by suffering. Everyone was tied up and we were all miserable.

I felt Great Spirit didn't love me, and kept saying, "Whoever that person is who deserves this, I'm not that person anymore!"

I was thinking about the world and what a mess it is—and how we are told that the Creator is perfect and that we were the ones who messed things up. I prayed and talked to Creator.

"Creator, aren't you responsible for your creation? How could it be all *our* fault? If you created it perfect like you, how could we make all these mistakes?"

Then I thought about what they say about free will and how that's the reason for the mess we're in, what we do with our free will. I said, "If I could be good all the time, I don't want free will. I'm not attached to it." I told Creator, "There have been all these worlds that have been destroyed and now we're at it again. Doesn't it mean something's not working?"

I said, "I'm just a little nothing, I know. Yet I have these feelings of needing a new and higher vibration. We've all suffered so much and for so long, I feel like we've earned a higher vibration—a much, much higher vibration. I feel like we've gone through all these slow evolutionary changes and now it's time to experience the big 'poof' of transformation into higher vibration, changing all this horrible suffering."

I told Creator, "They say you are perfect and don't make mistakes. I don't know if you are, and maybe you feel like we don't really make mistakes. I don't know, but when we are born with predation, when animals are born to eat one another, there is pain, suffering, and fear. Being in a world that's programmed with predation is what brings us to think that in order to survive we need to kill. It's so deep in us. It's such a solution to everything. 'Well, I guess we've got to go kill in order to survive.'"

I went on. "Creator, I don't know about a 'Creator,' whether there really is a Creator." I then heard a voice inside me say, "But there has to be something that's All-Good." I said to that voice, "I believe it, because I believe there is something All-Good inside me and inside everyone else."

I turned back to Creator. "I don't know whether there is a Creator, but I do know there is something that is All-Good," I said. "I just don't know at this point if that All-Good is going to win. But what I do know is that if it doesn't win, I want to go down with the All-Good."

"Creator," I said, finishing up. "I'm dying. I will not last a week with this pain. I will not last like this."

It was my darkest hour.

After some silence, I heard a voice say, "Well, Zelima, you have prayed to be an instrument of joy and to be allowed to work with others as a whole to create something that will definitely make a difference on Earth. You have prayed to make a difference on Earth."

The voice said, "It takes a lot of purification and a lot of work to be able to fulfill that intention. You want to do the work. This is what happens."

Then I remembered about "Shaman's Death" in the tradition of my Meso-American ancestors. I don't know if it's true in the north, but with my ancestors, before you can become a shaman, you have to go through Shaman's Death. The initiates don't know what it's like because the shaman doesn't share it. They bury you up to your head. Sometimes they put you in a hole and you have to stay there. You're ridiculed and spit upon. People mistreat you and try to drive you crazy. Shaman's Death is an experience of deep pain and suffering. Sometimes initiates don't make it through their Shaman's Death experience and actually die.

I had been through several of them. But this was the worst. I was losing weight again and even lost my dentures, so now my face was all wrinkled in.

I had to go into town with the humiliation of no teeth, and without my teeth I couldn't eat the home-made granola that Carol had been sending me. It was the only really healthy food I had to eat.[54] I also lost my wallet. The little money I had was in my pocket, but I lost the papers that were in my wallet. I couldn't find my dentures or my wallet.

But after talking to the Creator and drumming our pain, I felt better. I felt the truth of what I heard. Throughout the whole experience, I could hear my voices saying, "Zelima, we're here now. This is it. This is what you prepared for. This is it. We're in the time of Earth changes."

I realized as I was grieving my lost animals, my children, that people were losing children everywhere. We were all grieving with the great losses we were suffering through during these changing times. I remembered how a long time ago, when I asked why it was that I could feel when an earthquake or a hurricane or flood was coming, I was told, "If a rock falls on your toe, you're going to feel it. You're part of Earth. We're all one body and we're all going to feel it."

I could feel something major shifting on Earth. If I had a TV or radio and could hear what was going on in world, I might have been able to figure it out. But all I could do was feel the pain, face it, and release it—and know that it wasn't just my pain. This was happening around the world. We were all feeling the pain of Mother Earth and all who suffer upon her. By connecting with the pain we could help to release it. I had come to learn that.

Years earlier I had come to understand that *unreleased* pain was at the root of evil. It came to me through a poem about a dinosaur and the devil. The devil was standing behind the dinosaur, listening to her talk. She was saying "unreleased pain is at the root of evil."

The truth of this wisdom from the dinosaur was confirmed for me when I found the Devil Stone, a beautiful flat, shiny onyx-black stone with clear crystals in different places. The first face I saw when I picked up the Devil Stone had a horn, crystal teeth, and crystals beginning to form around the ear. I understood from this that the devil was beginning to want to tell the truth and to listen. When I turned the stone over, the face was sorrowful. The devil was suffering, entering into his pain. It was several months later when I saw the third face. This face was perfectly at peace, with crystals in his crown chakra. The devil had released his pain.

This Devil Stone that I found in the desert in a corner of Arizona told me so much about what was going on in the world! It told me about the transformation of evil, the devil, the collective evil in the world. I knew that by working to release my own pain, I was releasing the evil in me—helping the devil. And because I saw both suffering and crystals of transformation in the Devil Stone, I knew that others around the world were also working to release their pain, freeing the world of evil.

"Yes, I'm suffering," I thought to myself. "But the Stone People talk to me and I'm seeing miracles. All these stones are here because they have a purpose, like the Devil Stone, each one a gem, with its own knowledge and beauty."

It came to me that if I ever got Medicine Wheel going again, I would build a hut where humans could come to learn from the Stone People. It would be a round adobe hut, full of Stone People, a library of love and knowledge. A real meditation place where people would learn things they couldn't imagine.

FALL INTO WINTER

Towards the end of the summer, I was so happy to find myself on the phone with my friend Peter, my Super Shrink. I had felt such gratitude toward him again, after talking about him so much for the book, that I had a strong urge to re-connect. My friend Jill helped me find him, tracking him down in Germany! When he returned, we connected and Peter and I had several wonderful conversations before I got an urgent call sometime in October from Alexa, Peter's partner. Peter had suffered a massive heart attack and had been rushed to the hospital. Alexa pleaded with me to do whatever I could to help.

I dropped everything and immediately tried to connect with Peter and do an absent healing, the way the Stone People had been teaching me. I connected the divine in me with the divine in him. I connected my third eye with his. The healing energy flowed. At some point I saw him embrace the Life Force. I was so relieved! Peter was in a coma and his doctors weren't giving him much hope. But I told Alexa that it looked like Peter was healing—he had embraced the Life Force.

A few days later, however, I sensed that something had happened; Peter had gone through a crisis. When I talked to Alexa the next day, she said, "Really? The doctors haven't said anything." A day or two after this, I had a really hard time connecting with Peter. When I finally did, I felt his chest, the cuts in his heart and all that the bones had gone through. He's still in a lot of pain, I thought.

The next day, on October 22, at 2:25 a.m., Peter died. Alexa called around 4:00 a.m. to tell me. Through the deep sadness, I felt so glad that our last words had been, "I love you." But I started to wonder why he hadn't healed. I had seen him so clearly embrace the Life Force. What did that mean? It wasn't until several months later that it started coming together. I was doing absent healing on a cat named Bucky, who also embraced the Life Force. I felt sure that Bucky was going to heal because of that but he died, too. As Elise and I were talking about it, she reminded me of my experience with the light of death and the light of healing—how I came to understand that they are one and the same Light. Perhaps the Life Force is both the force of life on Earth and the force of life Beyond. Peter and Bucky were saying yes to the Great Life Force, the force that would go on after their bodies gave out.

When Alexa told me Peter had died, I felt his presence. But after a day or so, I couldn't sense him. From the very first time I met him and sensed a special bond, I had never felt disconnected from Peter—even during the long stretches when we were out of touch. Now I couldn't sense him at all. I felt so lost, felt such grief and sorrow. Until one day, a couple of weeks after he died, I woke up and suddenly realized I could feel Peter's presence again. I was so grateful to be reunited with my friend.

Fall was turning to winter and as the temperatures began to drop, I started worrying about my birds. I wasn't sure if I could survive another winter. But I knew there was no way my birds would make it. They had suffered so much through the last winter. So it was a huge relief to me when Elise told me that she and Carol would take care of them that winter. The only thing was that the earliest Elise could get there was the week before Thanksgiving. That's fine, I said. I was so happy and relieved to know my birds would have a warm place to be all winter.

Another nightmare was in store for us. It started a couple of weeks after Peter died, right around Election Day. I felt the evil energy that had swept through our little corner of the desert during the summer come through again.

I could feel it in myself. I was losing my temper. My car had broken down again and I had to go into town to get it fixed after feeding everyone and taking care of other chores. The animals were edgy and the birds very demanding. A week or two earlier, one of the Conure parrots, Pickle, had flown away. He just couldn't take it any longer. So it was now just Baby, Sunny, and Totzl (or Tootsie, as I called her) in one cage, with Shalu in the other.

Baby and Tootsie started shrieking. They were putting out these ear-splitting shrieks and wouldn't stop. It was driving me crazy so I grabbed Tootsie's tail to get her to stop, but she pulled away from me and I was left with three tail feathers in my hand. Things were getting out of control! I had to go into town to take care of my car and right before I left, Baby left her cage and flew out. She flew away so high, I knew she couldn't take it—and that she wasn't coming back.

When I finally got back from town, I was furious at the dogs because they had chased off a dog that I thought belonged to Mary. I wanted them to know how angry I was at that kind of behavior so they went to bed without dinner or treats. The temperature was dropping fast. I gathered a lot more blankets to cover Shalu's cage and then Tootsie and Sunny's cage, and finally went to bed, exhausted.

The next morning, when I took the covers off the bird cages, I started screaming. I ran outside, screaming, crying, gasping for air. There were feathers scattered all over Tootsie and Sunny's cage, blood splattered everywhere—and Sunny lay dead at the bottom.

Tootsie had killed him.

It took me a while to finally be able to breathe again and go back in the dome. When I got there, Tootsie was slumped over in the cage. I picked her up. She had no cuts, no sign that anything was wrong with her body. But I knew she was dying. Tootsie *loved* Sunny; they had always been so close. She was stricken with grief—grief and guilt at the horror of what had happened.

Tears streamed down my face, as I sat holding Tootsie, watching the life slowly go out of her. I thought about all the grief and sadness in my life and remembered my last conversation with Peter. We had talked about how life is so hard yet how love can heal all, love and forgiveness. Peter had been able to forgive everyone in his life, even Hitler. Holding Tootsie in my arms as she was dying made me remember Rita's father. I could not make any sense of that, a man whose job was to deny such horrible things dying in my arms without any cancer pain and with his third eye open. I remembered the way the words came to me: "Don't judge." There is so much you don't know. Don't judge.

Holding Tootsie, I told her that we do awful things to each other, but those awful things can sometimes lead us to change. I told her I knew she loved Sunny and felt awful about what happened. I told her she was forgiven and that I loved her. I told her all the things I felt in my heart, holding and petting her until she died, with no visible sign of the cause of death.

By the time Elise arrived two weeks later, there was only Shalu left to take home.

MIRACLE HEALINGS

During the fall, I began to experience the real power of the Stone People, seeing some of the miracles that I had been told would occur during these times of Earth changes, these times of great destruction and creation.

Earlier in the year I had begun doing absent healings on my friend Fern who had undergone knee replacement surgery. The only kind of absent healings I had done before this were on the phone, when I would connect with the person and try to send energy, or when I would do ceremonies for people.

I started by lying down in the dome and feeling the Light within me. With my third eye, I would start scanning for Fern on such and such a street in Tucson. I would go looking for her or sometimes she would just appear and then I would connect my third eye with hers and the Light would start buzzing. I could see the energy start going to her knee or wherever.

Very soon after I started doing this, I began working with the Stone Person that had given me all that love to give to Tigger. I placed my left hand over the Ancient One and could feel her vibrating as I did the absent healing. I noticed that when I was done with the healing this beautiful stone was sweating—even though it was the middle of winter!

This is when I really began to learn about absent healings. It was the ultimate in following the Path of the Little Sisters—it was *all* about being guided, allowing the Stone People to lead, obeying their instructions, as they had told me to do. I had to learn this lesson over and over again, as I tried to take the lead in sending energy to a particular place. No. All I had to do was be my real self, focus my intent on connecting the Divine in me with the Divine in the other, my third eye with the other's third eye, and then follow the energy that the Stone People would direct, working with them, my animal allies, and the Light.[56]

At the beginning I only worked with the Stone Person that sweats, placing my left hand over her. Later I started working with another Stone Person under my right hand. She was actually my oldest Stone Person friend. I found her years ago in Tucson on a very busy street and carried her home a long way even though she was heavy. I had her next to me on my bed for years.

In the fall, right after I got the call about Peter going to the hospital with a heart attack, I had heard that Bob, my dear friend and colleague from Golden Dawn days in Tucson, had been in the hospital for months after suffering cardiac arrest while exercising at the gym. Bob is a beautiful African-American man with a heart of gold, beloved by all his clients. I referred all my little children to him when I left Golden Dawn. Bob's brain had been deprived of oxygen so long during the heart attack that he was unable to move at will or speak from the anoxic brain injury.[55] His wife, Trena, a nurse, raised some funds and mortgaged their house to get the man she adored placed in a special rehabilitation center in Texas. When I asked Trena if I could do absent healings on Bob, she said yes, so I started working with him.

That same month, Elise asked if I would do absent healings for her friend, Maureen, a Catholic Sister, who had just been diagnosed with peritoneal cancer. Maureen and Carol had been the best of friends for over thirty years and Carol had gone up to New York to be with Maureen after they had operated on her and found tumors all over her abdomen, too diffused to remove. I started doing absent healings on Maureen, even though I didn't know exactly where she was at the beginning.

Moving into winter, I got other requests to do healings—for my friend Bobbie, who had been dealing with cancer for years, for a four-year-old Chinese girl named Min who wasn't able to talk, for Carol when she fell and suffered a double dislocation of her elbow and multiple fractures in her forearm, and for Margie who had thyroid problems. I had five or six people I was doing each day, and I started seeing miracles.

After working on Maureen for about two months, I had the feeling she was healing. The sessions with Maureen were so powerful. She got this Sacred Radiation, this beautiful thick yellow-bronze light that just came and enveloped her whole body, shimmering. Inside, Maureen started looking clear to me. After about the third month, I told Elise that I was pretty sure Maureen had healed and that I was going to stop doing healings on her because I had people on my waiting list who were really sick and needed help. Elise begged me to please keep the healings going until January 10, 2005, when Maureen was supposed to have the surgery to take out whatever tumors had hardened and could be removed. It was only about a week away, so I said fine.

At the end of the day of the surgery, Elise called to tell me everyone was astonished—the surgeon found *no* tumors in Maureen. A few days later, she called again to tell me that the pathology report showed no signs of *any* cancer cells. No one could believe it.[56] [See p. 219 for a chronicle of the absent healing Zelima did with Maureen.]

Margie had been on my waiting list. She had a goiter and other problems with her thyroid. She had gone through treatments, but they couldn't get rid of the goiter. I didn't know anything about goiters or the thyroid and had never done any healing work on them.[57]When I started working on her, I said to the Stone People, "I know nothing about this, so can I just turn it over to you?" Around two months later, Margie told me her goiter was gone! San Martín de Porres had come to help with her healings. She has since become a devoted follower of his.

With Bob, I kept sensing that he could heal even though one of his doctors at the special center in Texas thought he was in such bad shape that he suggested Trena sign "do not resuscitate" forms. Trena refused. Had she signed them, Bob would have died one night last December when he went into failure.[58] The same doctor had expressed concerns about Bob's cognitive abilities. But within a few weeks of starting the absent healings, Bob started to speak a few words ("I love you"), and to move limbs he couldn't move before because of the heterotopic ossification[59] in his hips. Severe bed sores that exposed his tail bone and ankle bone started to heal after we began working on them. At one point the bed sores on his ankle had been so bad, they wanted to amputate! Bob has continued to improve and is now talking. His speech therapist recently said his language had gone from being zero percent intelligible to eighty percent![60] Trena has been the most extraordinary partner. She has refused to accept any idea other than that her beloved husband will be back home and well again. She has moved mountains to make it so, and until we know the work is done, we'll keep doing the healings.[61]

I would begin the absent healings before dawn and usually finish around 9:00 a.m. Then, during the day, I had some very present healings to deal with—a couple of miraculous face-to-face healings that allowed me to see, with my own eyes, the power of the Stone People.

The first patient was rushed over one day in September by the same neighbors who owned Sassy. Their kitten had been sleeping under the tire of the pickup truck and they accidentally ran over it. When Misty's father handed the kitten over to me, the lower portion of his back leg was bare bone, all the skin, muscles, sinews, tissue, veins, everything was gone, and his belly was cut open with a wound coming up from the leg.

He was so badly hurt I had no idea what to do. His eyes had a look I've come to recognize—it's a swollen look that says, "I've suffered enough. I'm ready to go." I turned to Spirit for help. I connected with the Stone People and began sending the kitten healing energy. Within about twenty minutes, I could see the look in his eyes had changed. But could he survive? His lower back leg was nothing but bone and a large gash ran up his belly with who knows what kind of internal injuries since he was urinating blood.

But I brought him up to my bed—the only somewhat clear place in the little camper—and kept working with him, asking for guidance. When a liquid starting oozing out of the bone, I asked, "Should I try to stop this?" I heard, "No, the fluid will form a protective coating." I figured it would turn brown and somehow protect the bone. I was guided to use herbs in a different way, sprinkling them on the bone and putting slippery elm over them, making a crust. The next day, when I got ready to clean off the crusted herbs, I heard, "No, not yet." The day after that, I heard the same thing. It looked like a mess, all those herbs crusted on. I worried about infection. But I left it alone.

On the third day, I got a "Yes." I carefully cleaned off the herbs, and was stunned to see red flesh growing over the bone! I never dreamed flesh could grow back like that. Over the course of the next few days, I saw the skin and fur grow back. I knew that veins, muscles, and tendons were also growing because the kitten started to move his leg! This was truly a miracle. I started calling the kitty, *Milagro*.

But it didn't stop there. That little Milagro went on to heal completely. By the time Elise came to visit in November, there was no sign he had ever suffered *any* injury. No scar, no limp, no nothing.[62]

I was told it was the Stone People who gave me the knowledge about working with tissue and tendons to heal Milagro. My voices said, "Of course, Creator is behind everything, but the Stone People were given the knowledge about all physical things. They were created when Earth was created; they are the Ancient Ones with all the knowledge about Earth's physical life."

The Stone People have that knowledge and, although it's all unconscious, I have been learning from them. They are my library—I go to them, open my pores, and ask them to teach me whatever they know. One day I was given a beautiful vision of the intelligence of life underground, inside Mother Earth. I saw what happens in the process of decay, death, and dying. I realized the Ancestors, the Stone People, would be there, continuing to teach me as my own body decomposes, nourishing Mother Earth. The whole process emanated divinity.

And the most remarkable thing about all this is that *anyone* can learn from the Stone People. It's available to all who seek it.

A couple of months later, my neighbors brought me their two-month old puppy, Destiny. She had been sick for about two weeks and by the time they brought her to me her legs were atrophied, her stomach was hard as a rock with a bulge on her right rib. She was skin and bones, having not eaten anything for a while and from vomiting so much. Her nose was hot and her face was swollen with the look, "I've suffered enough, I'm ready to pass."

Again, I turned to the Stone People. From the symptoms, it looked like the puppy had lead poisoning.[63] I had experienced lead poisoning once before, years earlier, when I worked on a Golden Eagle at a wonderful refuge in Tucson, called Forever Wild Wildlife Rehabilitation Center. Someone had found him with his talons locked shut from lead poisoning. They tried medicine to open the talons but nothing worked. The only humane thing to do was to put him to sleep but no one wanted to do it. My friend Paula asked if she could try one more thing—and brought me in.

I had asked Linda to come help me because she knows a lot about animals and can communicate with them. Linda held the Golden Eagle upright by the wings, meditating on him while I went to work on his legs. As the energy flowed, the Golden Eagle fell asleep! It felt so sacred to be embracing this wild and beautiful being, his head resting on my chest as I worked on his talons. Slowly, as the energy flowed to him, his talons started releasing. Eventually, both talons opened and when they felt flexible enough, I asked Linda to gently set him down. When the eagle opened his eyes, he looked puzzled, gazing down at his open talons. Slowly, he started trying to use them, taking one step and then another. A woman came into the room at just that moment and called out to the others, "He's walking! He's walking!"

Soon after, the eagle was released back to the wild. Spirit energy is really good at anything that needs opening up.

So that's what I turned to as I began working with Destiny—that and the Stone People. As the energy started flowing, I could see Destiny look beyond me, her gaze going higher and higher above my head. All the animals I've worked on do this. They see my aura, and recognize the energy that's flowing through me. It's *Spirit*, they know, and right away they calm down so I can work on them. This way they respond is how I know animals are deeply spiritual beings.

Destiny was vomiting and vomiting. When they brought her to me I had just been getting ready to go into town to get water. I couldn't leave her, so I had to melt snow to clean up the messes. For more than a day, I didn't have the Lobelia I needed to stop the vomiting. Lobelia tastes awful, but after I pried Destiny's mouth open and gave her some, her little eyes looked at me like, "Oh, this is good." Later she was able to drink the thick gummy slippery elm tea I made with goat milk. She liked it and it nourished her. You can get through a famine if you have slippery elm.

But mostly, I used energy, working with the Stone People. That's what I was guided to do. Slowly, her little atrophied limbs started to stretch back out again, her hard stomach became soft, and she started eating and putting on weight.[64] It took a few weeks, but Destiny healed—another little miracle.

MEDICINE WHEEL

During the last few weeks of December I thought I was having some kind of stroke or brain malfunction. I recognize pain in my temples as a sign that floods are coming. But this pain was so intense, so severe, I had no idea it was connected to floods—until I heard about the tsunami.[65]

Reading about the tens of thousands of people who died, I knew we were witnessing the kinds of Earth changes—with massive destruction like we've never seen before—that I had seen in my visions.[66] But I also knew after witnessing all those miracles that a new healing energy had come upon the Earth.

That healing energy is now all over Mother Earth—and the wondrous thing about it is that it's available to *all* of us. Even if you know nothing about illness or healing, *you*, who are reading this book, can turn to the Stone People and help transmit this energy, changing the vibration on Mother Earth for the good of the whole.

I taught a little bit about this for the first time in April 2005, when I did a workshop at Santuario Sisterfarm, the ecospirituality center outside of San Antonio, Texas, that Elise and Carol co-founded with María. They had gotten some grant monies to offer healing workshops for social justice activists, especially latinas from the Borderlands. It was the first workshop I had done in several years and I was able to do it because Mary said she would take care of all my animals while I was gone. I celebrated my sixty-fifth birthday while I was there and met some beautiful people who came for a Little Sister's Sweat Lodge, a day-long workshop on healing, and a healing ceremony for Mother Earth.

I had made the mistake of having a little glass of wine during my birthday dinner. It made me really sick for several days and I ended up staying an extra three days to recover from the illness. My pancreas just can't take *any* alcohol, I realized. But Spirit was with me. During the times I was giving workshops and healings, I was able to gather the healing energy and do the work.[67]

As I was heading back home, Mary broke the news to me that a few days after I left my cat, *Vida Linda* (Beautiful Life), had found an open window and run away. They had searched and searched all over but couldn't find her. Vida Linda had been gone for five or six days, in the desert with no food or water! I was devastated. I didn't think I could face going back to that life without Vida Linda. Unlike my other cats who wandered off all the time, Vida Linda was always near me. She would never have run away if I had been there. I was haunted by the image of her being chased and eaten by a coyote. That's how her mother died—and, as a little kitten, she had witnessed it.

A few days after I got back, my voices told me to go to Mary's. When I got there, I started looking for Vida Linda. I followed my voices and the strong feelings that came into my body, feeling pulled in one direction and then another. I had walked some distance away from Mary's property and by now I was sobbing, wailing, "Vida Linda! Vida Linda!" In between sobs, I heard a weak, "Meow."

I look all around but didn't see anything. "Meow," again. It came from above! I looked up and there was Vida Linda, in a cedar tree. Elated beyond words, I climbed up the tree to get her. The top of her head was sunburned, so she must have been up there for a while. How she managed to survive all this time without starving or being eaten by a coyote, I don't know—except she's a good hunter and a good climber (at least going up).

The rest of my animal family was so happy to see Vida Linda when I brought her home. For days after I returned with Vida Linda they all seemed so content. We all felt it—that sense of "no matter how humble..." We were home and there was no place like it. Our home was where we all were. That was it.

I am still here, on this land, living in the small camper and dome tent with my animal family. The heat of summer is beginning to build. After that, I face another fall and winter—not knowing what will happen to me; not knowing what will happen to Mother Earth.

All I know is that I am here because of a reversal—a reversal in the legal description of a parcel of land that resulted in my going on a long Medicine Journey and into a Shamanic Death. From Micaela, the one who initiated me onto my sacred path, I learned that reversals are good, having something to do with achieving greater balance.

Ravens are coming up to my camper. They call me. I go out and they fly to where I am. I have been feeding them since I noticed that the cedar trees in the desert are no longer bearing berries. The birds are going hungry. So I go out to feed them and chant to them with my heart. I put whatever's in my heart in my chant and they pick up it, coming close to me even when I'm out there with one of my doggies.

Jesus has been visiting me. I feel the vibrations, the divinity entering my body and going deep into my soul. I have been seeing Jesus on the cross lately and thinking about all the preachers and people who say he's coming back to judge. The feeling comes to me so clearly: If Jesus were going to judge, he would have done it when he was on the cross, when he couldn't be anything but his truest self.

Yet when he was his truest self, Jesus said, *"Forgive them."*

What I know is this: The All Good has begun to penetrate into the world. It has come upon the Earth, and something is happening or getting ready to happen. Something we are not expecting, and something we know. The Stone People are here to guide us and they've been preparing for this for thousands and thousands of years. We are entering a battle in which we must not kill.

The words that Fermina spoke to me long ago are close to my heart. "The job of the human is to pray for every being on Earth." That's the job Spirit gave the human, "but the human is not doing it and it is causing great harm," she said.

From my little corner of the desert, I accept the job Spirit gave me. Every day, I pray for every being on Earth. Every day, I pray for Mother Earth.

I accept that my little Medicine Wheel may never come to life.

But I pray, with all my heart, that the Great Medicine Wheel, our Mother Earth, will come into new life. I pray that the pain and suffering of Mother Earth and all who live and dwell upon her will be released, restoring balance, and bringing all of us into our proper place in the sacred circle of life.

Mitakuye oyasin
All my relations

Chronicles of an Absent Healing

At the end of September 2004, Maureen, a Catholic Sister and immigration lawyer working with indigent immigrants and refugees in South Florida, was admitted to a hospital in New York with severe abdominal pains. She was in New York getting ready to fly overseas for her godson's wedding. Instead she was taken into surgery where the doctors found she had peritoneal cancer. It was inoperable: the tumors were too diffuse to remove. The doctors proposed an aggressive protocol of chemotherapy in the hopes of hardening the tumors sufficiently so that they might be removed in a series of successive surgeries, with chemo in between. Maureen was later told that she would also need to have a stent inserted because she would likely need chemotherapy for the rest of her life. A port for intravenous treatments was recommended.

Below is a recording of telephone conversations with Zelima or messages she left on the answering machine about her absent-healing work with Maureen.

October 10, 2004

I've been sending energy to Maureen. I don't know where she is but I said to my Stone Person, the one I heal with and that sweats, "You know where she is. Guide me." In the last few days, I felt both Great Spirit and Great Mystery going to Maureen.

Elise: *How do you distinguish between Great Spirit and Great Mystery?*

Great Mystery is the Creator of everything. She created Great Spirit as an equal to take care of the humans. Great Spirit comes in like sunlight...yellow light. Great Mystery, her color is black like Raven (although she can also put out light). That's why Raven represents her. She's both male and female, but somehow Great Mystery comes in female to me, although I know she's also male. She has Raven's translucent black color. Raven represents Great Mystery in all absent healings. I always call on Raven when I do healings, especially distant healings. When I feel Great Mystery I understand why she's called "Mystery."

Great Mystery went to Maureen. I felt Great Spirit and Great Mystery reaching Maureen, even though I didn't know where she was. But I turned to my Stone Person, my teacher, and said, "You know where she is. You'll guide the healing energy there."

October 12, 2004

The healings with Maureen are going wonderfully. I'm loving it!

Elise: *How do you do the healings?*

Well, first I prepare myself. I have my Stone Person with the face that sweats to my left. I put my left hand over her. I don't know much about computers but I've learned a little about how people use the mouse. I feel my hand going around, moving the stone like a mouse.* Since it's so cold now, I put a cloth over her to protect my hand from the cold. By the time I'm finished with the healings, the Stone Person is sweating! Once we're all set, I thank the ancestors, the Stone Person.

Then I clear my mind and call on Great Mystery, Great Spirit, Raven, and my animal allies. Whatever animal ally is going to work with me on the healing comes in. I thank each of them as they come in. Snake, Owl, and Eagle are my totems so they are always with me. Raven is always in any absent healing. He presides over all absent healings. And lately Ixchen, the Aztec Goddess of Medicine, has been there. And she's powerful! With these healings, I've ended up having Gorilla, Alligator, Mouse, and sometimes Elephant appear. The first time Kangaroo came in was with Bob. I've also had Butterfly, Iguana, Lizard, Cricket, Frog, and Turtle work with me. I say, "Thank you for coming in." Then I say, "This is for Maureen in Sleepy Hollow at Phelps Hospital." I let the Stone guide me, let my allies guide me, and we go to her. Usually the Stone Person comes in, saying, "Remember to follow. Don't try to lead." They always remind me.

I'll see a face and I'll say, "The Divine within me honors the Divine within you, and I give gratitude for this connection." I connect my third eye with her third eye and say, "My third eye connects with the third eye in you, and I give gratitude for this connection." It really is a beautiful feeling, that connection.

I can feel her. We work with her. I can feel the energy coming through me. I feel the Stone Person vibrating in my hand. My hand moves and I just watch and start to see what's happening. I see the Light. I see the energy and where it goes in the person's body. I feel it in myself and feel the strength of it, the power of it. I feel the Spirit, feel the allies. We worked on her solar plexus a lot today. She seems to be improving. There's been an improvement.

*Now my hand remains still, vibrating with the stone.

October 13, 2004

The Sacred Path cards are talking to me about Maureen. They show that she's getting her internal timing together, that she's going through a Shaman's Death—a death and rebirth. She's going through a process of expansion, which is good; it's needed for her healing. She'll be sharing what she's learning with others. Working in her favor is the Sacred Pipe—which stands for inner peace. It's already there. Unlimited vision—it's already in her. Prayers being answered. It's opening to all possibilities. Being at home with other realities, bridging all worlds, acknowledging the potential dreamer within, healing denial and blindness—all that's already coming through for her.

The challenge is being able to use the new abilities she's getting with courage, risking set backs while learning new skills, and letting go of old tools that did not work. She needs to acknowledge the new abilities and her right to take charge and use the new abilities. She's releasing a lot of stuff. It was beautiful, lots of light.

December 1, 2004

The healing for Maureen today was wonderful. I do it just about every day. This morning it was so clear. I think the fourth time I did a healing with her she got "Sacred Radiation." That's straight from the Creator. Today she got it again. Sacred Radiation!

My allies are animal spirits. When I do healing with Maureen, she usually gets Gorilla, Owl, Eagle, and others. Today, for the first time, Butterfly came in. In all the years I've done healing, this is the first time that Butterfly has come in. I'm not sure what it means, but it was beautiful.

I'm really happy with Maureen. When Sacred Radiation came in, it gave me a lot of hope. That is the Creator, the Holy Spirit, THE ONE that's coming. It's very powerful. I call it Sacred Radiation, because it just RA-DI-ATES!

Carol: *When the nurses and oncologists saw the results of Maureen's blood work, they were astonished. It went from 700 to 49!*

I believe it. Spirit can do anything. It reminds me of when I was doing a healing with someone who was very sick in the hospital. The nurse came in at some point and said, "Please don't use your cell phone." I said, "I don't have one." She went out. We continued the healing. Then she came back in again and said, "Our readings show you have a cell phone on." We didn't say anything about what I was doing. I just told her again that I didn't have a cell phone, and we laughed. I'm overjoyed about Maureen!

December 6, 2004

Most of Maureen's healings have been very powerful, but this one was so intense. "Whoa, Maureen!" She had the Sacred Radiation again—full force. And Butterfly came to her again. I have never worked with Butterfly before and am just getting to know her. She's very pleasant and light. She has a very good feeling.

Today with Maureen, it was so intense, first in her pelvic area. Then it moved up to her stomach and solar plexus and then to her heart and up her spine. She was just covered with it, her whole body, within and without. That's when I saw that Sacred Radiation again. It's ra-di-a-tion! It's thick light.

When that Sacred Radiation came for in Maureen, it was more intense than before. All I could say was "Thank you, thank you, thank you!" It's so awesome when you see this, gratitude just comes in.

December 7, 2004

Butterfly was with Maureen practically through the whole healing today. She's having her victory. Butterfly had never come to me before Maureen. But after I did the healing today with Maureen, I did one with Bobbie who's been sick for years. Butterfly went right into Bobbie's healing. Cancer also has been her battle. I got scared at first because there was this beautiful red light. Somewhere in my mind I thought it wasn't good. But it said, "Let me through." Then it was wonderful. Bobbie's going to have new vitality in her life. That's what I was told. It represented new vitality, the Life Force.

December 8, 2004

The healing was very light today, no heavy stuff. It was very, very light. Butterfly was just flying through it—just Butterfly and the Light.

December 10, 2004

The healings today were so powerful! I was shaking part of the time as the energy was flowing through me to the people. I think Maureen has healed already. Yesterday she was so clear. It was so clear in there. I get the feeling, I'm not sure because I've never seen this before, but I get the feeling that Maureen's already healed. I think she's healed already.

Carol: *Maureen for one chemo treatment was so sick she had to spend hours back at the hospital getting rehydrated intravenously. But for the third treatment, she had no nausea. Her sister Denise was with her for a week after this treatment and they went out to lunch every day, and Christmas shopping for the family. Every time I called, Maureen was out! I finally left a message with the person saying, "Tell Maureen this is Carol-who-stays-at-home." She went to the Metropolitan Museum and to a lecture on stem cell research. Now she is afraid that people will think she is okay and no one will continue to pray for her.*

December 19, 2004

Jesus came to help me with the healings. He chose the Owl feathers. It was so like him—always choosing the outcast!

January 3, 2005

That Maureen girl, I think she's going to be healthy. It was strong today. She got bombarded with energy. It was very clear, very clear. The energy went from her chest to her solar plexus to the pelvic area.

January 10, 2005

[Maureen was in surgery for three hours during the morning. Zelima called at 9:30 a.m. CST, and then again an hour later.]

First call: I've been doing the healings with Maureen. She looks good, at peace. There's power there.

Second call: I sent more energy to Maureen. Raven came and just called and called and called. Raven is always present in absent healings. Raven called and then left. That's a very powerful sign of a strong healing presence.

[Around 6:00 p.m. CST, Maureen's sister, Kathleen, called to say Maureen had come through the surgery and that the surgeon reported she had found *no* tumors. Kathleen said the surgeon couldn't believe it—she had never seen anything like it.]

January 14, 2005

[Maureen called at 7:17 p.m. CST and left this message on our answering machine.]

Hi, Carol. It's Maureen. Hi, Elise.

I'm calling because the pathologist's report has come back and she found *no live cancer cells* in anything that was submitted. So, I'm pleased to tell you I am a case where the doctor has not seen the likes before. She's been at it fifteen years. And I am—through prayer and Zelima's healing ceremonies—I have been cured! So, I want to thank you, and I want you to thank Zelima. I knew that it was astounding that the doctor couldn't see anything but now, today, this evening, I got a call with the pathologist's report finding that even through microscopes they can't see anything either. So, it's just phenomenal. Thank you, thank you, thank you.

PART TWO
HEALING WAYS

PART TWO: HEALING WAYS

Whether it is feeling the vibrations of a story about the honor of a snake, using an herbal recipe for treating allergies, or following instructions on how to gather energy from a tree, each of these ways will help you access the marvelous healing powers of Mother Earth.

ANIMAL STORIES

Sharing

To teach my doggies about living together and sharing, especially violent dogs I have saved from execution by the pound, I have them eat and sit in a circle to get their treats together. When Tigger had her puppies, I started training them right away. Whichever puppy sat quietly without jumping around on everyone else or trying to grab the snacks away from me would get the treat first. Gordito was the best. He sat right down, looking up sweetly, always getting to be number one. His little brother Frankie, on the other hand, was always jumping up for his treat, wanting to grab it away. But Frankie wanted to be good, so he started hanging out with Gordito. When Gordito would sit down, Frankie sat right next to him, doing just what Gordito did, trembling it was so hard for him to be still. He and Gordito got to be number one. But then Gordito died. Frankie got so scared—they had been partners in being good! Frankie tried hard. He wanted so much to be good, but it was a real struggle for him without Gordito; he couldn't quite do it.

So Juanita got to be the best. She would get a very serene look on her face and just stand in the background while the others were going, "Pant, pant, pant! Gimme that treat!" Juanita was number one for so long that Panchita noticed. She found a way to copy Juanita's expression and stand in the back. Her face started looking just like Juanita's. I could see her struggle to get it at first, but then she got it, that nonchalant look. So she got to be number one with Juanita, getting the treats first.

Loyalty

Everybody felt something was coming. At my neighbor's house there were about a dozen puppies, all sucking on two mothers who were starving, and a few other dogs who were also sick and starving. They all had worms, mucous coming out of their eyes, and ribs sticking out.

Onyx kept going over there, coming home with worms. I tied him, but Onyx was so miserable that I let him go as soon as he healed. Back he went. I couldn't make him stay home! I finally did a reading and it told me that he deeply loved a female over at my neighbor's. They were very closely bonded in a high spiritual love. That's what kept him going over there.

At some point, Onyx even stopped coming back to eat. I tried going over to feed him, taking him some chicken, which he loved. When he saw it in my hand, Onyx started coming over to me, but then stopped as if to say, "My friends can't have any..."

He looked at me. He had mucous in his eyes like the others. He started to back away. I went to grab him, to take him home to heal him, but he fought me. "No, I don't want to go," he was telling me, running to hide under a trailer.

The female he was with just lay there in a total depression, her poor babies pulling at her starving body, trying to nurse. It was awful. I decided to give Onyx three days. Then I was going to force him back home.

Something dreadful was in the air. Three of the puppies that had come to me from there kept having nightmares. On the third day, I went over with a leash to get Onyx. But it was too late. He had been shot along with all the others, puppies included.

Onyx knew that those dogs were in bad trouble but he chose to be there with his beloved. He chose to starve with them. The people who killed him had no idea what a beautiful being they destroyed.

Spirituality

When I was living in Arivaca in a little cottage, I was right next door to a cattle ranch. The cows and I were separated by nothing but a barbed wire fence. Almost every day, I would come out and play my drums. I noticed that there was a bull with the gentlest eyes that always had two calves next to him, on each side. They'd walk together like that, the bull taking care of them. I loved seeing them and later found out that the little calves' mother had been taken away to be slaughtered and that often, when the mothers are taken away to slaughter, the baby calves die. So, these little calves lived, being taken care of by the gentle bull.

I became friends with them and they would come over to the fence. We would spend time together. The calves were always snuggling against the bull. One day it struck me how much I was enjoying them, loving them—and I got scared because I knew what would eventually happen to them. But I felt the love we were sharing was just too beautiful to give up. So we kept visiting each other.

One morning while we were visiting, I heard a voice say, "Enjoy this moment. This will be the last time." I looked at them—at the bull with his gentle eyes, this beautiful being and these two little calves huddled against him, and I went crazy.

"Oh, no!" I started screaming. "Oh, no! Great Spirit! Help me! Great Spirit!"

I heard a voice say, "Get your drum."

I ran and got my drum. Then, the voice said, "Pray, and call upon their Deities."

I started to pray. I called upon their Deities. A female and a male, two oxen in one body, came to my mind's eye. I started drumming to them. I drummed and drummed and drummed, singing my chant, singing my heart to their Deities. Singing and drumming and praying to them.

I had my eyes closed. When I opened them, I saw that all the bulls and the cows in the field had come over to the fence. They were all lined up along the fence, except one, who stayed apart. I knew he was meant to be there, he was so very, very still.

Many times before I had drummed but the cows had never come over to the fence. When I finished the drumming, they all left, wandering off to other parts of the ranch.

I watched them go. It was the last time.

Honor

In the early 1970s, a friend took me to a place named Rattle Snake Gulch in California. I used to be deathly afraid of snakes, but I was beginning to be attracted to them. The only names of snakes I knew were "rattlesnake" and "cobra." "Look! There's a snake," I said to my friend. "Yeah, that's a Diamond-back," she answered.

I didn't know that a Diamondback was a rattler. It was the 1970s and everyone was spacey, including me. I wandered over to the snake and looked at her, getting within just a couple of feet. I started to put my palms up toward her, wanting to give her energy—I had just learned how to do that. The snake looked at me, and kept turning her head like she wanted to get away from me. I started to go after her, but she gave me a look like, "Don't you dare!"

So I went back to my friend and said, "Gee, she got mad at me." Explaining how she pulled away as I tried to give her energy, I asked, "What kind of snake was that, again?"

"A Diamondback," my friend said. "A Diamondback rattler."

"WHATTT? A *rattler*? I got that close to a rattlesnake?" I gasped in dis-belief, thinking what a fool I had been.

Later when I had the sense to think about it, I realized what had hap-pened. That snake had taught me about honor. She had honor—she was not about to kill a fool.

Gratitude

One day at Medicine Wheel, I was walking toward the tipi to do a cer-emony. I had six or seven dogs with me at the time. We were walking on the road when the dogs started barking. They had a snake surrounded by the bushes. "Get away!" I said, chasing them off. The snake was making an undulating movement. She kept trying to get up, but couldn't. She was sick.

The dogs had run off ahead, so I got closer to the snake—a rattler, I saw. "Are you okay, baby?" She gave me a look like "No…" So I went to her and I put my hands right over her. I could feel the healing energy flow out of me, and she stopped undulating. The energy kept coming, flowing into her. As it did, I kept repeating, "I'm not going to hurt you. I'm just giving you healing energy." The energy kept flowing, and then it stopped. I leaned down and said, "I hope you feel better, baby. I hope you feel better."

I continued walking, catching up with the dogs. We were gone for a while and then came back on the same road. I was by myself on one side of the road and the dogs were way ahead, running. All of a sudden I heard this shrill machine. It took me a while to realize there was no machine out here in the wilderness. It was this shriiiiiillll, high, loud machine noise. I looked around. "What could this be?"

I walked a few more steps and the noise got even shriller. Then, all of a sudden, I froze. I was on the right side of the road. The snake had appeared on the left and was standing straight up to my eye level! The shrieking noise was the rattle in her tail. The blood left me. We both stood still. She was looking right at me. Finally, these words came out of me, as a feeling of hurt caught up with my fear: "What are you doing? I *told* you I wasn't going to hurt you!" I turned around and walked away. She didn't follow or strike.

Later, I asked two medicine people, "What do you think that was all about?" They both said, "She wanted to give you a gift!"

"She wanted to give you a gift, to show you how strong she was after you healed her," they said. The fact that she was reared up like that meant she wasn't going to hurt you, they explained. If she had been coiled up, she would have been ready to strike.

I didn't know any of that, and for a time I felt I had just blown it, lost an incredible gift from a beautiful being. But now I feel sure that I actually did get it. I got the gift.

Trust

One night when I was in the Medicine Wheel house, I went into the kitchen for something. I had my little lamp and as I stepped towards the counter, I could see that there was a snake lying there, looking at me from the ground. I looked at the snake and then focused on letting her feel my vibration and on allowing myself to feel hers.

To do this, I had to get to my real place inside, open in love to this animal person, and show a desire to communicate. All these feelings send a vibration of respect. We humans have the luxury of being able to wander off from our real place. Animals don't. They have to be in their real place always in order to survive—so they can feel the vibrations of other creatures and know whether it's dangerous or safe.

As I spoke, I put the vibration in my voice so she could understand my words. They don't understand the words, but they feel the vibration in them. "If you want to stay, we're going to have to communicate," I said, letting her feel "communicate."

"Oh, okay," I could feel her say as she turned, giving me her back. That means, "I'm trusting you—you can trust me."

I knew it wasn't a rattlesnake but it looked like some other kind of very poisonous snake. "Thank you, but I still don't feel comfortable," I said.

"Oh," she said, starting to look around the room toward the door. Thinking she wanted to go out, I went to the door and opened it, saying "Do you want out, honey?"

"No..." she said.

I could tell she knew the house very well. She was very comfortable in it. There was a crack in the paneling of the wall. She went over to it and put her head in first, leaving half her body out. She just stayed perfectly still. "If you want to kill me, go ahead," she was saying.

I got up close to her. I saw that I could kill her right now if I wanted to. "That's okay, baby. I'm trusting." After I said these words, I watched her slowly coil back out. She looked right at me. "Okay?"

"Okay," I said. "Goodnight." She went her way and I went mine, back to my bedroom.

GATHERING HEALING ENERGY

Gathering healing energy from Mother Earth and Sky is our birthright. We all knew how to do it thousands of years ago. The way comes back in seconds. All you need to do is open yourself up and allow the healing energy to come in. You don't "pull" or "draw" the energy in. You just open your pores and it will flow. The energy is there, ready to enter. All you need to do is open to it.

Standing outside in bare feet on Mother Earth, gently focus your intention on opening the pores of the soles of your feet. It helps to say this four times: "I open the pores of the soles of my feet."

Let the healing energies of Mother Earth rise up and into you. Again, don't try to draw them into you; just let them seep naturally into you, as you open the pores of the soles of your feet.

Raise your arms and hold your hands out, palms up, to the sky, and gently focus your intention on opening the pores of the palms of your hands. Repeat four times: "I open the pores of the palms of my hands."

Let the healing energies in the air and from all the life around you and throughout the Universe flow into you through the open pores in the palms of your hands. Again, don't try to draw the energies into you. Just let the healing energy flow into you.

Finally, open your eyes wide, opening the pores of your eyes. Allow the energy of the sun, the stars, the moon, the cosmos to flow into you through your eyes, as you repeat four times: "I open the pores of my eyes." Open your eyes and let the healing energies of the Universe flow into you through your open eyes.

All life forms carry great intelligence. But trees do especially because they spend their entire lives, day and night, in rain, sleet, snow, and sun, in deep meditation. So they have much to impart. The key to communicating and gathering energy from a tree is to recognize the equality in the worth of all life, of the tree's life and your own.

To gather energy from a tree, place both hands gently on the trunk of the tree. If the tree has exposed roots, stand on these, barefoot. Center yourself and then say, "I realize that your life is worth as much as mine. And I ask that you give me of your energy so that I can help." This is very important. You must feel this, send this vibration to the tree. Then, open the pores of the palms of your hand and the soles of your feet, and let the energy flow in. Do not try to draw or pull it in.

When it feels like the energy has stopped flowing, usually in just a few minutes, let go. Do not stand there hugging the tree for an hour! Give thanks to the tree for the energy and for her beautiful being.

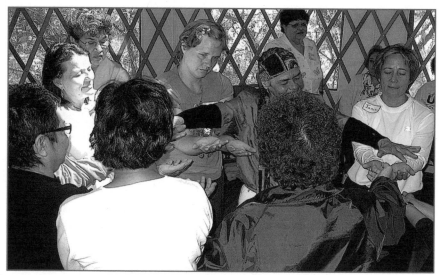

Zelima and workshop participants share energy.

Once you know how to gather energy by opening your pores, you don't have to say or repeat the phrase—all you need to do is just do it, open your pores, and the energy will flow in.

DANCE OF THE SOUL

This is a dance to heal Mother Earth and all who live and dwell upon her. It came to me after seeing something that happened in Australia years ago.

When I was in college in the 1970s, I saw a film about a place in Australia that had been totally devastated by humans. The Earth was parched and there was little vegetation. In the middle of this wasteland, a scrawny rooster and hen were stepping back and forth, back and forth. The pair was engaged in a mating dance, but it was no ordinary mating dance. The energy coming out of that rooster and hen had so much intensity and intention, they were not just dancing to mate, they were dancing to *live*, dancing for *life*—dancing as if *all* life depended on it.

Years later, I saw another film about Australia. It turned out to be about the very same place I had seen a decade or so earlier. But now, instead of it being a wasteland, the place was teeming with life! I couldn't believe it. Then I remembered, with gratitude, the rooster and the hen and their incredible dance for life.

Spirit guided me to teach a similar dance for humans—a dance that everyone can do for healing Mother Earth. It is urgently needed for these times of Earth changes. Mother Earth is incredibly stressed. She is trying to hold onto life and to continue to be life-giving in the face of great destruction. The Dance of the Soul is a healing dance. It is healing for Mother Earth, as well as for the people dancing, and all others who live and dwell upon Earth.

No special skill is needed to dance this dance—only the kind of intention and intensity and love for life that the rooster and hen put into their dance. It's a dance for Mother Earth—*as if all life depended on it.*

It is done in bare feet. Get centered. Move into your healing intention. To the beat of a drum, begin to move your body, placing each foot down gently on Mother Earth, knowing and feeling that each step you take in the dance is a prayer.

As you take each step, open the pores of the soles of your feet. Let the healing energies of Mother Earth rise into you. Know that each step you take is a prayer, a prayer to Spirit for healing Mother Earth and all creation.

Raise your arms as you move in this dance, and open the pores of the palms of your hands. Let the healing energies in the air and from the trees and plants and birds and throughout the Universe flow into you through the open pores in the palms of your hands.

Open your eyes wide as you move in this dance. Open your eyes to the stars and the moon, the sun and the planets. Open your eyes and let the healing energies of the cosmos flow into you through your open eyes. Let the healing energy flow into and through you.

All of this energy joins with the energy of Mother Earth, intensifying the healing power. Dance on Mother Earth as if all life depended on it. Know that each step you take is a prayer. *Mitakuye oyasin.*

WORKING WITH THE STONE PEOPLE

The Ancient Ones are speaking, coming forth to help the Human People at this time of Earth changes. They have been preparing for this moment for thousands and thousands of years. They are the masters of transformation. They are constantly changing—moving from sand to mountain and mountain to sand. They hold a healing vibration for us and for Mother Earth that we can help to release by placing Stone People who have chosen to play this role in our lives on our altars or in other sacred places. Also by holding and gently caressing the Stone People.

If you feel drawn to picking up a stone, it is probably a Stone Person calling you, inviting communication and collaboration in sharing and releasing this healing energy. The mantra for entering into the Stone Person's healing energy and for releasing it to the planet is this: "See what happens when you softly, gently, and tenderly touch a stone." The words must be said in that order: softly, gently, and tenderly.

Begin by connecting with your own essential self. Get to a real place within yourself. Then, holding the Stone Person in your hand, enter into the feeling of "softly." Softly, softly, softly caress the stone with your thumb.

When you feel like you've gotten the touch of "softly," enter into "gently." Gently, gently, gently caress the stone. When you've got a sense of the feeling of "gently," focus on combining "softly" with "gently." See what happens when you softly *and* gently touch a stone.

When those energies are moving, enter into the feeling of "tenderly." Tenderly, tenderly, tenderly caress the stone. When you've got that feeling, combine all three. See what happens when you softly, gently, and tenderly touch a stone.

You will know if you have entered into the vibration if you feel yourself in a deep meditative place and experience a profound sense of peace. Know that it is this healing peace that is being released to the world, and that you are participating in it with the Stone People.

WORKING WITH THE LIGHT

The key to working with the Light is to activate the Light that is within you, not try to draw it in from outside.[68] I learned to work with the Light from Jesus, who started coming to me when I was home from the hospital after being told I had pancreatic cancer that had progressed to the liver. I was told to use the Light to heal myself. You can work with the Light in the way I will describe regardless of whether it is physical, emotional, or mental/psychological pain you are feeling.

Center yourself. Get to your real self. Then go inside yourself to the place of dis-ease. This is not about visualization. Go to the real place within where you feel pain, darkness, tightness, however the dis-ease is presenting itself. Confront the pain. Just look at it and see what is there. Then say, repeating, "The Light is within you. The Light is within you. The Light is within you. The Light is within you." Know that the Light is within each and every cell of your body. Repeat the phrase until you see the Light within activated.

Once that happens, then focus on going *inside* the place of dis-ease. Recognize that the pain, the discomfort, is not separate from you. It is you. You are it. Then say, repeating, "The Light is within me. The Light is within me. The Light is within me. The Light is within me."

I usually feel a calmness and serenity right away. But the release generally comes the next day. I'll recognize that something got released or I feel less pain. I work with the Light in other areas, as well, like resentments or anger I might find inside myself. I do this a little differently.

I center myself and go inside to that place where the resentment or anger lies. I look at it and feel it. I try to go to those places where feelings I may have denied are lodged. Then I say, "I own this feeling. And because I own it, I can walk it to the Divine within me." Then I just walk it to the Divine Light within. Sometimes I feel the Divine is behind it; sometimes I'm face to face with the Divine. Either way, the feelings change. The feelings get transformed.

Herbal Remedies

Years ago when I first started having visions of these times of Earth changes, I was told that I would need to learn to heal without herbs because there would be times when even healing herbs wouldn't be available. I've found myself in that situation several times these past two years in the desert and have relied on working with the Stone People and the Light to get me through.

But there are a few herbal remedies I have used over the years that I want to share. Unfortunately some of the most powerful plants and herbs, gifts of Mother Earth, have been taken away from us. For example, ephedra, a wonderful medicine for healing asthma and allergies, has been pretty much taken off the market and is hard to get these days.[69]

Mother Earth's most powerful medicines, like tobacco and ephedra, are sacred and need to be used carefully. They *will* cause harm if abused. But they are powerful and sacred gifts from Mother Earth that should not be denied the people and the animals.

To bring the full power of the medicine into these remedies, I always do ceremony.

Before you make any of these medicines, create a clean space and smudge it with the smoke of cedar or sage. Place the ingredients you're going to use on the counter and smudge them, giving thanks to each one. Give thanks to the plant and to Mother Earth and the Creator for giving us these beautiful healing medicines. Keep working with the cedar or sage as you go. Ask for guidance as you make the medicine. They are much more powerful if you let yourself be guided in making them. When you're ready, mix the ingredients, and create the medicine. Then cedar or sage it when you're done, again, giving thanks to Mother Earth and the Creator.

Agua Florida (Flower water)

All *curanderas* use *agua florida*, a healing cologne, for a variety of things. It's available in any *botánica* (Latino pharmacy) and is used for all manner of things, from hangovers to strokes. It is usually splashed/slapped onto the inside of a person's elbows, chest, back of the neck, and back.

Allergy Medicine

This medicine works wonders on people who suffer allergies, hay fever, and congestion.

Colt's foot (dried)
Ephedra or Ma huang (even better) (dried best, but can use powder)
Hyssop (dried)
Blue violet or violet (dried)
Lobelia (dried)
Licorice root (powder)

Mix equal parts of all herbs in a bag. Store the mixture in a glass or ceramic jar. Shake the ingredients each time before you take it to make sure it is well mixed. Boil water, place one teaspoon of the mixture per cup, and add water (don't boil the herbs). Steep for seven minutes, covered. Strain and serve. It's best to make a large jar of the tea and sip it several times throughout the day, placing it by your bedside to sip at night.

Your symptoms will decrease and the allergy will never be as serious again. I was terribly allergic to animals at one point. Spirit guided me to these herbs. For years, the allergies were gone. Every once in a while I'll get symptoms. All I have to do is take this tea and the allergies go away.

Asthma

Coffee enemas, usually more than one, help stop asthma attacks. Use coffee instead of water in the enema bag. A friend of a woman who was having an asthma attack called me. The woman had spent the previous night in the hospital and didn't want to go back. I gave her two coffee enemas and a healing by my fireplace. I later found out she went dancing that night. The allergy tea is also good for treating asthma.

Brain Tumors

Juice fresh Concord grapes and create a poultice (you can use Concord grape juice from a health food store, but it's not as good as fresh grapes). No matter what area of the brain is affected, put the poultice at the base of the brain. Keep changing it. You'll know it's working when you see blisters. They'll be drawing out toxins.

Cancer or Nourishment

Sip as a tea made from one teaspoon of slippery elm to one cup of hot water. It's very good for cancer. It soothes and pulls out toxins.

Cold

Slippery elm tea or a ginger tea made with fresh ginger root, a little cayenne, honey, and lemon. The allergy tea is also sometimes effective with colds.

Headache

There is nothing better for a headache than a coffee enema. Use coffee instead of water in the enema bag. With migraines it sometimes takes more than one. When you finish one enema, do another.

Nausea

Take aloe vera juice, scraped fresh from the inside of the leaf. Be careful not to use any of the yellowish juice. Blend with a little bit of apple juice to mask the flavor.

Poison Oak/Poison Ivy/Acne

Make a strong tea of goldenseal root powder, at least a teaspoon or more per cup of hot water. Steep for about a half hour. Strain and then wash it over the infected areas. You have to keep doing this as the liquid dries on your skin. If the tea alone isn't enough to heal, sprinkle some of the goldenseal root powder over the affected areas right after washing with the tea.

Salt Bath

This is a wonderful purifier—physical, emotional, spiritual—drawing out toxins of all kinds. First, pour sea salt in a medium to large bowl and add just enough water to create a paste. Ideally, you will want to place the bowl outside all day to gather energy from the sun and all night to absorb moonlight, praying as you place the bowl on Mother Earth. When it's time for the bath, fill the tub with hot water ankle high. Have the recipient stand in the water—as hot as she can tolerate. Before you begin the salt bath, the bather needs to get all wet. Then, begin the salt bath by rubbing her arms vigorously, to and fro, with the salt paste. Rub her entire body, including her head and hair. When you're done, have her shower to wash off the salt. *Do not remove the plug until after she showers.* When you pull the plug, it is very important for the person to watch the water drain until it all goes down the drain. Afterwards, it is good to soak in a warm tub for a while.

Soft Tissue Infections

½ raw potato, grated
½ raw onion, grated

Blend these together, nice and juicy, and apply as a poultice. If pus begins to come out, don't squeeze! Just let it drain naturally. My teacher Mildred Jackson taught me this one when a client came to me with her labia so infected she could only walk with her legs apart. It worked wonders; in two and a half days the swelling was gone. I've also used this poultice for people with tooth abscesses, having them take 1000mg of Vitamin C and two capsules of goldenseal and myrrh three times a day, as well.

For other kinds of infection, like a little girl I treated with an infection on the back of her ear, I use raw aloe vera. Cut a leaf in half and apply the jelly side wherever there is infection. Tape it on, if necessary. Refresh regularly until the infection is gone.

Sore Throat

This remedy came to me when I was living in Medicine Wheel. It was a freezing winter and I woke up with a terrible sore throat. Spirit guided me to get up, put more wood in the stove, and then to get each of these ingredients. Within an hour or two of taking these cough drops, my sore throat was gone.

Slippery elm powder (lots of it)
Ginger powder
Licorice root powder
Comfrey leaf or root powder (leaf better)
Cayenne pepper (African is what I like most, very powerful)

Honey

Lemon juice

Slippery elm powder is the main ingredient that will make the dough, with ginger powder being the next main ingredient. Use lesser and equal parts of licorice and comfrey and add cayenne pepper to taste (cayenne does a lot of healing, so it's good to add as much as you can handle).

Mix the dry ingredients together, beginning with lots of slippery elm, but leaving some aside to add later to get the consistency you want. Add honey to sweeten and then work in the lemon juice, but not so much that you'll have to use three pounds of slippery elm. You want to create a consistency that will allow you to make nice small jelly-like balls. Not too hard, but hard enough to suck on for a while. Keep tasting it to see how it feels in your body.

I went to see my mother one time because she was sick. She had a terrible cough, so I offered her some of these cough drops. My mother refused, saying, "It looks like dog food." That night, I put some in a dish near her and went to bed. Pretty soon I didn't hear her coughing. It seems Mami ate some dog food that night.

Stomach Aches/Ulcers

Drink the juice of a fresh leaf of aloe vera blended with a little bit of apple juice (to mask the flavor). A little lemon juice in water is a favorite Nicaraguan recipe for stomachaches, even for ulcers. And any kind of mint, sipped as a tea, does wonders for the stomach.

Vomiting

To induce or stop vomiting, add a cup of hot water to a teaspoon of lobelia. Steep for at least seven minutes, preferably ten.

PRAYER FOR LOVE
This prayer came to me after September 11, 2001.

O, Great One,
We ask that your Light shine Bright
Within us
As we pray for
Divine Intervention
And Divine Solution
In our World
That Love Triumph
Healing All
Everybody, Everything
And we ask that this prayer
Be joined with all those
Who are praying for this
Consciously, Subconsciously, and Unconsciously.

Mitakuye oyasin
All my relations

END NOTES

[1] Exemplars of this during the last century are Sri Aurobindo and Mother Mirra, who wrote and spoke of the coming of a new humanity, the "sun-eyed children of a marvelous dawn," and forged their own cellular changes through the practice of Integral Yoga, as well as Jesuit Pierre Teilhard de Chardin, who wrote about the "emergent human" coming into mystical union with the Divine through immersion in the Universe and its unfolding story. I am grateful to Francis Rothluebber, former Director of Colombiere Center, for introducing me to Sri Aurobindo and Mother Mirra and for sponsoring the workshop in Idyllwild, California, where I first met Zelima. [For more information about the retreat center, which has been re-envisioned and renamed, Spirit Mountain Retreat, and is now directed by Esther Kennedy, O.P., please see www.spiritmountainretreat.org.]

[2] See Timothy Ferris, THE WHOLE SHEBANG, New York: Touchstone, 1997, pp. 269-270: "Classical physics assumes *locality*—that is, it assumes that changes in systems are caused by direct physical contact…. [whereas] quantum systems are said to exhibit *nonlocality*. They act like an intimately connected whole, regardless of whether their parts are far removed from each other."

[3] Sister M. Nazareth Briare was a much beloved member of the Dominican Order of San Rafael, California. She entered religious life as Maria Elizabeth Briare in 1911, taking the name Sister Nazareth, and began teaching in 1912. She taught music in various schools until 1927 and then taught grades 5-8 in a number of Dominican schools, including St. Dominic's, until 1969. Her necrology states that in "most of these missions she was either the superior of the house or the principal of the school and in some cases both." Sister Nazareth died on December 20, 1973. A year earlier, she had suffered a stroke and when she was admitted to the hospital, it was discovered that she had cancer. "Because Sister Nazareth had never mentioned her illness, it came as a surprise to her sisters," the necrology says.

[4] In the summer of 1969, homosexual patrons of Stonewall Bar in Greenwich Village, New York, fought back when city police raided it for the second time in a week. The spontaneous resistance to police oppression provoked other confrontations, bringing new visibility to the "love that has no name" and the injustices suffered by gay and lesbian people. Stonewall is widely credited with sparking the national gay and lesbian civil rights movement.

[5] Before he died of a heart attack on October 22, 2004, Peter Rogers, Ph.D., read this chapter of the book and wrote to me [Elise D. García]: "My speech 'defect' is technically called hyperrhinolalia and is characterized by that nasal quality often associated with a cleft palate. And cleft palates are often associated with a harelip, which Zelima assumed I had operated on. The reality is that I was born with a congenital paralyzed uvula, which also results in nasal speech. I did have an operation in New York, in my

twenties, which is called a Pharyngeal Flap and helps me redirect air forward through my mouth and speak more clearly."

[6] Peter observed about this that "times were very different thirty-five years ago, and therapists had more autonomy to work with clients as they saw fit. The state of California didn't even have a licensing board until a few years later. Also there were no mandatory reporting statutes in those days. If I were seeing Zelima today, I would be required to report her violent behavior toward Lee's children, and Child Protective Services would have gotten involved."

[7] In an interview conducted on August 22, 2004, Peter said he was trained in gestalt therapy and was "very influenced by the existential psychotherapy movement." As a result, he said, "dialogue came naturally to me as a way of trying to get all the personalities working together. This is often thought about in pathological way, but it's not uncommon for abused children to learn to dissociate and to have a secret playmate who they confide in—and that's how I saw her different personalities. There were parts that had some real value that we could access with real dialogue." Peter said that at the time he treated Zelima, he was interested in the work of psychiatrist R.D. Laing, "who had a different kind of perspective on what we called madness in those days. He was interested in exploring and finding positive aspects and strength in that. Zelima was in pretty bad shape. A lot of people thought she was crazy. The best thing I did was to tell her she was not crazy. I allowed her to stay with her experience and not be scared by it, and work it through. She was able to work through some very difficult things quickly because she was ready to deal with them. So much of long-term work is gaining trust and losing defenses—preparation work. With Zelima, she went into full participation right away. She was very courageous. That's the first thing that comes to mind—her courage and her willingness to go to very scary places. She literally confronted her own demons. It was a privilege to work with her in that respect."

[8] Peter remembered "Zelima teasing me about my skinny ankles inside my cowboy boots."

[9] Peter wrote, "My birth name is Rosenbaum, and yes, my mother, fearing anti-Semitism, requested that we change our surname when we became citizens. They allowed me to choose a new surname, the only proviso being that it start with the letter "R." And it is true that I was a childhood fan of Roy Rogers, and consequently chose that for our new "American Name.""

[10] The results of the interviews that Zelima and others conducted were published in Bell, A. & Weinberg, M. (1978). HOMOSEXUALITIES: A STUDY OF DIVERSITIES AMONG MEN AND WOMEN. New York: Simon & Schuster.

[11] Glen S. Dumke was Chancellor of the California State Colleges from 1962-1976 and Chancellor of the California State Universities and Colleges from 1977-1983.

¹² "These little girls were probably orphans or children of starving mothers," Zelima says.

¹³ Interestingly, the Mandala Project describes a mandala as "a model for the organizational structure of life itself—a cosmic diagram that reminds us of our relation to the infinite, the world that extends both beyond and within our bodies and minds." www.mandalaproject.org

¹⁴ In 1974, the Women's Collective in Oakland published a book of Zelima's poetry. Titled SOY (I am), the book is currently out of print.

¹⁵ The Runes are a Norse system of guidance and divination, using an alphabetic script developed by peoples of Northern Europe beginning in the first century. The I Ching, or Book of Changes, is an ancient Chinese guide whose origins date as far back as 2800 B.C. The Gong Yee Fot Choy, another Chinese divination system, uses thirty-two cards of a regular playing deck for revealing information about wishes.

¹⁶ From the Historical Museum of Southern Florida, "The Afro-Cuban Orisha religion, sometimes referred to as 'Santería,' is the product of the encounter between Yoruba Orisha worship and the popular practices of Spanish Catholicism in colonial Cuba. Enslaved Africans juxtaposed their beliefs and customs with those imposed by the Spanish colonists to give birth to a new interpretation of their traditional religion." www.historical-museum.org

¹⁷ On March 19, 1974, Inez García was raped by Luis Castillo while being held down by 300-pound Miguel Jimenez. Inez shot and killed Jimenez when a knife was thrown at her. Castillo went free, but Inez was sentenced to five years to life for murder. The California Coalition for Women Prisoners website notes: Inez García was convicted of murder and spent two years in prison, [California Institution for Women], before her conviction was reversed on appeal. Inez and her supporters fought for the understanding that women have a right to defend themselves against rape and her victory in court confirmed that right…. We want to take this chance to say we remember what she did and thank her for standing up!" www.womenprisoners.org

¹⁸ Angela Davis had herself been freed from prison just two years earlier, after serving eighteen months in jail on charges of being a conspirator in the abortive kidnapping and escape of George Jackson, a young revolutionary and one of the "Soledad (Prison) Brothers" whose cause Angela had been championing in trying to improve prison conditions. Angela was cleared of all charges. Now a philosophy professor at the University of California at Santa Cruz, Angela has continued to be involved in prison reform, exposing the racism that is endemic to the U.S. prison system.

¹⁹ Susan B. Jordan, National Lawyers Guild News, S.F. Bay Area Chapter, November 2002.

²⁰ "I didn't know after that glorious sun that I was going to end up here, in this tiny camper, sleeping with dog hairs!" Zelima laughed as she relayed this story.

²¹ Inspired by the title (and content) of Marcus J. Borg's book, MEETING JESUS AGAIN FOR THE FIRST TIME.

²² Interestingly, Ixchen is the name of Nicaragua's foremost women's support center. Established in 1989, it has served more than two million Nicaraguan women from ten centers located around the country, providing health and social services, as well as legal assistance, particularly in cases involving domestic violence. For more about the organization, see their website at www.ibw.com.ni/~ixchen.

²³ Mildred Jackson was a pioneer in the alternative healing movement, starting in the early 1960s, when the kind of herbalism and hands-on body work she did was either vilified or ridiculed by the established medical community. She is a real hero of the movement. Mildred's book was published in 1975 and reprinted in 1997.

²⁴ Thomas Banyacya died on February 6, 1999, at the age of 89. He is recognized as a leading messenger "for nonviolence and the spiritual reawakening necessary to change the course of human history off of the path towards total destruction and onto the path towards true peace and harmony among all life," according to an unsigned article that appears on numerous websites. The article goes on to note, "Inspired by the great Hopi Elder Yukiuma whom he regarded as 'The Hopi Gandhi', Banyacya spent seven years in prison in the 1940's because of his steadfast conscientious objection to registering for military service." The atomic bombings of Hiroshima and Nagasaki were seen by the Hopi spiritual leaders as a fulfillment of their ancient prophecies about "the gourd of ashes falling on the Earth two times." In December of 1948, diverse Hopi leaders "met for the first time in history to compare their previously secret knowledge as per their ancient instructions handed down through the generations," according to the article. "Banyacya was commissioned at that meeting to bring to the outside world the Message of Peace and the warnings for humanity revealed at this meeting…. Devoting himself totally to this mission, he still lived a simple lifestyle and he and his family survived as best they could in the traditional ways with some help from the minimal donations of people who supported his work."

²⁵ According to the above article, "Banyacya felt that his life's mission was fulfilled, after decades of unsuccessful attempts, when he was able to bring the Hopi message and spokesmen to the United Nations (the 'house of mica' predicted by the Hopi prophecies)." He delivered the message in 1992 and 1993 at a U.N. gathering of global indigenous leaders when 1993 was designated as the International Year of the World's Indigenous Peoples and 1995-2004 as the International Decade of the World's Indigenous Peoples. "His message was simple yet still inscrutable to the mind of 'Western Civilization', that all of the problems of modern society are rooted in an error in human thinking clouded by attachments to the world of material comforts and that to solve all of these problems we only have to reawaken spiritually to the innate human/spiritual relationship to all life as our relations, and to all people as one human race," the article notes. "He was convinced that the simple spiritually focused lifestyle is the only one which will survive in these times of increasing wars, violence and even natural disasters brought on by this error in human thinking. His life was an inspiration, for so very many people, to respect the ancient wisdom of the traditional

indigenous cultures of our beloved Mother Earth. Decades before scientists recognized the currently evident signs of global climate change he was warning that the actions of industrial society would bring on the calamities we now see all around the world with increasingly devastating storms, earthquakes, etc."

26 For a comprehensive treatment of the very recent and scandalous history of U.S. government and corporate complicity in exploiting the land and the people of the Big Mountain-Black Mesa area, see the article by historian and author Judith Nies, "The Black Mesa Syndrome: Indian Lands, Black Coal," in the summer 1998 issue of ORION MAGAZINE, http://www.oriononline.org/pages/om/archive_om/Nies.html

27 Judith Nies writes in her ORION article, "Today, thirty years after the strip mining for coal began, the cities have the energy they were promised, but the Hopi and Navajo nations are not rich—that part of the plan proved ephemeral. Instead, Black Mesa has suffered human rights abuses and ecological devastation; the Hopi water supply is drying up; thousands of archeological sites have been destroyed; and, unbeknownst to most Americans, twelve thousand Navajos have been removed from their lands—the largest removal of Indians in the United States since the 1880s."

28 Chakras, from the Sanskrit term meaning "wheels," are energy vortexes located throughout our bodies. There are seven main chakras which distribute life energy throughout the body, mind, and emotions. The sixth, or third-eye chakra, located just above the space between the eyes, corresponds to our sense of intuition and nonjudgmental self-awareness.

29 In a June 5, 2005 interview, Rita Arauz, an internationally acclaimed AIDS activist in Nicaragua, said this about her father: "I felt very moved by what happened at his death. I understand what it means and it was a relief to me that my father was able to achieve that level. But I also was not surprised. He always was a fair man, good to everybody. People who worked for him, including farmers on the land, remember his goodness. His only incongruency was being part of Somoza regime."

30 Medicine Wheel was built in the high desert, some 5,700 feet above sea level, near the town of St. Johns. The area is characterized by snowy subfreezing winters and desert-hot summers. White sand and red clay soils are dotted with sage brush and cedar; rocks and stones abound; and deep gullies and wide washes are carved into the bare hills. Powerful desert winds regularly whip across the landscape, stirring up dust storms. With no electricity or running water, the living conditions at Medicine Wheel were primitive by modern standards. But whatever was lacking in amenities was made up for by the big sky, offering expansive views into the distance by day and intimate blackness, resplendent with stars, by night.

31 In recent decades, people like Dorothy MacLean of the Findhorn community in Scotland and Machaelle Small Wright of Perelandra in Virginia, among others, have shared the ways in which they have been able to communicate with the natural world, bringing forth challenging and inspiring messages. When Dorothy MacLean was first guided to attune to nature in the spring of 1963, she heard the words, as she relates in

THE FINDHORN GARDEN, "Seek into the glorious realms of nature with sympathy and understanding, knowing that these beings are of the Light, willing to help, but suspicious of humans and on the lookout for the false, the snags."

32 The Secret Dakini Oracle cards that Zelima has used over the years were created by Nik Douglas and Penny Slinger, who write, "The Dakinis are the guardians of the deeper mysteries of the self, and it is through them that the secrets of inner transformation are opened." See THE TANTRIC DAKINI ORACLE (Rochester, Vermont: Destiny Books, 2003).

33 Describing her experience of the ceremonies, a friend of Zelima's named Liz, said, "It was a very deep time of prayer to Great Spirit and of becoming more and more conscious of why we are here and what our purpose is. I remember during the dancing that we could actually feel ourselves meeting with other forms of creation energetically, and dancing together. It's an experience you have, with no proof—just the powerful sense that you're dancing with the cedar trees, the birds, and the animals. Perhaps the most dramatic was the sense of dancing with the trees because you don't expect them to move or to find yourself moved in response to them, whereas with animals or birds, you expect some reciprocity. You don't expect that with bushes and trees. But when it happens, it's so obvious. It's right there, incontrovertibly."

34 Zelima's experience is very much akin to descriptions of shamanic journeying or psychonavigation as described by students of shamanism, including Joseph Campbell, Sandra Ingerman, Michael Harner, John Perkins, Alberto Villoldo, and others. "An experience of another whole realm of consciousness," as Campbell says. Joseph Campbell with Bill Moyers, THE POWER OF MYTH (New York: Doubleday, 1988), p. 87.

35 A student of Zelima's named Fern described the classes: "I signed up for a class called Ancient Healing. There was a group of about fifteen to twenty women in the class. Zelima introduced herself and told us she would tell us things that would really change our lives. She drummed, and the drumming opened my heart. I just became so receptive to everything that she had to share with us from that moment on. Zelima said that the drumming changes the energy and will open our hearts and help us to feel and get out of who we are and just be with Spirit. So that was the first class—the drumming, a little introduction to the ancient ways of healing, allowing the energy to come in by opening your pores to the sun and to moon and to stars. They just went on and on, with more lessons each time. It was wonderful! I had just felt so stagnated and I remember coming home feeling charged with life again. It was an opening. She opened the doors. I've had juvenile arthritis since I was ten months old. My hands at the time I met her were not as bad as they are now, but the arthritis never stopped the energy from flowing through. I don't have strength to help a lot of people but she taught me how to gather the energy and I use it to work with my little animals. When my hands started becoming in the crippled state, I never thought that I could be of service like that again. But it has allowed me to know that it really doesn't matter what shape you're in because when Spirit works through you, you can heal with your eyes. So with these things I've come to learn and grow."

[36] There are numerous stories about San Martín de Porres that tell of similar responses on his part. In one of these, when Brother Martín discovered mice tearing up the bedding and gowns he used for the sick in the priory infirmary, he told Brother Mouse that he would bring them all food each day if they would just stay in the garden and out of the infirmary. For a wonderful collection of such stories and insights into the meaning of San Martín's friendship with all animals, his medicinal-plant growing, and love for the Earth and the poor, see MARTIN DE PORRES: A SAINT OF THE AMERICAS by Brian J. Pierce, O.P. (Ligouri Publications, 2004).

[37] The Independent Catholic Churches International was formed in 1980. Most member churches "are descended from the Old Catholic Church of Utrecht, which broke with Rome in the 1870's over the dogmas of Vatican I, including that of the infallibility of the Pope," according to the church's website. The Independent Catholic Church "upholds the ancient tradition of the independence and interdependence rather than hierarchy of bishops. Our members have carefully guarded the Catholicity of our faith and the validity of our Apostolic Succession." The church's motto, drawn from St. Augustine of Hippo, is: "In essentials, unity; in nonessentials, diversity; in all things, charity." The Independent Catholic Church accepts vocations "without regard to gender, marital status, sexual orientation, race, cultural origin or citizenship." www.independentcatholics.org

[38] Zelima did not know the biopsy results for at least a week. She called me [Elise] a day or two after she left the hospital to say she had some "bad news," but that I shouldn't be upset because she was okay with it. The bad news was that she had been diagnosed with pancreatic cancer that had progressed to the liver. She called again on December 15 to say, "There is a strong beautiful Light inside me—it's either an intense, powerful healing or I'm getting ready to cross over. I can't tell the difference. It's either the beginning of the end or the beginning of the beginning. I feel all lit up from head to toe. It's an incredibly beautiful feeling! I've never felt anything like it." On December 18, she called to tell me about her continuing work with the Light, saying, "I think I'm healing." Her son wasn't so sanguine. Zelima said, "My son was the first one the doctor talked to after looking at me. The doctor said nothing could be done. My son thinks I'm not facing reality when I tell him I'm going to try to heal myself. He said it would be a miracle if I healed myself. I told him I believe in miracles, but that if I do go, I'd be happy."

[39] Zelima is guided each step of the way in creating Medicine Necklaces, which become charged with Earth's energy and the particular intent that goes into its making. Every aspect of the Medicine Necklace is suffused with meaning, energy, and intent, including the particular stones chosen, the number of knots tied, the beads and images painted on them, etc. They are created in a prayerful trance and then she does a ceremony so the Medicine Necklace picks up the vibration of the Earth, the sun, the moon, the stars. The energy stays locked in the necklace and can be recharged again and again. Zelima has a few stories about people sensing the energy from the Medicine Necklaces as a heat on their bodies when they ran into trouble—getting caught in a whirlpool in one case and losing brakes going downhill in another—until they were safe.

[40] Evolution biologist and futurist Elisabet Sahtouris writes that a rock "could see the whole world as nothing more than its own dance, its endless transformation into living creatures and back into rock. Try for yourself the exercise of looking out over your world and seeing all of it—the landscape, the sea and sky, the creatures, yourself and your fellow humans, their airplanes, their cities, the furniture in your house, this book in your hands—all as no more and no less than rock rearranged." Elisabet Sahtouris, EARTHDANCE: LIVING SYSTEMS IN EVOLUTION (Lincoln, NE: University Press, 2000), p. 307.

[41] On November 11, 2003, I began a two-day trek from San Antonio to St. Johns to see Zelima and capture her story. I hadn't seen her since her ordination. Although we talked at least once every couple of weeks, nothing prepared me for what I saw. The large strong woman I remembered with long black hair was now diminutive, wearing clothes from a thrift store that fit preteens. The living conditions were harsh. Red clay dust settled everywhere—inside the dome, the camper and on everything around the campsite. In just three days, my nose, throat, and lungs were clogged. Although winter hadn't yet fully set in, I had a hard time staying warm in my down sleeping bag at night. Cooking on the stovetop in the tiny camper was a major chore, as was cleaning up after it, drawing cold rust-colored water from the well to scrub pots and wash dishes. Using the bathroom meant going out behind a shrub with a roll of toilet paper and a shovel. After four exhausting days and nights of sharing Zelima's life on the land, I was astounded at how she had managed to survive, coming to the land as weak as she was—and I worried how she would make it through the winter.

[42] Zelima called on November 23, 2003. She said it was so cold, she moved into the camper for a couple of days, keeping the burner on the stovetop lit for warmth. But she ran out of propane in two days and couldn't afford to replace it. The birds were in danger of freezing. Even though she had stayed up as late as she could to keep the wood stove going and banked it for the night before going over to the camper, the fire was out by early morning when she went back in. She had covered the bird cages with layers of blankets but it wasn't enough. "The birds cannot take it," she told me. "The water in their cage was frozen when I got over there. I mean frozen. We had a windstorm and the camper was rocking back and forth. I started to get scared and began praying. I asked the wind, 'Please be gentle with us if you're going to take us.' My fear went away, but then I felt so bad about the puppies, being outside in that wind and cold. It's very intense. I'm running out of food and water but I have to wait until Wednesday when my check comes in to go into town. I'm on the edge of despair."

[43] According to the National Institute on Aging, "A body temperature below 96° F may seem like just a couple of degrees below the body's normal temperature of 98.6° F. It can be dangerous. It may cause an irregular heartbeat leading to heart problems and death." www.niapublications.org

[44] On December 27, Zelima called, telling me in a very calm voice, "Something is happening. The Light comes to me every morning. Here I am a woman in the wilderness. It feels like I'm going through an intense initiation. Last night the winds were whistling like crazy. The animals were so scared. Three cats had their arms around me. We were snuggled real close. I started praying and the Light came inside. My prayers

calmed me and then they got calm. I can't believe I'm still alive and feeling so calm. I'm down to a size one. I don't think I would still be alive if the Light didn't come to me every day. When the Light comes, it doesn't matter how anxious I'm feeling, or how much pain I'm in, I get calm and feel all right. I'm now convinced people can heal from anything. I'm my own guinea pig."

[45] Zelima had to replace her cell phone service soon after she got there because she could not get a signal from the previous provider. Less than a year later she had to replace the phone that came with the new service because it had stopped working as a result of damage caused by condensation from the constant freezing and thawing.

[46] Zelima wasn't the only one affected by her story. As I began working with the details of Zelima's life and traumatic childhood, I found myself feeling sick to my stomach. I would get a knot in my solar plexus and feel haunted by the stories she told long after I would hang up the phone or leave the computer. I discovered how to deal with this one day when I felt drawn to go outside and open myself up to Earth's energies. Walking out barefoot, I opened the pores of the soles of my feet and the pores of the palms of my hands. Also opening the pores of my eyes, I allowed the energies of Mother Earth and Sky to flow into me. Soon, I felt a release. It became a ritual every time I worked on difficult parts of the book, especially in those first chapters. In time, I found the healing energies of the Mesquite tree in the yard to be exactly what I needed to get through them.

[47] Zelima based her calculations on 1,673 square feet of improvements comprising the home and cabin and a low-end construction cost of $11 per square foot, for a 1986 value of $18,403. Using interest rates a friend derived from the Federal Reserve, she applied a 5.4% average interest compounded annually from December 1986 through December 2003, bringing the total owed to $44,995. In her letter, Zelima told Jack Brown that she also thought it fair for him to compensate her for fifteen years' worth of taxes she paid on the improvements until the tax assessor finally straightened out the records in 2002, thanks to the efforts of her friend, Liz. ("I almost lost the land around this time because I was so far behind in tax payments," Zelima said. "Liz did a wonderful job of organizing a fundraising effort and so many of my friends contributed generously.") Calculating the extra taxes at an average of $85 per year brought the total figure to $46,270.

[48] Zelima said, "I never rejected getting back any part of Medicine Wheel. Why would I do that? I had just pleaded with him to try to get the full eighty acres since the lands were ceremonially connected and I had buildings on both parcels."

[49] In a March 20, 2004 interview, Tammi described the unusual circumstances under which she had come to buy Medicine Wheel in 1995. Tammi said she was looking to buy the forty acres next door when she saw the unusual building and went over to look at it. "I loved it!" she said. "I could tell no one lived there," so she found out who owned the place and drove to his house. It wasn't on the market but it turned out the owner had no idea there were any buildings on the land. He had bought the forty-acre parcel a few years earlier for $7,000 from a friend who had financial problems and

needed to sell. Curious, he went to the land to see what Tammi was talking about. "He freaked out," Tammi said. "He heard it was a healing place and when he saw it, he was scared of it." The man told Tammi he would sell it to her for the same amount she was planning to buy the land next door—$13,000. "It hadn't been lived in, but it wasn't in bad shape. I just had to do a lot of clean up. It's gorgeous," Tammi said. "Everyone who comes loves it."

[50] These are the same photographs that appear in this book.

[51] The website address was www.arizonansforjustice.org.

[52] Senator Brown declined to respond to numerous attempts to be interviewed for the book. On September 22, 2004, Carol Coston, OP and I faxed a letter to him, which noted, "On June 9, 2004, we began efforts to try to secure an interview with you concerning a book we will be publishing about the life of one of your constituents, the Rev. Zelima Xochiquetzál, who resides in St. Johns, Ariz. As we noted in that letter, 'In the telling of her life story, Zelima relates an incident involving you in your occupation as a Realtor.' ... We have followed-up on this written request with several phone calls, an email, and the names and contact information for people who could testify to our character and work. On August 19, we spoke with your secretary ... indicating that we were at a loss as to what additional steps we could take to try to secure your side of this story. We noted that while it is your right, obviously, to decline to be interviewed, we just wanted to be sure you were fully aware that the story Zelima tells paints a very unflattering picture for anyone, but especially for a public servant. Denise said she would relay this information to you, as well as our willingness to schedule the interview at a time convenient to you."

[53] I am reminded by Zelima's cry to the Creator of the beautiful words written by renowned Latin American theologian Ivone Gebara, a Brazilian Sister of Our Lady: "Praying is not just making requests; it is being present, being intimately part of the body of the universe, the human body, and the bodies of those who are dear to us— the bodies we love." Ivone Gebara, LONGING FOR RUNNING WATER: ECOFEMINISM AND LIBERATION (Minneapolis: Augsburg Fortress, 1999), p.120.

[54] Carol Coston began to send Zelima other foods she made, as well, including soups made from ingredients harvested from our organic garden. Zelima was astonished at the difference the food made in her body. After having been in significant pain for several weeks, and then getting a care package from Carol, she said, "I noticed a difference in how I felt when I ate the granola. I felt more clarity. Then the little beans yesterday. I had been dragging, and I started feeling more energy. Then that chaya and garbanzo soup last night! It was the first night I had *no* pain. I went from excruciating pain to no pain. I notice these things when I do healing. I know the healing feeling of the Earth very well. But this is the food. I have never felt my pancreas in that way before. My pancreas felt nourished. I think my pancreas was starving, withering from a lack of real food. Carol has a sacred gift. It's the food and the gift of the healer. She's so unpretentious about it, that's what makes it even stronger! She's a healer." Using a play on the word *curandera*, we started calling Carol the "Foodandera."

[55] "The diminished oxygen supply can cause serious impairments in cognitive skills, as well as in physical, psychological and other functions. Recovery can occur in many cases, but it depends largely on the parts of the brain affected, and its pace and extent are unpredictable." Family Caregiver Alliance www.caregiver.org

[56] In THE FIELD, Lynne McTaggart does a brilliant job of presenting the evidence being gathered by physicists around the world, working on the edges of quantum physics, about the existence of a Zero-Point Field—a "heaving sea of energy" that connects everything in the universe in a single resonant field. The Zero-Point Field makes sense of supernatural phenomena like absent healing and the power of prayer. See Lynne McTaggart, THE FIELD: THE QUEST FOR THE SECRET FORCE OF THE UNIVERSE (New York: Quill, 2003).

[57] A goiter is a "noncancerous enlargement of the thyroid gland, visible as a swelling at the front of the neck, that is often associated with iodine deficiency," according to The American Heritage Stedman's Medical Dictionary.

[58] According to Trena, the doctor who encouraged her to sign the "do not resuscitate" (DNR) forms explained that "Bob had his accident over a year ago and we do not know how much he understands and he will be on an air mattress for the rest of his life." Characterizing this as a "miracle," Trena said that "Bob went into respiratory failure while in the intensive care unit in Texas. The same doctor tried to reach me that night. However, the hospital was calling me in Arizona instead of where I was in Texas. If I had signed the DNR and they had reached me, my husband would be dead from a mucous plug causing his respiratory problem. It needed to be suctioned."

[59] "Heterotopic ossification is a phenomenon in which new bone is formed in tissues that do not normally ossify.... When the extent of heterotopic ossification is of such magnitude that limitation of joint motion occurs, heterotopic ossification may interfere with activities of daily living such as sitting and dressing of the lower extremities or cause abnormal skin pressure areas." www.med.harvard.edu

[60] Trena adds that the psychologist doing neuro feedback work with Bob is "excited" because "Bob understands more than what people are giving him credit for."

[61] "Zelima has been the glue that has kept me together," Trena says. "I love it when she tells me that Bob will be having new abilities, and then I see them appear."

[62] In an interview on Nov. 21, 2004, Zelima's neighbor, Misty, said, "The kitty was under the truck. It's a large truck. We ran it over. It let out a high-pitched scream. The truck ran over its leg, and it was ripped all the way to its belly—a big slice open. We took him to Zelima." Misty's father said he was sure when he handed the kitten to Zelima that it would probably die very soon. "Zelima started doing the healing," Misty said. "It was like magic! Every day he was showing improvement. Two weeks later, we stopped by. The flesh was closing, fur growing back. That was a miracle.

Now you can't even see a scar! The way she put her heart into that kitty, we said, go ahead, that's your baby."

[63] Misty later told Zelima that her grandmother said the dogs had dug up a dog that had been buried after it had been shot. Zelima thinks the puppy was poisoned eating meat near the lead bullet.

[64] On Dec. 5, 2004, Zelima called to report on Destiny's progress. "Last night she drank water by herself. I've been spoon feeding her. My bed is the intensive care unit. I'm rubbing her tummy now and she's listening. She lets me know by moaning if I should go deeper. She is also turning to let me know where to touch her. Her nose isn't real hot as it was, but until it gets cool as a cucumber, she's not out of the woods."

[65] After the devastating tsunami, there was a rash of stories in the news about the strange phenomenon being observed that while tens of thousands of humans died, very few animals did. Report after report spoke of speculation about a "sixth sense" that animals must have that warned them of the impending danger. In a January 4, 2005 online article, The National Geographic wrote, "Alan Rabinowitz, director for science and exploration at the Bronx Zoo-based Wildlife Conservation Society in New York, says that animals can sense impending danger by detecting subtle or abrupt shifts in the environment. 'Earthquakes bring vibrational changes on land and in water while storms cause electromagnetic changes in the atmosphere,' he said. 'Some animals have acute sense of hearing and smell that allow them to determine something coming towards them long before humans might know that something is there.' … At one time humans also had this sixth sense, Rabinowitz said, but lost the ability when it was no longer needed or used." Zelima's clear sense that we already have entered a time of Earth changes suggests that we humans may do well to re-hone this ability to perceive Earth changes, an ability Zelima clearly possesses.

[66] According to January 7, 2005 online article in The National Geographic, "The earthquake that generated the great Indian Ocean tsunami of 2004 is estimated to have released the energy of 23,000 Hiroshima-type atomic bombs, according to the U.S. Geological Survey (USGS). Giant forces that had been building up deep in the Earth for hundreds of years were released suddenly on December 26, shaking the ground violently and unleashing a series of killer waves that sped across the Indian Ocean at the speed of a jet airliner. By the end of the day more than 150,000 people were dead or missing and millions more were homeless in 11 countries, making it perhaps the most destructive tsunami in history."

[67] Before each of the three major events, Zelima was doubled over in pain and vomiting. I pleaded with her to let me cancel; everyone would understand. But she said, "Let me try to gather some energy." She would then head down to the creek, near some tall cypress trees and a beautiful outcropping of rock, and emerge some forty or fifty minutes later, ready to go. No one who came ever suspected she had been so violently ill just before they arrived. It stumped me, too.

[68] This represented a very subtle but significant shift for me [Elise]. During much of the time Zelima was dealing with her pancreatic problem, I was dealing with a sudden loss of balance and hearing in one ear. I remember talking to Zelima one day about how I was trying to draw healing light into my vestibular and cochlear nerves, visualizing them bathed in and surrounded by Light. Without passing any judgment on what I was doing, she simply said, "What I try to do is activate the Light that is already within." It totally transformed the way I thought about the healing process.

[69] The Bush administration finalized its ban on ephedra on February 6, 2004, but on April 14, 2005, a court in Utah lifted the ban to allow low doses.